"*Inner Drives* is a wise, beautifully written, extraordinary tool for writers in all fields. I will be recommending it to screenwriters with whom we are working and to the screenwriting students that I mentor through the USC filmic writing program. "

Lynn Hendee, Producer, *In My Country, Ender's Game*

"In this seminal work, Pamela Jaye Smith explains how to enrich your work, and possibly even your life, through a profound understanding of how myths work and what they reveal about our humanity."

Pamela Wallace, producer, Oscar-winning co-screenwriter of *Witness*

"Pamela Jaye Smith goes deep into the universal unconscious with her immense knowledge of myths. Her approach to scripts is unique and essential, whether you're writing the Great American Screenplay or an episode of a popular TV show."

Ellen Sandler, Emmy-nominated co-executive producer, *Everybody Loves Raymond*

"I have personally had the privilege of listening to Pamela Smith's lectures on character and the chakras, and found them to be a one-of-a-kind experience, a fresh look at ancient wisdom that is all her own."

Lindsay Crouse, actress *The Insider, Buffy the Vampire Slayer, Providence, Hack, Dragnet*

"In *Inner Drives*, Pamela Jaye Smith links the motivations of the characters to the source of those motivations, and thereby reveals the true source of a great character's real power. I highly recommend it."

James Bonnet, screenwriter and author of *Stealing Fire from the Gods: A Dynamic New Story Model for Writers and Filmmakers*

"In remarkably clear prose, Ms. Smith blows away the cobwebs of conventional thinking. She opens a window to fresh breezes of mythological truth, freeing our imaginations, and enabling us to create with greater clarity and power."

James D. Pasternak, director, producer, teacher

"Smith delves into that oft-ignored world of what to do between all those inciting incidents and turning points. She leads us so effortlessly through the delicious nexus of spiritualism and story."

Sheila Gallien
Sheila worked alongside Oscar-nominee William Broyles, Jr. on numerous films including *Cast Away, Unfaithful*, and *Entrapment*

"You might just as well drink rocket fuel as use this book for character development… that's the effect it will have. Congrats, Pamela, on a revolutionary work for writers which combines a very old concept with modern writer's craft."

Michael Thunder, writer's coach and script analyst

"In *Inner Drives*, author Pamela Jaye Smith has laid out a mind-boggling mythic menu that all scriptwriters and novelists should keep within easy reach when they need to add that extra compelling layer of depth to their projects."

Kathie Fong Yoneda, development specialist/author of *The Script-Selling Game: A Hollywood Insider's Look at Getting Your Script Sold and Produced*

"Pamela Jaye Smith coalesces mythology, psychology, the body, and plenty of arts and culture references in the making of this utterly unique, very valuable book, reminding us that a character's inner world cannot be ignored in creating a compelling outer-world story."

Brad Schreiber, Vice President
Storytech Literary Consulting; Author, *What Are You Laughing At?*

"Pamela Jaye Smith's ground-breaking book is the first to connect the exciting field of subtle energy and esoteric anatomy with a character's motivation, style, and archetype. By showing how the chakra system affects behavior, she offers writers new pathways to creating authentic, multi-dimensional, and unforgettable personalities. "

Celeste Allegrea Adams
Author, *Keepers of the Dream*; Creatrix Studio

"I always think visually when writing… what I can see and hear. Getting into the character's head *before* you type, before the words hit the paper, is helpful."

Steve Finly, screenwriter
Shadow Warriors, Blackheart, Wishful Thinking

"Pamela Jaye Smith reminds us eloquently that the deepest motivations of human beings have little to do with logic. In fact, as the old philosopher said, logic is a method of achieving high confidence in the wrong conclusions. If you take Pamela's book to heart, your characters may be stubbornly wrong-headed, but they won't be hollow."

Gerald Everett-Jones, writer-producer, La Puerta Productions
Co-author of *Real World Digital Video*

"Reading *Inner Drives* is like attending a week-long intensive seminar on mythology, psychology, physiology, and spirituality all rolled into one. The end result is a fascinating and enlightening guide to the depths of human behavior and motivation that will help any reader create unforgettable, and totally relatable, characters."

Marie Jones, Associate Reviewer, *bookideas.com/Absolutewrite.com*

"Smith's visionary *Inner Drives* is a welcome addition to the art. It gets to the heart of character creation and delves deep into motivation. Should be soundly applauded by actors, writers, and film directors."

Derek Pell, Editor-in-Chief, *www.dingbatmag.com*

"It is a breakthrough resource that clearly outlines an accessible, hands-on approach that will empower your life and/or writing. Certainly it is cliche to say this is a must read, but somewhere on Mt. Olympus Zeus is saying, 'Hmm, so that's why I did that?' "

Devorah Cutler-Rubenstein, President
Noble House Entertainment & The Script Broker

$\mathcal{I}$nner $\mathcal{D}$rives

How to Write and Create Characters Using the Eight Classic Centers of Motivation

Pamela Jaye Smith

LEARNING
RESOURCES
CENTRE
HAVERING
COLLEGE

Published by Michael Wiese Productions
11288 Ventura Boulevard
Suite #621
Studio City, CA 91604
(818) 379-8799, (818) 986-3408 (FAX).
mw@mwp.com
www.mwp.com

Cover design by MWP
Interior design by William Morosi
Copyedited by Paul Norlen
Printed by McNaughton & Gunn

Manufactured in the United States of America

Library of Congress Cataloging-in-Publication Data

Smith, Pamela Jaye, 1948-
  Inner drives : how to write and create characters using the eight
classic centers of motivation / Pamela Jaye Smith.
       p. cm.
  Includes bibliographical references.
  ISBN 1-932907-03-3
 1. Motion picture authorship. 2. Characters and characteristics in
literature 3. Motivation (Psychology) in literature. I. Title.
  PN1996.S58 2005
  808.3'97--dc22

2004025917

Dedication

To Dr. Linda Seger, friend and mentor. With many thanks for her continual guidance and generosity, both personal and professional. Linda helped me grow my MYTHWORKS consulting, speaking, and writing business. She has been instrumental in sending me around the world to write and give seminars. Plus, her enthusiastic introductions and endorsement opened the doors to help get this book published.

To Georgia Lambert, Wisdom teacher and inspiration. Her impressive range of knowledge and outstanding ability to impart it to her students gave me a great example on applying the ancient Wisdoms to our modern lives and storytelling.

To Monty Hayes McMillan, dearest friend, fellow adventurer, and astute puppetmaster. He was there from the beginning, saw the vision, and always provided excellent backup.

Contents

Acknowledgments

First of all, much gratitude to my four close classmates through our long years of Mystery School training: Brian Dyer, Geffrey von Gerlach, Tom Gibson, and Hilary Sloan. Their clever senses of humor often had us doubled over in delighted laughter in the midst of grasping fascinating new esoteric information, and somehow that made the lessons stick all the better. After all, learning should be fun, right?

Thanks to Michael Wiese, Ken Lee, Bill Morosi, Paul Norlen, and the entire staff at Michael Wiese Productions, for their enthusiastic acceptance and assistance in making this book possible.

Many thanks to my Content Contributors: Brian Dyer — for information on musicals and theatre; Aurora Miller — for her input on video and computer games (I certainly could not have done those sections without her youthful perspective and timeless perceptions); Monty Hayes McMillan — for information and insights on matters military and adventurous; Georgia Lambert, Geffrey von Gerlach, and Dr. Claire O' Neill — for their insights into esoteric anatomy and its practical applications.

Feedback and suggestions from many generous people were invaluable in crafting this book full of esoteric information into, hopefully, something accessible to all. Special gratitude to Jill Gurr, Deborah Nikkel, Steven A. Finly, Bruce Logan, Brian Wilson, Mario Bernheim, Monty Hayes McMillan, Judith Claire, and Brian Dyer.

For years worth of encouragement to my writer-self: Monty Hayes McMillan, Sherry Garrett, Paula Lewis, Meg Logan (who first said, "Pammy, you should write a book about this!"), and all the MYTHWORKS clients and seminar attendees who continually asked, "When's your book coming out?"

For helping start my esoteric studies: my grandmother Burt Fox Smith, Craig Lovell, Raja Rao, Sri Krishna Menon, and Carl and LaVerne McMillan.

Many thanks to my fantastic Career Coach, Judith Claire. Her insights and wisdom are supportive, practical guides to professional progress.

For advice, referrals, and seminar support: Renee Wayne Golden, Kathie Fong Yoneda, Donie Nelson, Garrison Hack, and Sue Terry.

And, to all those seekers and teachers who have carried on the Wisdom through all cultures, all times, all places.

$\mathcal{F}$oreword

In every industry, there are those people who contribute something so unique and original, so important and so wise, that they ground and deepen the work that we all do. Pamela Jaye Smith is one of those people.

I have watched Pamela's work in the film industry blossom and grow for at least a decade. I've sat in on her seminars, learned more about her work as a myth consultant, and even team-consulted with her on several myth-oriented projects. And yes, I've had the pleasure of reading this book.

Pamela is smart. She's insightful. And she has carved out a very unique niche — to look at the deepest mythologies that determine who we are and why we behave as we do, and then to show how they relate to story and character. She makes all of this accessible, while never dumbing anything down.

We know that characters drive the story. Pamela helps us understand what drives the characters. She looks at what we're made of — physically, psychologically, spiritually — and how that motivates us, and makes us do what we do. In this book are many examples of well-known characters from films, books, and operas; we might wonder how any writer could create characters as rich as those. Pamela will show you how.

You will deepen your characters through your familiarity with her perceptions.

With humor and style, Pamela takes the character to its basic physical, psychological, and spiritual drives, showing how to construct the character from the inside out. Not only does she look at the character's problems and yearnings, at what is invisible and often unconscious, but also at ways to externalize these through clothes, gestures, surroundings, styles of speech, physical actions, and even phobias and flaws. And she's always filled with hope — with the possibilities of character transformations as the character changes and grows.

Being with Pamela for any amount of time, whether through a book or in one of her seminars or in a one-to-one, always makes me rise to another level of insight. Besides being one of the wisest people I know, she's also one of the most gracious, and carries with her the classiness that we might think of as the best of authentic Southern charm. Yes, she's a Southerner, from Texas, and, besides all this, she can be very funny. I can guarantee that you will have some good laughs and many insights as you read this book.

Inner Drives gives you an opportunity to study, practice, observe, and feel your way into these concepts. It's a book to be read, re-read, studied, experimented with, played with, and used as a guide to create more dynamic, truthful, insightful, deep, profound, and unforgettable characters.

Dr. Linda Seger
Script Consultant and Author, *Making a Good Script Great*

Introduction

Why does the Terminator growl "I'll be back" in *The Terminator*?

Why does Stanley Kowalski bellow "Stellaaaaaaaa!" in *A Streetcar Named Desire*?

Why does Rocky Balboa train and fight against all odds in *Rocky*?

Why does Norma Rae climb up on that factory table and take a stand for her fellow workers in *Norma Rae*?

Why does William Wallace sacrifice his very life for freedom in *Braveheart*?

Why is John Nash so obsessed with mathematics in *A Beautiful Mind*?

What keeps Frodo Baggins on the road to Mount Doom in *The Lord of the Rings*?

Why does the Dalai Lama of Tibet choose flight rather than fight in *Kundun*?

It's motivation, motivation, motivation — each of a different type.

And in a twist on the first rule of real estate — location, location, location — our motivations, and those of the characters we create, do have actual locations. They are the Centers of Motivation, or the *chakras*, as they've been called for thousands of years. The Eight Classic Centers of Motivation are each a focus of physical, psychological, and philosophical concentration which both affect and respond to how we act, feel, and think. They determine our Inner Drives.

This book will give you a working familiarity with tried-and-true ancient tools of character portrayal. You will learn:

- the mythology and history of the Centers
- the characteristics and function of each Center
- how to use each Center in character development and portrayal, including backstory and "ghosts"
- how to plot movement through the Centers for character arcing
- how to position differences between Centers for dramatic conflict
- how to infuse your story with the varied emotions of the Centers
- how to structure your story with believable turning points, revelations, and resolutions
- as a bonus, you'll also learn a tremendous amount about yourself and others in your "real life"

From the Greek Perseus rescuing Andromeda, to the Norse Brunhilde and her Valkyries, to the Maori trickster Maui, effective art in every time and culture makes use of these Centers of Motivation to portray a character's position, yearnings, attempts to grow, temptations to fall, and ultimate success or failure. Many artists do this intuitively yet unconsciously by tapping into what Carl Jung called our "collective unconscious." That's what being an artist is truly about — accessing the higher forms of thought and emotions and bringing them down into physical reality for the rest of us. However, by consciously applying this information based on the Centers of Motivation you can be ever so much more effective in the expression of your own writing, directing, acting, design, and artistry.

Once you have read this book and have become familiar with each of the human body's Eight Classic Centers of Motivation and their unique functions, then you too will be able to use this timeless knowledge to craft much more dynamic and believable characters, just as myth-makers have done with great effectiveness for thousands of years.

Whether you are a Writer, Director, Actor, Development Exec, Designer, or any other type of Storyteller, knowing how to use the Centers of Motivation and the Inner Drives can help you create a powerful, character-driven piece by:

- creating dynamic, authentic characters
- knowing your characters' true motivations
- constructing believable internal character conflict
- enriching the character arc
- creating greater distinction between characters
- enhancing dramatic conflict among characters
- using an actor's "business" to powerfully portray character
- selecting wardrobe to reveal character traits
- designing sets that reflect character conflicts and changes
- learning some very interesting things about yourself and others

So what are these Inner Drives, these Eight Classic Centers of Motivation?

This book deals mainly with the Centers as they relate to character motivation and development, but it's helpful to first get an understanding of what they are and how they work. This ancient system of physiology, psychology, and philosophy has been used by many cultures in many times all around the world to analyze, heal, motivate, entertain, instruct, and inspire humans. Various chapters of this book go into greater detail both about the basis of this knowledge and about how you can use it to your advantage.

The Centers of Motivation are bundles of actual physical nerves and their associated endocrine glands which affect us physically and emotionally through the particular hormones secreted by those glands: sex hormones from the Sacral Center, stress hormones from the Root Center, etc.

Often called *chakras* (a Sanskrit word meaning "wheel"), these Centers are part of the ancient disciplines of yoga, acupuncture, *chi*, energy work, and chiropractic and are gaining more credence every day as modern science develops the instruments to perceive and measure their effects.

The Centers of Motivation are also said to have *etheric* (ee-ther´-ic) counterparts which influence us as well. This etheric body is seen as a web or net lying just outside the physical body; you can see this depicted in medical charts for chiropractic and Oriental medicine. It is the pattern or blueprint into which the atoms of the material world gather to create the physical form of "you." It is said to be the connection between the gross physical and the hyper-physical (metaphysical) worlds, or between physiology and philosophy if you will.

This system of influence works both from the philosophical-to-psychological-to-physical as well as in the other direction from physical-to-psychological-to-philosophical. Many spiritual disciplines train devotees to use their conscious Will to affect their Centers and thus their thoughts, emotions, and physical being.

No one can teach you art. You either have it or you don't. But craft can be mastered. That's where our actual work comes in. "Work?!!?", you shudder, "But I'm an *artist*, my creativity is supposed to just come flowing down from the gods in perfect form." Right. The artist by nature taps into that marvelous realm of inspiration but we bring it down via our own equipment and influences and sometimes those aren't quite perfect, so any help we can get is welcome.

Contrary to some writing teachers who promise "No bothersome theory" and all practicality, I want you to grasp the theory behind the practice. This way, you can keep repeating it because you will understand the principles. It's like the difference between giving a hungry person a fish or teaching her how to fish. I want you to be able not only to fish in the wilds, but also to be able to construct a fish farm and raise the little critters yourselves.

Or in another analogy, I want you to be not just passengers on the airplane of artistic creativity, and not just pilots who can fly the planes, but the aeronautical engineers who can actually design and build the things. You will need to put on your Creative Scientist hat and your Creative Engineer hat here for a little while, but I promise you it will be worth it.

Once you have mastered the information in this book you'll know not only when to plot certain actions, which is where most writing books stop (Inciting Incident on this page, Turning Point on that page), but you will know *what* to do, *why* to do it, and *how* to back it up with appropriate character motivation.

As an added bonus, you can also use this system for self-analysis and self-directed growth, to analyze others as individuals and in groups, and to become more effective participants in those fascinating stories which are our real lives. Plus, you can more fully weave your personal experiences into your art.

The Eight Classic Centers of Motivation and their expressions are:
- Root Center   Sheer Survival, connection to physical form
- Sacral Center   Sex, Fear, Money

    Solar Plexus (a dual Center with diverse expressions)
    - Lower   Personal Power, Greed, Individuality, Exclusivity
    - Higher   Aspiration, Brotherhood, Inclusivity
- Heart Center   Unconditional Love for all humanity
- Throat Center   Conscious Creativity, Communication
- Ajna Center   Balance and Integration of all the Centers
- Crown Center   Connection with higher realms of Energy

The characters in the opening questions of this chapter are, at the story points mentioned, operating from these various Centers:
- Root Center   The Terminator
- Sacral Center   Stanley Kowalski

    Solar Plexus:
    - Lower   Rocky Balboa
    - Higher   Norma Rae
- Heart Center   William Wallace
- Throat Center   John Nash
- Ajna Center   Frodo Baggins
- Crown Center   The Dalai Lama

The best way to use this book is to read it all the way through, then go back and begin applying the information. Section One gives background and explanation of the Inner Drives through the Centers of Motivation, Section Two explains the individual Centers, and Section Three is about how to use the Inner Drives within and between characters, and in various combinations.

The Centers descriptions in Section Two show in detail how a character focused in a particular Center of Motivation will look, sound, feel, act, and react according to their Inner Drives. You will be able to use these insights to make your characters more complex, to create vivid backstories, to plot out opposing attitudes in the characters, and to flush out their personas via other characters who challenge their moods, thoughts, ideals, likes, dislikes, actions, etc. Doing this for each of your characters will make for much more interesting interplay and will help each character dramatically reveal things about themselves and the other characters with whom they interact.

As you progress through this book you'll begin to perceive where some character problems are the result of a scattered focus, or unclear motivation. Selecting a main Center of Motivation will help integrate your characters and make them that much more authentic. Think of the difference in effectiveness between *Spiderman* and the *Hulk* movies of 2003.

Section Three is about movement between and among the Centers for individuals as well as groups of characters. Just as we experience different moods throughout a day, your created characters won't necessarily stay on one Center throughout a story. In fact, it's much more interesting to see how they move about and meet the challenges of different Centers of Motivation. Rocky for instance starts out in a very bleak and defeated Root Center; he's barely getting by in most areas of his life. Throughout the movie he struggles and fights his way up to personal expression, victory, recognition, and rewards at the Lower Solar Plexus.

Norma Rae starts out in a flawed Sacral Center, rather repressed, typically fearful of the bosses and the system, and financially strapped. She rises above this, finds her own voice and strength at the Lower Solar Plexus, and takes a valiant stand for her fellow workers when she climbs up on the table, holds aloft the "Union" sign (a perfect Aspirational Solar Plexus slogan), and inspires others to take a stand for what is correct and good.

Just as dramatic conflict is created by the moves a single character makes up and down their own Centers, conflict is also created as characters interact with other characters on different Centers from themselves. Frodo Baggins, who eventually makes his way to an Ajna Center focus, is buffeted about on his mission by the various Centers of his compatriots (Sam's Lower Solar Plexus buddies-forever loyalty), his allies (including the noble Aragorn at the Higher Solar Plexus and Boromir's self-serving and fatally competitive Lower Solar Plexus), and by the fierce opposition (the Root Center zombie Uruk-hai and the evil dropped-Ajna Saruman).

Sometimes there's no conflict between characters because both are on the same Center in the same way. By moving one of the characters to a different Center or to a more diverse part of each Center's spectrum you can add considerable dramatic conflict. Think of Obi Wan Kenobi and Darth Vader in *Star Wars*, both of whom are on an Ajna Center but are operating from totally diverse sides.

For internal conflict, a character who's torn between their own Centers makes for very good drama. Each Center has its high/low, dark/light, focused/scattered expressions so you have wide latitude to build characters with dramatic conflict yet internal integrity. Two good examples are Charlie Sheen's Bud Fox in *Wall Street* and Spiderman in that eponymous movie.

Creating effective ensembles of characters will be greatly helped by using the Centers of Motivation to be sure every individual's Inner Drives are unique and that your characters all mesh dramatically with each other for effective conflicts and resolutions.

Both men and women in romantic relationships tend to stereotype and be stereotyped, often to their confusion and detriment. We'll explore how these impositions of patterns make for relevant and poignant stories.

Sometimes a character will do what I call "Raising the Dragon" and will make an entire run up the Centers of Motivation. We'll explore this in the films *Groundhog Day, Jacob's Ladder,* and *Under Siege.*

Using these Eight Classic Centers of Motivation and the Inner Drives you will be able to analyze your characters, develop them from the inside out, craft their challenges and growth, and fine tune each character's path through your story. Then you too, like the myth-makers of old, will be able to create dynamic, authentic, and memorable characters. I hope you find this journey informative, inspiring, and fulfilling.

Explaining the Inner Drives

I.

1.
What Are the Inner Drives?

The Terminator, Stanley Kowalski, Rocky and Norma Rae, William Wallace, Rick and Ilsa... they all act differently one from the other. Why? Inner Drives, motivation. What's at the center of their motivation? Emotions, mostly. What affects our emotions? Is it bio-rhythms? The phases of the moon? The amount of caffeine in that double cappuccino? Well, yes, maybe some of all of that. But deeper down it's a question of, to use the old hippie phrase, "Where you're coming from."

Some of the most creative answers to these questions come from what's called the Ancient Wisdom or the teachings of the Mystery Schools, those sometimes secret enclaves of philosophers and scientists who helped craft myths, stories, and religious systems to keep alive the facts and philosophies of the eternal verities. Influences of the Mystery Schools can be found in Tibet, ancient Egypt, Persian Mithraism, Greek Eleusinian rites, Druid rituals, Gnostic Christianity (a la *The Da Vinci Code*), Medieval Alchemists, Rosicrucians, the Masons, and others. Unlike shamanism, which uses the emotions to access altered states, these systems are mentally based and consciously created; they are about gaining control rather than losing control. For example:

High in the wind-swept Tibetan Himalayas, student priests with shaved heads and wide eyes stare in fascination around a large stone slab with holes in each corner for the blood and body fluids. As has been done for thousands of years, their anatomy teacher directs the dissection of a human corpse and instructs the students in the interconnected workings of the body, mind, and spirit.

Hieroglyphs on Egyptian ruins show embalmers and medical practitioners; the proportions of some Egyptian temples are said to reflect the human anatomy, even down to brain structure.

Ancient Maori mythology names various parts of the brain to reflect their actual functions, which were only discovered by modern science in the last few decades.

Students of yoga and the martial arts spend endless hours, days, and years learning to master the functions of the physical body through awareness and manipulation of certain forms of energy focused in specific areas of their bodies.

From Native Americans to Medieval Alchemists, from the authors of the Bible's book of Revelations and the sacred Hindu *Vedas*, and many many more, the system of the Centers of Motivation is an effective tradition of character analysis, motivation, and healing used around the world under many different names. Whether we call them chakras, Centers of Motivation, Inner Drives, Fields of Psychological Focus, layers of the Hierarchical Pyramid of Motivation... these metaphorical representations of the actual endocrine glands and actual hormones explain the driving engines of our humanity, as science is now proving. The endocrine system is where and how we process information from the world around us and within us, whether it's fight-or-flight adrenaline kicked off by stress or the love-drug oxytocin stimulated by physical intimacy.

Knowledge about the Centers of Motivation, home of the Inner Drives, is more prevalent today than ever, so you may already be familiar with the chakras. There are a number of approaches to the system so you'll find some information out in the marketplace that may differ somewhat from what's in this book. Some systems are presented for elementary study, some for more advanced students. Some are more for physical health and mastery and other more esoteric systems are for personal and spiritual growth and initiation. Few of the other systems you may come across will be incorrect. The trick, as with any system, be it exercising for ballet versus boxing, or training to sing rap versus opera, is to work with dedication in the one you've selected for that particular project. The basic principles will be the same and your previous knowledge should easily apply here.

The Eight Classic Centers of Motivation and their relevant concepts are:
- Root Center   Sheer Survival, connection to physical form
- Sacral Center   Sex, Fear, Money
  Solar Plexus
    - Lower   Personal Power, Greed, Exclusivity, Individuality
    - Higher   Aspiration, Brotherhood, Inclusive
- Heart Center   Unconditional Love for all humanity
- Throat Center   Conscious Creativity, Communication
- Ajna Center   Balance and Integration of all the Centers
- Crown Center   Connection with higher realms of energy

There may be many doors and windows into and out of a building, but if only one is open, that's the one that everything must use. In the same way, the Centers of Motivation (chakras) are doorways and windows into and out of our Selves. Just where a character's awareness is currently focused in the Centers along the spine is a determining factor of who they are, how they act and react from moment to moment. It will determine both their motives and their methods, in varying degrees.

Since everything that exists has its own identity and hence a "body", this system of Centers also holds true for relationships, organizations, corporations (which are granted individual human status in U.S. law), events, cultures, nations, and the species of humanity. Some of the more ancient mythic systems have even identified Centers of the planets, the solar system, and beyond.

These Inner Drives, the Centers of Motivation, or chakras, are expressive of and are based upon physiology, psychology, and philosophy.

Understanding the functions of these very different Centers of Motivation will give you good, solid workable tools for dramatic characterizations. Your characters will have internal integrity of drive and goals, strengths and weaknesses, fears and hopes. A character's arc will make sense according to his or her own Inner Drives. You'll have a solid foundation from which to draw for the character's "ghost", that backstory event that has somehow scarred a character and which we later discover to be a hidden motivator for their current actions. For instance, in *Lethal Weapon* the "ghost" of Mel Gibson's character is the death of his wife. In *A Beautiful Mind* John Nash's "ghost" is his mental illness which actually creates ghost people in his troubled mind.

After exploring each of the Centers, you will have the information to create dramatic situations by juxtaposing characters operating from conflicting Centers, craft an individual character's style of speech and physical "business" to reflect their deepest motivations, and use the symbolism of each Center to trigger a specific audience response about each character.

Plus, you'll be able to answer the actor's eternal plea, "What's my motivation?!"

As a bonus you'll also learn more about yourself and others and why we all act and react the way we do. As with all really good storytelling, you'll be holding a mirror up in which we the audience can, if we dare, learn more about ourselves as we journey with your characters through their story.

The Centers of Motivation in Physiology, Psychology, and Philosophy

"Human nature being what it is, a character is always more than just a set of consistencies. People are illogical and unpredictable. They do things that surprise us, startle us, change all our preconceived ideas about them. Many of these characteristics we learn about after knowing someone for a long time. These are the details that are not readily apparent, but that we find particularly compelling, that draw us toward certain people. In the same way, these paradoxes often form the basis for creating a fascinating and unique character."

Dr. Linda Seger, *Creating Unforgettable Characters*

The most dynamic characters are multi-dimensional. Many writing books, teachers, coaches, and consultants urge you to know the character's "backstory." What's their birth order? Family religion? Where'd they go to school and were they a bully or a teacher's pet? What is their overriding fear, hope, strength, weakness? What are they hiding? What's their "ghost"? These kinds of profiles can indeed be helpful in crafting characters.

Even a character as seemingly simple as Indiana Jones in *Raiders of the Lost Ark* has these aspects well-developed. We know his physiology: his physical prowess and stamina are very strong; he's a can-do, athletic kinda guy. We learn about his psychological phobias: snakes and romantic commitment; both complicate his progress through the story. We know his philosophy as an archaeologist: respect for the distant past and integrity towards the profession. We can suppose he's not a fascist since he has such an obvious distaste for Nazis.

In these next sections we'll explore how the Centers of Motivation are based on very real human nature and how they express underlying truths. In the rest of the book you'll learn how to apply these principles to your own characters and stories.

The Centers Explained via Physiology

German philosopher Friedrich Nietzche observed that "The aesthetics of art is nothing but applied physiology." One wonders if he knew how specifically correct he was.

Have you ever had acupuncture? Been to a chiropractor? Done yoga? Studied martial arts? Seen a Jet Li or Jackie Chan movie? Watched Xena: Warrior Princess bounce around her steel *chakram* or paralyze people with a touch to the throat? Something all these have in common is a familiarity with and use of the chakra system. But it isn't just an ancient Oriental system, nor has its wisdom been limited to physicians or warriors.

Chakra is a Sanskrit word meaning "wheel": the motion of *prana* (vitality or life energy) in, through, and around each of these Centers is said to spin like a wheel. To a person with psychic vision they are said to look like little whirlwinds or spirals with the small end at the spinal column and the larger open end turned out away from the body. In the Bible the prophet Ezekiel reported seeing wheels within wheels, which is very similar to a description of a chakra from the ancient Vedic scriptures of a wheel turning upon itself. Each of these Centers is a place where your actual physical body's nervous system gathers into a *ganglia*, or grouping of nerves, and connects to an endocrine gland which produces certain hormones which bring about changes in your body, your emotions, and your mind.

You can find these groupings of nerves on charts of the nervous system in an anatomy book; chiropractor's charts will also show the gatherings with illustrations of how each nexus affects other parts of the body.

Acupuncture, acupressure, chiropractic, Ayurvedic, and Oriental medicine have used these physical Centers and the corresponding glands for thousands of years to analyze and treat imbalances in the human body, emotions, mind, and spirit. These empirical and practical sciences recognize and use the invisible net of energy which sustains the human form. This net lying just outside the physical body is called the *etheric* body and is the pattern or blueprint into which the atoms of the material world gather to create the physical form of "you." The flow of energy through this network can become blocked because of injury, illness, or impinging psychological reasons. Among other things, these healing practices are said to unblock the stuck *chi* or energy and allow it to flow more freely in and through the Centers of Motivation, which promotes healing and increased well-being.

How can working on invisible patterns affect the physical form? The actual physical material of your stomach lining is replaced every seven days, so a chronic stomach problem is the result of a *pattern* in this etheric body. An obvious example of this system in action is the healing of a wound. Some flesh has been lost, cells move in to replace them, the wound is healed and — *voila*, your skin is back. You don't have sick or wounded atoms or molecules, you have sick or wounded patterns into which those molecules form. This is why mind-control, bio-feedback, and cognitive behaviour modification can create seemingly miraculous healings — they work on the etheric patterns rather than on the physical stuff. A lot of genetic research is working in what seems to be a parallel track to analyze and sometimes alter the instructions for cell formation.

This etheric net system can also explain that weird phenomenon of phantom-limb sensations where an amputee can still "feel" and "move" the missing part of their body. Only the physical matter is gone; the pattern is still there. Brain research and consciousness studies are making fascinating inroads along these lines but the hard sciences still haven't answered some of the more basic questions addressed by the esoteric sciences.

Note in the first *Matrix* film that when Neo wakes up naked in his cradle he's got a series of wires plugged into his spine? They're all along his Centers/chakras, feeding him the sensation of being out in a "real" world. The big one that he pulls out from the base of his skull is in a spot often called "The Mouthpiece of God." That whole first *Matrix* movie is full of bits and bobs of esoteric information and philosophy.

The etheric network and its focal points are also used in the martial arts for devastating blows, and martial artists balance their center of gravity in a chakra called the *dan tien*. The Vulcan Death Grip (also used to dramatic effectiveness by Xena: Warrior Princess) uses the Eagle-Wind point on the etheric network to immobilize a nerve Center. Handy information to have, yes?

What's this got to do with Stanley Kowalski yelling "Stellaaaaa!" in *A Streetcar Named Desire* or William Wallace sacrificing himself for freedom in *Braveheart*? The body-mind-soul-spirit connection is a lot more solid than the last five hundred years of rational Western thinking have allowed. The endocrine glands are material-world expressions of the Centers of Motivation and are directly related to the type of personality characteristics associated with that Center. Knowing how these work will help you build strong characters with internal integrity and dramatic conflict whether you are a Writer, Director, Actor, or Designer.

Modern science is daily showing us more and more evidence of how body chemistry influences states of consciousness, from depression to mystical religious experience, something the wise ones in every system have always known and used. Drums, smoke, music, incense, dance, sex, drugs, intoxicating drinks, fasting, chanting, poses and positions — all aspects of ritual are ultimately based on how the physical body works to co-create certain states of mind and spirit.

One of the primary purposes of meditation training is to learn to consciously control the mechanisms of the physical body. Think of that test for Tibetan monks — while sitting in a snow bank they had to be able to dry wet sheets draped over their naked bodies. Now that's mind control. Esoteric teachers promise that the practice of meditation will actually change the brain chemistry of the devotee and modern brain science can now measure those actual changes.

There's a whole other fascinating realm of how people specially trained to do so can affect other people's Centers for good or for ill. Just think of that grade-school game of telling someone how ill they look until, sure enough, they go home sick. There's a sequence in Lawrence Durrell's *Alexandria Quartet* novels where a rather mischievous fellow bets he can create a love affair between two strangers and proceeds to privately tell each of them that the other is secretly crazy about them. The two do fall madly, heart-racingly in love, based solely on their imagination's affect on their emotions and body.

From tribal shamanism to Aldous Huxley's "doors of perception", from mother-child bonding to hyper-aggression, from deep depression to states of ecstasy — all these moods and states of being are dependent to a great deal upon the influence of hormones secreted by the endocrine glands which are influenced by the Centers of Motivation of the etheric body, which in turn are motivated by the Self, consciously or unconsciously. In your case, the character's Centers will be controlled by you, their creator.

Recent brain studies have shown that the same brain activity occurs whether someone smells something foul or simply sees someone else's expression when they smell something foul. Watch someone bite a lemon and your mouth scrunches up. Watch someone yawn and you're soon yawning, too. Listen to someone laugh and it's hard not to at least smile. Science is now validating what story-tellers have known for aeons: even from a distance or in a make-believe situation, other people's actions can have a dramatic affect on us. It's part of the mechanics of how theatre, movies, music, and art work.

The Centers Explained via Psychology

You can't "see" an Oedipal complex, but you can see the nexus of nerves between the Lumbar Vertebrae #4 and #5 which forms the physical basis for the Sacral Center, where Sex-Fear-Money live and from which the Oedipus complex might be said to spring.

The medieval system of character analysis, based on the theories of Hippocrates the Father of Medicine, attributed four types of humours to four personalities: sanguine (cheerful), splenic (melancholic), phlegmatic (calm), and bilious (ill-tempered). These were closely tied in with the endocrine glands, but the system was not as precise or extensive as the Centers system.

Psychologist Abraham Maslow constructed a Psychological Motivation Pyramid which reflects the distribution of the Centers in humanity today. The majority of people are at the bottom of the pyramid, concerned about physical survival. As individuals move up through needs for companionship towards self-actualization, the pyramid narrows and becomes rather rarefied towards the top. Rather than a continued climb upwards, however, the Wisdom Teachings show individuals hopping all over the place as we aspire to alleviate our pain, learn new information, put it to use, are pleased with ourselves, backslide, aspire again, learn anew, etc. Chapters in Section Three of this book will explore those Character Arcings and Center Transfers.

Early twentieth-century Austrian psychiatrist Dr. Sigmund Freud argued that it's all either pain or pleasure, the libido (sex drive), the hidden Id. A rather limited view of humanity. Although he was right about a few of the lower Centers, it's not the whole picture by any means. Some interesting new research is identifying the actual brain regions where the libido resides and is shedding new light on broader implications of Freud's work that he probably didn't even realize.

Behaviorism sees simple survival as the basic motivation for actions. Whereas Freud saw gaining pleasure and/or avoiding pain as the motivation behind all actions, Austrian psychiatrist Alfred Adler posited the motivation of personal Will, taking a note from German philosophers Nietzsche and Schopenhauer. Rocky Balboa is a great example of strong personal Will.

Swiss psychiatrist, symbolist, alchemist, and mystic Dr. Carl Jung proposed a more comprehensive approach to analysis that took into account the collective unconscious and its archetypes: that sea of energy, thought-forms, and emotional-forms in which we all swim throughout our lives and dreams. Only our physical bodies belong to us alone. Our emotional, mental, and spiritual bodies are said to share territory and substance with each other, with the past, and perhaps even with the future and other dimensions — which is one explanation of how Jung's collective unconscious, as well as some psychic phenomena and synchronicity, may work.

Other systems of analysis are the Meyers-Briggs and Enneagrams, both of which use versions of archetypes, which can be seen as personifications of the Centers of Motivation.

A current fad in therapy is that there are only four emotions: glad, sad, mad, and fear. A 1998 Ohio State University study identified fifteen basic desires and values.

Dr. Candace Pert's book *The Molecules of Emotion* recounts the Nobel Prize-winning discovery of how our entire bodies, not just our brains, are wired to receive the chemical signals from hormones and thus affect us emotionally. Dr. Thomas R. Damasio's *Descartes' Error: Emotion, Reason and the Human Brain* connects the mind and the brain with emotions and actions in a revealing new view of our physiological-psychological matrix that reflects the ancient philosophies.

CAT scans, PET scans, Magnetic Resonance Imagery (MRIs) and ever-increasing intricacy of in-depth neurophysical and neurochemical analyses reveal how the various systems of the body act, react, and interact with each other and with that ineffable thing called mind, or consciousness. Science is beginning to explain much of what we used to think was beyond the realm of science and into the realm of the emotional, the psychic, the spiritual. This isn't to say Western science explains away these experiences but rather that it explains them according to modern instruments and systems. The ancient Wisdom Teachings have been doing that for aeons using metaphors and myths for the general public and more scientific terminology (often in Sanskrit, the ancient language of the Hindus) for the initiates of their Mystery Schools.

Modern pop psychology with visualization techniques, neuro-linguistic re-programming, and meditation-for-money-love-and-Mercedes-Benzes operates within the parameters of a couple of specific Centers, as we shall see.

Whether consciously or not, practitioners of physical and psychological arts and sciences have used the inter-relations of the Centers for thousands of years to affect changes in the bodies, minds, and souls of themselves and fellow humans.

They have most often communicated this information through myths.

The Centers Expressed via Philosophy, Myth, and Art

Myths are the stories we tell ourselves to explain the world around us and within us.

Wisdom Teachings throughout the world acknowledge these seven Centers of focused energy within man and the cosmos. The seven planets, the seven steps of ancient Persia's Mithraic religious system, the seven notches on the Siberian shamanic tree, the seven-stepped Babylonian ziggurat, the seven candles of the Jewish Menorah, the seven Churches in the Book of Revelation... all are delineations and representations of these energy patterns that influence human activity and define our personalities.

Prana, the very energy of life itself, is said to enter the human body and activate various Centers according to a person's level of consciousness and physical health. How your character acts, reacts, and interacts with life will be determined by where on the Center system you have their awareness most often and most strongly focused. This can and does change quite often according to what's going on in both their inner and outer worlds, but there's usually a predominant Center of Focus for a character at any one time.

The goal of most spiritual systems (but not necessarily religions, which often get bogged down in bureaucracy and separatism) is to have us consciously uplift our Center of Focus to the highest frequency and to have all the other Centers operating under the directing Will of the overshadowing spiritual soul, god/goddess, higher energies, whatever terminology a person uses to express that-which-is-greater-than-self. Interestingly enough the Heart Center is higher in frequency than some of the Centers which are higher up in placement on the physical body. Like the Crown Center, the Heart Center is not an aspect of the personality, the individual separate self, but is rather considered an aspect of the soul. We'll see more about this in the sections on each Center.

Many stories of a hero's journey are symbolic of a trip up and down these various Centers of Motivation or states of consciousness. The Greek tales of both Hercules and Ulysses follow this pattern; once you know the symbols of each Center their fantastic adventures take on deeper meaning. In the movies *Groundhog Day, Jacob's Ladder,* and *Under Siege* the heroes likewise do a Centers run, which we'll look at more closely in the chapter in Section Three, "Mythic Structure: Raising The Dragon."

Ishtar, the Assyro-Babylonian Goddess of Love and War, had to pass through seven gates and give up seven items of her regency, goddesshood, and identity and become stark naked on her way to the underworld.

During the annual pilgrimage or *hajj* to Mecca, Moslems make seven circumambulations of the Ka'bah and also run seven times between Mt. Safa and Mt. Marwah.

The Dance of the Seven Veils is often interpreted as a passage of the consciousness through the seven Centers of Motivation, which are said to have protective webbing separating one from the other.

Twelfth-century Persian mathematician and poet Omar Khayyam writes in his *Rubaiyat* about the various aspects of enlightenment and initiation into higher levels of consciousness. The book is ancient Wisdom disguised as gorgeous poetry about love, drinking, philosophy, and death. This particular quatrain specifically addresses the rise of one's awareness through the seven Centers or Gates, where the Root Center is the grounding to Earth, the Crown Center is Saturn, and each ganglia of nerves (a Center/chakra) is symbolized as a Knot:

> *Up from Earth's Center through the Seventh Gate*
> *I rose, and on the Throne of Saturn sate,*
> *And many Knots unravel'd by the Road;*
> *But not the Knot of Human Death and Fate.*
> *The Rubaiyat,* Omar Khayyam

Many of the beasts or half-beast/half-man creatures of folklore and myth are symbols of a particular Center of Motivation. You'll see more of that as we explore the individual Centers.

The iconography of the Christian saints also reveals knowledge of the chakras. Saint Michael is shown on foot with his sword piercing the heart of the dragon whereas Saint George is shown mounted on horseback with his lance piercing the throat of the dragon, and there's usually a damsel in distress somewhere in the background, often in a cave (the thalamus or "bridal chamber" in the head).

Each saint's imagery carries symbolic meaning about the soul's approach to the energies and dangers of the physical world.

Some schools of thought pose a connection among Shakespeare, Sir Francis Bacon, and the Rosicrucians and see many esoteric truths (as well as great drama and comedy) in the sonnets and plays of the Bard of Avon.

In Bela Bartok's opera about Bluebeard, the curious wife Judith ignored the warnings, opened seven Doors to the Soul, and discovered some other ugly things along the way.

In *The Lord of the Rings*, the city of Minas Tirith has seven levels with a gate between each one and a tree at the summit. How much more symbolic can you get?

A great many myths are stories specifically crafted to guide the seeker along the Path of Wisdom from Center to Center with tips about how best to conquer and control each of the Centers. They are couched in such a way as to be simply good stories as well as guidebooks and were invaluable methods to pass along the ancient truths back when very few people were literate or able to study in the Mystery Schools.

So why do we even have these Centers of Motivation, these various Inner Drivers? In the Mystery Schools it is said that the life energy of humanity was supposed to be focused in the head but that it dropped to the Root Center at the base of the spine where the desire to be alive in a physical form manifests as Sheer Survival. This is one of the great Falls and is referred to in the Judeo-Christian story of the serpent tempting Eve in the Garden of Eden. Interestingly enough, the problem there wasn't about sex, but eating. Actually, it was about a lot of things and is a fascinating concept that has been explored at great length by mythologists, anthropologists, sociologists, philosophers, and theologians for millennia. A number of books and articles have been written about the various Falls in various cultures. I myself have written one titled "Beware the Ides of March, or, Legends of the Falls"; the article is available through the MYTHWORKS website.

In Greco-Roman mythology the Fall is echoed in the story of the vain Narcissus falling into his own reflection. Aesop tells the fable of a greedy dog who, catching his own reflection in a stream and wanting the bigger bone in the mouth of that dog down there in the water, dropped the very real bone from his own mouth, and in a fit of avarice plunged into the water and drowned.

The Hindu Vedic system has Shiva, the masculine aspect of the kundalini energy (the principle of intelligence), at *Sahasrara*, the Crown Center, and Shakti, the feminine aspect, "fallen" into *Muladhara*, the Root Center. The union of Shiva and Shakti is similar to the Christian concept of the Church as the bride of Christ. In any case, it's about opposite poles and the magnetic field between them. We'll see how this can apply to your stories in Section Three, "Mythic Structure: Centers Transfers."

The medical symbol of the *caduceus* is a direct reference to the energies of the chakra system: the staff is the spinal column and the serpents are the two currents of energy twining up and down it. In Sanskrit the feminine current is named *Ida* and the masculine one *Pingala*. Where they cross in their spiraling up the spinal column we find the major Centers of Motivation.

Religious and spiritual arts consistently use the symbolisms of the chakras to portray various stages of enlightenment: the open hearts of Catholic Jesus and Mary (Heart Center), Buddha's topknot (Crown Center), the stigmata of saints (the Centers in the palms of the hands are related to the Heart Center). Hindu and Tibetan iconography as well as Catholic and Episcopal rituals have specific colors and symbols for specific seasons, events, gods, and goddesses. Even so-called modern art often has elements of the esoteric, as evidenced by Wassily Kandinsky and some of his compatriots who used the proportions of so-called sacred geometry and attempted to portray the concepts and qualities behind physical appearance. His book *Concerning the Spiritual in Art* explains it quite well.

This esoteric anatomy is reflected in other art pieces as well, such as the Celtic harp, spiral staircases, mazes, Klingon warbirds and Minbari White Star ships, which mimic the ventricles of the brain.

Music composed by initiates of the Mystery Schools is specifically designed to affect the listener in certain Centers. Most music will do that anyway; just think of the different effects on your body of marching songs, rock and roll, a spiritual, or an intricate Haydn symphony. Some composers are more obvious about the influence of the ancient Wisdom and if you know what to look for you can find arcane secrets in the librettos of many operas. Puccini's *Turandot* is said to contain clues to heights of personal initiation and Richard Wagner's *Parsifal* is replete with references to fallen kundalini (the fallen vamp-babe Kundry) and all sorts of self-initiation steps. There's even a rumour that Mozart was assassinated for making public such esoteric secrets in *The Magic Flute*.

Architecture employing the Wisdom Teachings has a very dynamic affect on the individual, be it the evocative mystery of Stonehenge in England, the intricacies of Angkor Wat in Cambodia, the Mesoamerican pyramid temples, or the use of the Golden Mean in Europe's Gothic cathedrals.

Many early dramas were designed to convey spiritual truths. The Mystery Schools in particular used ceremony and dramatization to involve the watcher and take them through a cathartic experience, often focusing on different Centers as the Initiate proceeded through the system. The rituals of the Persian religion of Mithra did this as do most religious and spiritual systems, be they shamanic traditions, Yoruba trance dances, Masonry, or the High Mass of Catholic and Anglican Churches.

In essence, all really good storytelling (as opposed to simple entertainment) conveys some higher truth. That's what makes it good — it reveals something universal to all of humanity through the dramatic conflicts and resolutions of individual characters.

By learning how to use the Eight Classic Centers of Motivation to craft your characters and your stories, you will be tapping into a timeless system of powerful communication and inspiration.

2.
$\mathcal{H}$ow to Use the Inner Drives Centers of Motivation Profiles

So how can you use these Centers of Motivation to create unique and memorable characters? Section Two will give you a solid familiarity with each of the Centers and offer you opportunities to practice working with the Inner Drives. Each Center Chapter begins with "The Theory" and lots of examples to help you understand the concepts and how they are applied, then offers "The Practice" with exercises for your characters and for yourself.

In explaining the Centers from which a character's Inner Drives spring, we begin at the very bottom. In the earliest stages of formation of an embryo there is a tiny clump of cells called the *kanda* knot from which the spinal column unfolds upwards. The development of the various Centers up around the rising spinal column is reflected in the psychological growth of an individual, as well as in other living units such as groups, civilizations, species, and, it is theorized, the cosmos.

You may have heard that "Ontology Recapitulates Phylogeny" which means that the growth process of the individual goes through the growth process of life: the human embryo goes through the various stages of evolution from single-cell organism to gilled fish to tailed amphibian to mammal with opposable thumbs. So too humans ideally move up through the Centers of Motivation as they grow from an infant learning to survive in the physical world (Root Center), go through puberty (Sacral Center), reject family and strive to become individuals (Lower Solar Plexus Center), learn to take responsibility for others (Aspirational Solar Plexus Center), develop mental abilities and choose a profession (Throat Center), etc.

The higher a person goes in their main Center of Motivation, the more influence that will have on their own lower Centers. This dynamic offers marvelous opportunities for character change. Section Three on "Mythic Structure" explores this in greater detail.

Coming-of-age stories can make particular use of this natural progress in starting a character out on a lower Center and then following their struggles to move to higher Centers, such as in *My Life As a Dog* and *Fast Times at Ridgemont High*.

Horror stories and war stories often take characters from higher levels and force them into lower Centers where they spend time and energy simply trying to survive, such as in *Scream* and *The Thin Red Line*. Some stories have heroes who hit all of the Centers, such as *Groundhog Day* and *Under Siege*. These variations and others are covered in the chapters on Mythic Structure.

Below are explanations of what you will find in the Centers chapters and how to use that information.

A. The Theory

This Section in each Center chapter includes:
- Motivation
- Location
- Endocrine Glands & Hormones
- Mythic Meaning
- Archetypes
- Symbols
- Planets & Astrological Signs
- Colors, Shapes, Materials
- Clothing
- Styles of Speech
- Physical Actions
- Foibles, Phobias, Foods
- Wounds & Deaths
- Examples

You can refer back to these explanations as you go through the various chapters.

Motivation — tells you each Center's "log-line," a quick explanation of what it's about.

Location — tells you where on the physical body the Center/chakra lies.

Endocrine Glands & Hormones — a layman's look at how these physical chemical factories of our bodies work, which gland is stimulated by each Center, and the effects of the hormones it produces.

Mythic Meaning — mythic characters, stories, and themes based on the particular level of consciousness associated with each Center of Motivation. Once you've become familiar with the Centers you will be able to see their influence in many other myths and stories.

Archetypes — these universal personality patterns have been used by creators of myth to personify the energy and behavior of individual Centers. When a person aligns with an Archetype they are said to become infused with the energy of that overarching universal personality type. Thus if a person wants to be a more effective warrior they could consciously align with the Warrior Archetype and tap into that pattern of honor, courage, compassion, and self-sacrifice for the greater good.

By aligning your characters with Archetypes you will not only give them more authenticity but you will also have a more direct link to the rest of us humans who have embedded within us an intuitive understanding of and familiarity with the powerful Archetypes.

Symbols — the shorthand of human communication. Modern scientific technology reveals more every day about where and how in the brain we process symbols, colors, and sounds. There are specific areas inside our heads that "light up" when we see a square, a sphere, a triangle. This is physical proof of what the myth-makers have always known: There is a universal language above and beyond words and it can be used in stories, art, architecture, and music to affect and influence people, regardless of their cultural or educational background.

Symbols drawn from a number of systems can be used in your characters' dialogue, actions, names, costumes, set dressing, collections, etc. to strengthen your audience's usually unconscious but nonetheless affective association of a character with a particular Center. What the audience will be conscious of is how "authentic" your characters seem.

Planets & Astrological Signs — make good background enrichment for the story itself and can also be woven into character names, costumes, collections, and environments. It's also a fun revelation-through-dialogue to have a character spouting off astrological signs, interpretations, tendencies, etc. Stella comments on Stanley's sign in *A Streetcar Named Desire* (he's a Capricorn).

Some signs show up in a couple of Centers: if you're familiar with astrology you'll know that each of the twelve signs of the zodiac has various expressions. People will nod knowingly to learn that the orderly person is a Libra or that the sneaky sex addict is a Scorpio. These stereotypes seem to hold some truths; plus, they are familiar to a great many in your audience so using them will help make yet another connection to your characters' backstories and background.

Colors, Shapes, Materials, & Clothing — enhance a character's personality through the use of costumes, sets, and surroundings. These sections will be particularly valuable for novelists, directors, and designers.

Even in a screenplay, where most of the visuals are left to the director and production designer, the screenwriter can use scene descriptions to build in a look that supports a particular Center, be it a sterile laboratory, a busy police station, or a romantic bathroom full of candles.

Dressing the Terminator in black biker leathers tells us something completely different about this character than the stylish, sexy outfits Julia Roberts wears in *Pretty Woman*. And look at the differences in attire between Miss Roberts in the former film and her look in *Erin Brockovich*. You might dress your *femme fatale* in slinky red but probably not in flowery pastel pink, and a hero in pink is pretty unthinkable, unless he's *Mrs. Doubtfire*.

Your descriptions of places can also benefit from use of shapes and colors specific to particular chakras. In Linda Seger's book *Advanced Screenwriting* she draws attention to the use of moisture and dryness in *The English Patient*, where moisture is emotional and sensual, i.e. Sacral.

Styles of Speech — when based on a character's dominant Center greatly enhance the power of what they're saying. Think of the difference between Gary Cooper's laconic Lower Solar Plexus "Yup" and the mathematical Throat Center blathering of John Nash in *A Beautiful Mind*. Think also of the difference between the lyrical and rhythmic Throat Center dialogue of *Shakespeare in Love* and the Root Center utterances of *Predator*.

In a brief example, look at the differences in these sentences:

I *think* we should do this.   Throat Center (conscious creativity)
I *believe* we should do this. Heart Center (higher aspirations)
I *want* us to do this.   Solar Plexus Center (personal will and power)
I *need* for us to do this.   Sacral Center (sex, fear, money)
I *must* do this!   Root Center (sheer survival)

Present tense implies authority: "I want to talk to you." Use of past tense, gerunds, or intransitive words implies a position of inferiority: "I was wondering if I could have a word with you."

Physical Actions — will be quite different according to the Center of Focus. A Throat-Centered character might pick at their throat, rub their neck, loosen a collar, etc. A Lower Solar Plexus person could hook thumbs over their belt, place hands on hips, draw their hands continually in towards that area. A person struck by jealousy might double over and clench their pain into their Sacral Center.

Depending on their focus, a character will walk heavy on their heels, or spring off from their toes, or swagger, etc. One of the best ways to see the differences here is to compare the same actor in two different roles. Think of Anthony Hopkins in *Remains of the Day* with a suppressed Sacral Center and the same Mr.

Hopkins prowling in *Silence of the Lambs*, playing an Ajna Center dropped down to the Root Center. Another wide-ranging example would be Meryl Streep playing the graceful, self-contained Throat Centered Isak Dinesen in *Out of Africa* versus her role as the hesitant, plain, Lower Solar Plexus lower-class religious mom in *A Cry in the Dark*.

Descriptions of how a character moves will give the director and actors powerful insights into that character. Certainly the novelist has room, and the obligation, to be very descriptive and to draw pictures with their words. The screenwriter's job is just the opposite: to draw a vivid picture with as few words as possible.

This is where the creative use of vivid words, including descriptive verbs, gerunds, adjectives, and adverbs can be of immense help. Will you have your characters striding, mincing, or strolling across a room? Will they mix a drink furiously or sensuously? This section of the Centers profiles helps you describe your characters' actions in ways that will draw them with clarity and intensity... even if they are a befuddled and meek person.

Try walking across a room with different centers of gravity: your head, your chest, your Sacral Center. You can feel for yourself that there's a decidedly different gait and posture for each one. In fact, in the security industry there's an addition to fingerprints and iris recognition — a new security device will analyze the gait (walking style) of potential perps.

Foibles, Phobias, Foods — reflect the fact that just as a change in our chemical balance (via coffee, Prozac, St. John's Wort, marijuana, etc.) changes the way we move and act, so too will changes in the predominance of a particular Center and its internal chemicals affect the way your characters move and act.

Aligning a character's illnesses, ailments, phobias, tendencies, and moods to their main Center of Motivation will enhance the authenticity of their own internal antagonist. A clean-freak, a claustrophobe, and someone with acrophobia can each be expressing different Centers.

The goals of addicts will be different at each Center: comfort at the Sacral, control at the Solar Plexus, perfection at the Throat.

Phobias make for such fascinating characters, be it Indiana Jones and those snakes, or Jimmy Stewart's vertigo. Illnesses are also excellent dramatic devices, whether it's *Camille's* consumption or the Ebola of *Outbreak*.

And what are your characters going to eat? Food scenes can reveal so very much about characters. Think of the exceptionally sensual eating-in-bed scene from

Tom Jones. Then there's Kathleen Turner's lovelorn Joan in *Romancing the Stone* comforting herself with ice cream. A wonderful food bit occurs in *Amadeus* when Salieri offers Mrs. Mozart the candied chestnuts called Nipples of Venus, white mounds tipped with chocolate; her low-cut dress forms her body into a reflection of the candies.

Wounds & Deaths — "Live by the sword, die by the sword." A character's Wounds and Death, like a character's opponent, should be worthy and be in alignment with the character's goals and challenges in life. No Bambi versus Godzilla, please. You wouldn't want Colonel Kurtz to actually die of malaria in *Apocalypse Now*; much better he gets his head chopped off like the sacrificial bull. So unless you're going for the ironic or the comic (*Fargo*), you'll want a character's demise to fit their desires.

For interesting examples you could view John Wayne's movies, after you've read this book so you can make the connections between the Centers and his Wounds and Deaths. In *The Sands of Iwo Jima* he's a tough sergeant who gets shot in the heart, from behind, after exclaiming with heartfelt sincerity and excitement what a great day he's having. In *The Shootist* he's a man at the beginning of the twentieth century trying to phase out of his old way of life, but his past won't let him change; he's got cancer, symbolic if you will of old things, inappropriate things, alien things. Or how about Charlton Heston in *Midway*: his hand is burned and he can't shake hands with his son (tiny Centers in the palms of the hand connect with the Heart Center).

If the character is a bad person, have the wound on the left side (left in Latin is *sinistra*). If a good person, on the right.

Examples — illustrate the expression of each of the Centers of Motivation in people's lives and activities, in works of art, history, current events, and storytelling throughout the ages. These will serve as reference points for you to get your own story into a good Centers alignment.

B. The Practice

Each Center Chapter includes suggestions both to get you the creator "into the mood" and suggestions on how to use the information to craft your characters more solidly on the selected Center.

1. FOR YOUR CHARACTERS

Here you will create Character Profiles with specific descriptions, qualities, actions, dialogue, etc. selected from aspects listed in each category of the Center Chapters.

Character Profile — uses aspects from as many categories of the profiles as possible for each character: colors, clothes, styles of action, etc. You won't use each and every aspect from a category for each character, but rather will select an aspect here, a quality there, up to a couple of pages worth of information. This is how you will keep your characters unique: the qualities you select and the way you combine them with other aspects will be uniquely yours.

Keep in mind that many aspects have a positive side and a negative side. The "Sliding Scale" Chapter in the "Mythic Structure" section explains this in detail. If you're building a dark character you would take an aspect to its most destructive and separative, then back off towards the Center of the scale until it feels natural for that character. Play with the Sliding Scales until you have a character who resonates with an internal truth; until you feel they have moved from stereotype to archetype.

For instance, the Terminator in the first movie is on the dark side of the Root Center, but Ripley in *Alien(s)* and the businessmen in *Deliverance* have all been thrust into the Root Center and are simply trying to survive. Yes, they act violently and kill, but the motives are radically different.

Photos — of actors you visualize portraying your characters in an appropriate pose, clothing, and action are helpful to some people in their creative process. For instance, if you're creating a Throat Center character, you might select a photo of Ralph Fiennes in his role in *Quiz Show* or Russell Crowe in *A Beautiful Mind*. If you aren't writing with a particular performer in mind, find a generic person from a magazine or newspaper who resembles your character. Draw it if you must. But draw it in the appropriate style: sensuously for Sacral, neatly for Throat, etc.

Profile Collage — like most designers do, you too could create a separate collage for each character which would include photos, clippings, and drawings of the type of clothes, collections, styles, fabrics, etc. that signify their Center.

You could also create a large collage with all your main characters on it to show how unique each one is and how they compare to and relate with each other.

The ID Statement — though we're told not to have our dialogue "on the nose," there are certain times when people just simply must say what they mean and what they are about. For each of your pivotal characters (and that can be a main, secondary, or tertiary character) it's sometimes important for them to come right out and say where they're coming from. E.g. "I'm just trying to survive here," "Don't you understand; I need you," "Stelllaaaaaaaa!," "For Scotland and for freedom!" Even if the character is oblique about the ID Statement, you the creator should know what it is so your characters' words come from their home truth.

Note Cards — are valuable distillations of character. Create a note card for each character, listing the main characteristics selected from the categories for their Center. Construct and decorate the cards as appropriate: suggestions appear in each Center.

Washes — an effective way to analyze and adjust each of the characters in your story is to read through the piece as if you were that particular character. See that all their actions and dialogue are in alignment with the selected Inner Drives characteristics. Actors often complain that, "My character wouldn't say or do that." So do this ahead of time. Read the work aloud to hear how it sounds. Perform the actions to see if they feel right. Set up a reading with colleagues, or professional actors if possible, then sit back, observe, and take notes. That will really give you a sense of whether or not you have created unique motivation, voice, and action for each individual in your story.

Add — your own assessments to the EXAMPLES. Write on the pages. Add to my lists. The more you actively work with the Centers, the more adept you will become at using them until it's simply second nature for you.

2. FOR YOURSELF

Whether doing your first write-through or tweaking the latest draft with individual "washes," you can get in the mood of the appropriate Center by wearing the clothes, eating the food, playing the music, watching the movies, and so forth of that particular Center. This can give you a working familiarity with those Centers where you ordinarily may not spend much time. Yet to be a facile creator of character you need to know a lot about various different types of characters.

This exercise will help immensely because it will allow you to walk that mile in the other person's shoes, or boots, or ballet slippers, or....

Watch the Movies, Shows, etc. — have a media marathon and steep yourself in the frequency of that Center.

Read the Books — observe patterns of speech, styles of writing, visual descriptions, and how they project your selected Center of Motivation.

Walk the Walk, Talk the Talk — so here's a challenge for you. Though most writers are not actors — at least not on purpose — it is generally agreed that if you understand what an actor must do with the words and directions you give them you will be a better writer. Writers and directors are encouraged to take acting classes, and one of the best ways to find out if your project is working is to have a live reading so you can see and hear your written words come to life through the actors' words and actions.

Get a jump on this valuable process by practicing one of the oldest disciplines in the Mystery Schools and the Wisdom Teachings — *Acting As If*. One of the best ways to train for anything, be it a piano concert or a golf game, is to practice it in your mind and to *Act As If* you have already reached the pinnacle of accomplishment. The marketplace is crowded with variations on this theme in any number of arenas, from team sports, to losing weight, to manifesting a soul mate.

Here's how to use the *As If* principle in your creation of characters. Read this book all the way through, then begin an experiment that will last eight weeks. For one week at a time become focused in one particular Center of Motivation and its Inner Drives. Dress, eat, move, talk, think, and feel as would, for instance, a Root Centered person or a Sacral Centered person.

You will also be the Observer, taking note of your own feelings and reactions and the comments and actions of others.

Now you might say, "But gosh, I can't be going around killing people or seducing everyone" (although depending on the level of stress in your life you might well like to at times). True. But what you can do is project the particular frequency of a Center. And it does work.

When I was studying this aspect of the Wisdom Teachings we had the same assignment and during the time we were doing a Warrior (Lower Solar Plexus) focus I attended a formal event at the elegant, high-fancy Biltmore Hotel in downtown L.A. So there I was in a foo-foo girly dress, with curly hair and high heels, accompanied by a handsome friend in a tuxedo who'd broken his foot and was on crutches. A nice young bellhop kindly helped my friend and me onto an elevator. As he turned to leave, the bellhop said to my friend (who actually has a warrior-military background), "Take care, have a nice evening." Then he turned to me, stood up straight, said "Good evening, sir," and *saluted me*!

As the elevator doors closed, my friend, who knew I was doing these studies and practices, turned to me with astonishment and said, "Wow, that Wisdom stuff really works." Yes, it does.

The more you understand these Centers of Motivation from personal experience, the better you can use them to create unique, believable, authentic characters.

This exercise is much more effective if you *do not tell anyone* what you are doing! Yes, I know I had told my friend, and everyone in our classes knew we were doing it, but the world at large did not. You want to gauge the results of your actions, not the effects of your telling people about your actions. Besides, talking about something before it happens can diffuse the energy. Stay silent, hold your focus, be observant.

So give it a try. A Center a week. It'll be fun and informative, with the extra benefit of deepening and honing your skills as a storyteller and creator of great characters.

3. ANALYZING THE WALK/TALK EXERCISE

The third section helps further explore your own experience in each Center. This will help you understand and create believable characters on each Center because you will have not only "lived" it but you will have analyzed it and absorbed that knowledge.

After you have done the WALK/TALK exercise, complete this analysis. You might redo this in your computer so you can fill it out separately for each Center and for the second, third or more times that you WALK/TALK a Center.

Walk/Talk Exercise Analysis Questions
- What difficulties did you have in assuming this frequency?
- What memories did it bring up for you?
- How did you deal with them? Forgiveness, reconciliation, denial?
- What negative qualities related to this Center did you identify within yourself? Within others?
- If you choose to transmute those negative aspects, how will you go about that?
- What positive qualities related to this Center did you identify within yourself? Within others?
- If you choose to enhance those positive aspects, how will you go about that?
- How did others react to you? Give at least three accounts.
- What did others say to you? Recount at least three comments.
- Identify three individuals and/or their words or actions that you came into contact with who were on this Center during your experiment.
- Name three situations or events in your immediate environment that seem to be on this same Center of Motivation.
- Name three movies or media events/products on this Center.
- Name three situations or events in the larger environment — such as your city or state, your country or the world at large — that seem to be on this Center.
- If you could bring more balance into one of these situations, how would you do that?

C. Conclusion

Let's move now into our exploration of each of the Centers of Motivation, home of the Inner Drives.

The Eight Classic Centers of Motivation

II.

3.
Root Center

Why does the Terminator growl, "I'll be back"? Because he's programmed to kill and will not stop until that mission is completed.

A killing machine is scary because there's no way to stop or deflect it with human logic, reasoning, or emotion. Only physical action will deter it. If you're doing a Battling Demons story, creating a character out to kill, or one who is the target of a killer, this section is for you.

As movie critic Joe Bob Briggs often opined about some chop-socky, fu-fighting films, there is "no plot to get in the way of the action." Think *Kill Bill* or *The Replacement Killers*. You, however, will of course want to have a fabulous plot, but always remember that for certain characters at certain times in your story, it is really only about sheer survival, either theirs or someone else's.

A. The Theory

MOTIVATION: SHEER SURVIVAL

- The drive to be in a physical body and to stay alive: physical survival, animal nature, instinct, robotic
- The desire to connect with the actual earth
- The need to be grounded, to be in touch with the physical
- The cold rage to kill and destroy
- The desperate drive to survive at all costs when life is threatened
- The later phase of life associated with destruction and decay, which are necessary for new life to arise

LOCATION

Base of the spine, at the end of the coccyx (tail bone) where the bones curve inward.

ENDOCRINE GLANDS & HORMONES

Luschka's Gland or the *Coccygeal Gland* is a tiny gland whose function is not yet fully determined by Western science, but it is listed in *Gray's Anatomy*. In the Wisdom tradition this pebble-like little gland is often called The Stone and can be seen in the symbolism of the stone over Jesus' burial cave and in the stones of sacrificial altars. When in the course of treading the Path of Enlightenment an individual reaches a certain stage and reunites all the higher Centers, this stone (Luschka's

Gland) is said to dissolve or to roll away, thereby liberating the kundalini energy formerly trapped in matter so that it can ascend up the spinal column.

The *Adrenal Glands*. You know that tingle that prickles all through your body at the instant of a shock or stress? The hormone adrenaline is for fight-or-flight and gets everything ready to spring into action. What's more essential to survival than that?! In an anxiety situation the adrenaline is pumped into your system; in a pleasure situation it's reduced and dissipates.

Caffeine stimulates the adrenal glands. So does stress. One of the problems of modern humanity is that we have no immediate relief for the excess adrenaline which our lifestyle continually pumps into our system. This excess remains and contributes to symptoms of stress such as high blood pressure, digestive problems, nervous tensions, etc.

The problem is especially acute in high-stress situations such as police work, military engagements, fire and medical emergencies, politics and diplomacy under deadlines and terrorist threats, the self-induced stress of some businesses striving to prove their importance (hey, it ain't brain surgery, guys... unless of course it actually is brain surgery, which is probably pretty tense), and the common incidents of everyday modern life: backfiring cars, too many phones ringing at once, too many children needing attention, scholastic pressures, work deadlines, traffic, etc. The end result of unrelieved stress can be a gnawing, edgy feeling that just won't go away. It frays the temper and makes life generally uncomfortable.

A person can become addicted to the adrenaline rush; down that path can lie bungee jumpers or serial killers, depending on the ethics of the individual.

Like the so-called Reptilian System in the brain, which is a remnant of our earlier development and closely related to our reptilian ancestry, some activities of the Root Center, such as territorial aggression, are sometimes seen as outdated in modern times. Yet they remain a part of our biology and influence our daily lives.

Studies connecting violent TV, music, and video games to actual violence note that the pacing and content of the images actually increase the release of adrenaline and the corticosteroids, also stress-related chemicals, by triggering the brain through the optic nerves, ears, and other sensory organs. Without a parallel release from the body of these self-produced fight-or-flight chemicals, the stress builds up until the person is compelled to an act of violence simply to rebalance their own chemistry. Think of beating war drums before battle or the pep rallies before the big game; if those warriors or players then never went into battle and drained off all that hyped-up adrenaline you'd have a really unruly bunch on your hands. This might go a bit towards explaining soccer hooligan- ism — too much energy build-up among the fans with not enough release, so, hey, let's go bash some heads and break some things.

A Rand Corporation study found that "weathering," the stress of living in pov- erty, neglect, and deprivation, contributed significantly to poor health but they didn't know why. Perhaps part of the answer lies in the effect on and by the Centers.

Blood tests showed that a chemical called Interleukin-6 sharply increases in the blood of stressed caregivers compared with the blood of others in the test. Previous studies have associated IL-6 with several diseases, including heart disease, arthritis, osteoporosis, type-2 diabetes, and certain cancers. Some stress is good for us and does help us get things done. Its effectiveness lies on a bell curve known as the Yerkes-Dodson Law. As stress increases, so does performance and efficiency, but only up to a point. If the stress continues beyond that point, performance and efficiency fall off.

The trick for a character's personal growth is to connect this lower Center with its higher counterpart, the Crown Center, and to string it up with all the other Centers into a fully activated, integrated system of energy. However, for good story-telling it's great to have this Root Center as prime motivator for a charac- ter such as the killer couple in *Natural Born Killers* and John Travolta's character in *Pulp Fiction*. Sometimes the story itself is about this Root Center and its effects, such as *Road Warrior*, *Deliverance*, and *The River Wild*.

MYTHIC MEANING

The Root Center is a fascinating state of consciousness because we both need it and need to rise above it. It is our doorway into physical existence as the fetus unfolds from the *kanda knot* to become the complete human being.

It is also considered the foundation of duality because two main lines of *chi*, or the energy field of the body, begin here: the masculine and the feminine. In the medical symbol of the caduceus, you usually see two serpents twining up around a staff which represents the spinal column. The serpents are these two currents of kundalini (personal life force) power, called in Sanskrit the *Ida* (feminine) and the *Pingala* (masculine). This polarity will manifest itself in the full spectrum of the masculine/feminine differences, from gender to political systems, from protons (+) and electrons (-) to silence (feminine and receptive) and sound (mas- culine and energetic).

In Greco-Roman myth the first feat of Hercules involved two snakes. While Herc was still an infant in his cradle, the jealous queen goddess Hera, supremely annoyed that her husband Zeus had made love to the lovely mortal Alcmena, sent two serpents to slay the result of that affair. Hercules here is Everyman and the two snakes at his cradle symbolize these two energy currents, which if accessed without proper preparation can fry the self, just as plugging your toaster into the power pole on the street would have disastrous results for the toaster. But Baby Herc grasps the two snakes and immobilizes them, bringing them under his control.

One of the reasons the Walt Disney animated feature *Hercules* may not have been very successful is that they tampered with the mythic truth of the story and made Herc the son of Zeus and Hera. He is supposed to be half-mortal, half-god. Zeus represents that Crown chakra divine energy and his earthly mom Alcmena represents the basic physical matter of the Root chakra. Since most humans are at times quite torn between their higher and lower natures we can identify more with a half-breed Herc than with simply a young god in exile.

Another part of the serpent symbolism involves fallen energy, but in a slightly different way. There are many, many stories to explain the presence of evil in the world. A lot of them put the blame on mankind (or womankind) itself, though some more skeptical systems put the blame on petulant gods or simply a tragic twist of fate.

> *Oh, Thou, who Man of baser Earth didst make,*
> *And who with Eden didst devise the Snake;*
> *For all the Sin wherewith the Face of Man*
> *Is blacken'd, Man's Forgiveness give — and take!*
> The Rubaiyat, Omar Khayyam

In the it's-our-fault original sin stories the typical scenario involves a higher degree of mankind falling into the lower levels of the physical world through a variety of missteps, from pride to greed to curiosity. Tales of Atlantis often attribute its destruction to the misdeeds of the Atlanteans themselves. Many creation myths have a somewhat rebellious mankind dropping down into this world from the sky-world to explore or to escape.

In the Wisdom Teachings Spirit is said to have fallen into its reflection in Matter and become trapped there. This concept is mythologized in the Hindu Vedic representation of the separation of the god and goddess Shiva and Shakti. Since the Root Center represents the densest form of Matter (Shakti), and since the doorway to the higher realms of spirit is said to be at the Crown Center (Shiva), these two Centers symbolize in physical form the fall of Spirit into Matter. You could see it as the drop of our consciousness from a full awareness of our spiritual heritage and identity to having become totally preoccupied and identified with matter and excessive materialism.

One positive side of this so-called Fall is the comforting sense of belonging, of being grounded.

In the Bible (Genesis 6:2) it's written that "the sons of God looked upon the daughters of men and saw that they were fair and went in unto them." Sons of God = Spirit. Daughters of men = Matter. The drop by sexual congress and interbreeding of more advanced beings with animal-man is the subject of much mythology and science fiction. In the first *Star Trek* TV series wasn't Captain Kirk just always boffing those alien women? The movies and TV series *Star Gate* and *X-Files* have made long runs on this idea of gods and humans interacting. However, one might well look at the theories of our having been seeded by alien races or being the result of genetic experiments in light of this idea of it being a difference in consciousness rather than a difference in DNA.

The cold-blooded demonic villains of myth and legend personify this lowest Center, including such creatures as Echidna, the mother of all monsters from the Greek system, although the TV series *Hercules* gave her a more human and motherly spin. The black and bloody death goddess Kali in the Hindu system represents aspects of this dark and deadly side of the circle of life.

Andromeda in the Greek's Perseus and Andromeda myth is a gentler version of this Center. Her mother, Queen Cassiopeia (the status quo), offended the gods with her vanity and in payment was ordered to sacrifice her virgin daughter to a sea serpent (the old forces of nature). Beautiful Andromeda (virgin matter) is chained to a rock wearing all the family jewels to be gobbled up by the sea monster. Luckily for her the hero Perseus (the soul) just happens to be flying by on his way home from slaying the snake-haired gorgon Medusa. He falls instantly in love with Andromeda, slays the serpent, and carries the lovely princess off to be his bride. A perfect story of the Soul rescuing fallen Spirit trapped in Matter. Later versions include Saint George and the Dragon and all those chivalric tales of knights rescuing virgins from dragons.

A recent version of this story is played out in the movie *Titanic* where the proud vain mother is intent on sacrificing her daughter Rose to the old establishment a la the rich fiancé Billy Zane. Jack is Perseus come to snatch her away to freedom. There's even that scene in the movie where Rose is perched on the bow, hanging out above the ocean, wearing the family jewels just as Andromeda in the myth is chained atop the rocky sea cliff, bedecked in the royal jewels.

In the movie *Under Siege* when Chief Ryback (Steven Segal) is trapped in the walk-in freezer and blows away the door to escape, it's a version of rolling away the (Luschka's gland) Stone blocking the cave. He then goes on to make his way up the other Centers, as we'll see in the "Raising the Dragon" chapter.

In the Jewish mystical system of the Kaballah the Great Serpent winds its way down the Tree of Life from Kether the Crown Center to Malkuth the Root Center. The spiritual path of evolution then moves back up through these energy fields from Malkuth to Kether.

You could also view Einstein's physics formula of $E=mc^2$ in this light, where energy (Crown Center) and matter (Root Center) are on either ends of the spectrum, with light or consciousness as the determining factor of the relationship between the two.

ARCHETYPES

Assassins — From the crafty to the foolish, martyrs, and suicide bombers.

Earth Goddess — She whose cauldron pours forth plenty, like the Celtic Ceridwin with her cauldron of plenty and the Greek Demeter with her Horn of Plenty.

Heroes and Heroines Who Face Monsters — In this category you have those trapped in matter and threatened by monsters, such as Shakti, Andromeda, Brunhilde, Sleeping Beauty, and the like. You also have heroes who find their lives in danger and must fight for survival. Lots of warriors fit this Archetype when in the midst of battle, be they Beowulf, Theseus, or Neo in *Matrix*.

Monsters — In this category are the Cyclopes, Minotaurs, and Harpies of Greek myth, Grendel of the Beowolf legends, the Frankenstein monster, and the legions of zombies and demons found in many pantheistic systems. The Hindu goddess Kali with her black skin, blood-dripping jaws, jewelry made of skulls, and fierce demeanor is the embodiment of death and destruction. The *Yamaduts* in the film *Ghost* are creatures who scurry away the souls of unprepared or wicked dead.

Rescuers — Though they may usually function at a higher Center (Aspirational Solar Plexus), when in action rescuing people from life-threatening situations, rescue workers are operating in the Root Center.

Survivalists — As you might suppose.

Symbols

Cauldron, Horn of Plenty — Just as the Root Center is the doorway for the soul to come into a physical body, so too are these womb-like containers the source of food and plenty, the passageway from one realm into another.

Dragon, Serpent — Almost every culture has a serpent, snake, or dragon as a major deity, from Quetzalcoatl of Meso- and South America to the Chinese dragon, to the Aborigine's Rainbow Serpent, Christianity's Satan, and Islam's *shaitan*. The dragon or serpent symbolizes the kundalini energy, the energy of fire in matter, fire by friction. Recall the sandworms in Frank Herbert's *Dune* series, the David Lynch film, and the subsequent Italian mini-series. Incidentally, there is a lot of esoteric meaning in Herbert's books and if read as "true myths" you can have lots of fun searching out the symbolism and often the outright delineation of Wisdom truths.

Remember in the section just above we learned about the separation and fall of energy or spirit into matter. The coiled serpent (especially if it's coiled around a tree or a staff) represents the fallen kundalini energy which humanity is attempting to raise back up into the head where it belongs. The symbolism resides in the Garden of Eden story, the knights-slaying-dragons stories, the magicians' battle between Moses and the Egyptian priests with their staffs, and most folk tales about a snake, dragon, or lizard. In the first *Terminator* film, Sarah Connor's pet is an iguana named Pugsley.

The medical symbol of the caduceus represents the spinal column in the staff and the kundalini energy in the two snakes twining up it. Some caducei only have one snake; presumably that's merely an unknowing design element rather than a statement about the imbalance in the function of that company or service.

Winged serpents and flying dragons have a different symbolism related to the Crown Center, but just remember that a wingless coiled serpent, dragon, lizard, etc. is usually symbolic of the Root Center.

Frozen Realms — Often the lowest Center is represented by ice. Cold, lifeless, frozen into inactivity, this is a real down side to the Root Center. In stories this symbolism plays out in the original book and some of the movies of *Frankenstein*, where both the monster and the doctor end up perishing in the sere, frozen wastes of the Arctic. In *Under Siege* Chief Ryback is trapped in a freezer aboard the ship but escapes by blasting his way out. Rocky beats up frozen beef carcasses while training for his big fight.

Mad Machines — From Frankenstein to the Terminator, from *Metropolis* to *The Matrix*, machines-gone-mad exemplify a drop from a Throat Center creation to Root Center misuse.

Ring of Fire — The kundalini energy residing in the Root Center is called the Fire of Matter, Fire by Friction, Heat without Light. When consciousness is trapped down here not much can happen: remember it's about sheer survival.

In Norse mythology the warrior princess-goddess Brunhilde is put to sleep on a rock surrounded by a Ring of Fire for disobeying her father, king god Wodin. Only a noble knight will be able to break through the fire and rouse her with a kiss. This is a pretty blatant reference to the Root Center with both the Stone and the Ring of Fire. Other versions of the Ring of Fire have a character surrounded by bramble bushes (Sleeping Beauty), locked in a tower (Rapunzel), or the like.

Skull — A symbol of death, it is also connected with the Crown Center. Skulls crowd the landscape in *The Terminator* films. From the very opening you know the movie is going to be about killing, death, and possibly survival.

Stone — Because the actual gland of this Center is like a little pebble, its symbol is a stone. Some examples are the stone that sealed Jesus' tomb, the stone cliff to which Andromeda was chained, and the rocks upon which Sleeping Beauty and the Norse goddess Brunhilde were laid to slumber, just as the soul is said to be asleep from having fallen down to the lowest, densest Center of pure physicality.

PLANET

Saturn — In mythology and symbolism this planet is associated with contraction, limitation, sorrow, death, and endings. It is Father Time, and eventually all human bodies must succumb to time and the pull of earth. The influence of Saturn is about foundations, about actually being alive in a physical body. It's about *dharma*, the Hindu concept of earthly, everyday duties. Saturn is also called Lord Karma because it brings around unfinished business, both positive and negative.

A character in the Root Center under this influence would be having to deal with her illusions and give them up in order to survive. The death of the Ego allows the true Self to thrive.

ASTROLOGICAL SIGNS

Capricorn & Scorpio — Both of these signs are associated with death, endings, dark secrecy, hidden things and motives.

COLORS, SHAPES, MATERIALS

- Black
- Brown
- Dark earth tones
- Dark shades
- Rusted, corrupted metallics
- Reptile skins in furniture, hangings, decor
- Animal skins
- Shredded, distressed fabrics
- Shattered glass
- Trash and junk
- Boulders, large rocks, especially blocking an entrance
- Ring of Fire
- Thorns
- Ice
- Gloomy and overcast skies
- Fences, especially entrapping barriers
- Metals
- Steely dangerous machines

CLOTHING

- Reptile and animal skins in boots, belts, vests, etc.
- Tattoos, scarification
- Torn and tattered clothing
- Ropes, chains
- Skulls, crossbones

Note the Terminator's clothes — chains, leathers and Gargoyle sunglasses. In the beginning of *Terminator II* the Terminator starts out stark naked, then acquires biker leathers, weapons, and a motorcycle, all through violence; all very Root Center.

And on the lighter side:
- Natural fibers, hemp, raw primitive "hippie look"
- Leaves, barks
- Open weaves, like nets, traps

STYLES OF SPEECH

- Simple
- Short declarative sentences
- Words would be solid, grounded, material, hard, tough, thick, congested

- Also dark, sharp, heavy, thunderous
- Think Rambo, Road Warrior "Come see me", and Terminator "I'll be back"

Remember that in story-telling this character is probably either in a life-threatening situation or causing life-threatening situations for others. This is about survival, not philosophy. As Kyle Reese explains to Sarah Connor in *The Terminator*, creatures or machines operating from a Root Center focus cannot be reasoned with.

PHYSICAL ACTIONS

A character grounded in the Root Center will be very grounded in their actions.

- They'll have their feet firmly planted
- They'll be touching solid ground or solid objects as often as possible — rooting themselves to the earth and matter
- On the positive side of the spectrum, Yoda-esque
- They'd clench their fists in front of the groin area
- They'd walk almost with a stomping motion
- Their gait will be heaviest on their heels, not pushing off with their toes
- They could scurry about, lizard-like, like the Gollum/Smeagol character in *The Lord of the Rings*
- Or they could move sinuously, like a serpent
- They'd sit solid and hard
- Or constantly swaying, hypnotically cobra-like (just be consistent within the styles)
- Desperate and frantic if the victim
- Cold and deliberate if the perpetrator
- Tearing up, squashing, destroying things
- Jerky, robot-like movements

FOIBLES, PHOBIAS, FOODS

- Pulls wings off flies (just kidding... no, actually, that would be correct)
- Clumsy — if on the down side of this Center
- Lame, paralyzed — down side again
- Claustrophobia
- Unwashed
- Jittery limbs and twitches — too much adrenaline
- Hemorrhoids

- Raw foods
- Bloody foods
- Coffee, teas, stimulants (affecting the adrenals)

Remedies for an over-stressed Root Center person could include cutting back on caffeine, doing vigorous exercise to burn off the excess stress chemicals, and getting reflexology or massages.

WOUNDS & DEATHS

The wounds of a Root Center person could be paralysis below the waist, blown-out athlete's knees, gout, being cut off at the feet, or suffering a broken or bruised tailbone.

Typical Root Center deaths would be by avalanche, smothering, freezing, trapped in a cave, sunk into quicksand, or swirled into a whirlpool.

That old medieval and horror movie standby of impalement is certainly Root Center.

EXAMPLES

Characters

Do keep in mind that a character will often move around on the Tree of Life, or chakra system, just as do real humans and we'll explore all this in Section Three on "Mythic Structure." But at times, a character will remain entirely on one Center throughout a story, like Freddy Krueger in the endless *Nightmares on Elm Street*. Then there's Jason, Darth Vader, Smeagol, and the Uruk-hai and Orcs in *The Lord of the Rings*, Agent Smith and his ilk in *The Matrix* films.

Not all movies or characters on a Root Center are serious. Check out *Tank Girl*. I often show clips from this film to illustrate the Root Center. It's definitely about sheer survival but it's also light, clever, and funny. There's a great clip where our heroine played by Lori Petty is rockin' and rollin' down a dirt road in her tank, which is all decked out with a TV set, a barbecue grill, a recliner, and a full bar. She's roasting a hot-dog, sipping a martini, and steering the tank after the bad guys, meanwhile chatting on the radio with her girlfriend about what they'll wear to the next battle. It's definitely Root Center but it's done with great good humor.

In *Moulin Rouge* Nicole Kidman's courtesan/singer/dancer Satine character is dragged down from her tandem Throat/Sacral Centers into her Root Center as she struggles to stay alive. Here the Root Center takes on a pathos that lends to the poignancy of the drama.

In Douglas Adams's classic *The Hitchhiker's Guide to the Galaxy* the people and robots of the planet Krikkit are so Root Centered and xenophobic that their opinion about the entire rest of the Galaxy is "It'll have to go" and they set about doing just that.

Arnold Schwarzenneger's character in the *Terminator* movies makes a Centers progression. In the first film he is solidly Root Center, determined to kill Sarah Connor and prevent the birth of her son John. In the second film, so the story goes, Arnie wanted to play the good guy, not the bad guy, so though he portrays the same individual, this time the character is operating from a higher Center, the Aspirational Solar Plexus and at times, the Heart Center. T-2 takes his place at the Root Center.

Films

Alien(s)

Armageddon

Boondock Saints — in the methods; but the motives of these two Irish brothers is ASP, to rid the neighborhood of bad guys

Death Wish

Deep Impact

Deliverance

Gangs of New York

The Great Escape

Independence Day

Kill Bill (especially Vol. 1)

Leaving Las Vegas —sliding down from Sacral/Throat

The Lord of the Rings

Natural Born Killers

Nightmare(s) on Elm Street

Papillion

The Passion of the Christ

The Poseidon Adventure

Predator(s)

Pulp Fiction

Rambo(s)

The Replacement Killers

The River Wild

Road Warrior(s)

Saving Private Ryan

Tank Girl

Terminator

Texas Chainsaw Massacre(s)

Titus

The Verdict

Warriors (Walter Hill's)

Horror films are almost always on a Root Center focus, though there may be any number of characters within the story that operate on other Centers. The demons and icky bad things are almost always Root Center characters.

Musicals, Opera, Ballet & Theatre

Götterdämmerung or *Twilight of the Gods*, Richard Wagner's opera, resonates with Root Center frequency as the corrupted reign of the Norse gods comes to an end, and the next era begins, that of human love... which interestingly takes us up to the next Center, the Sacral.

La Boheme — Puccini's characters are propelled to a Root Center by poverty, illness, or conflict. Marcello and Rudolfo are starving artists teetering on the freezing brink of eviction. In a vivid example of the conscious creativity of the Throat Center falling to Root Center, their philosopher friend Colline even burns one of his manuscripts to create a little warmth. And then there's the heroine, that sickly girl Mimi who coughs her fatal way into the star-crossed lover's hall of fame.

Le Sacre du Printemps (The Rite of Spring) — In this ballet a maiden dances herself to death to ensure fertility of the earth.

Les Miserables

Little Shop of Horrors

Rent — a contemporary *La Boheme*

Rocky Horror Picture Show

Sweeney Todd, The Demon Barber of Fleet Street

Titus Andronicus is all Root Center activities. Julie Taymor's film of Shakespeare's play is a fabulously stylistic approach to a lot of bloody mayhem.

Books

Clive Barker's and a lot of Stephen King's works are very, very Root Centered, as are most horror stories.

The Grapes of Wrath

Heart of Darkness

The *Left Behind* series

The Perfect Storm

Survival and disaster stories

Games

The *Grand Theft Auto* video games are blatantly about death-dealing, murder, mayhem, and trying to survive. They also fit into the next chakra, the Sacral.

Slaughtersport

Splatterhouse

Technocop

Music
Atonal
Chants
Drumming
Ring dances, stomps, techno, simple steps
Simple driving repetitive beats

Historical
Some of the most terrifying warriors have been those firmly dedicated to killing, sometimes to save their country or to honor their god, but nonetheless, in the heat of battle these guys and girls have been very caught up in the blood-lust of slaughter and mayhem. A few famous groups come to mind such as the Berserkers of Norse legend who wore bear skins, blood, and little else and the Amok warriors of the Malay archipelago whose name has come to mean a killing frenzy.

Natural disasters toss people down into the Root Center. Some of our most powerful myths are about these disasters: the sinking of Atlantis, the floods of Manu and Noah, the Mesoamerican Jaguar Wind, and the tragic prophecies of the Hopi and Black Elk.

Current Events
Assassins. Well, those boys and girls are still hard at work in their new guise as terrorists, psychopathic and serial killers. Unfortunately, many people today are born into a Root Center life in the Third World or are thrust into it because of war, famine, disease, and disasters. Others in the developed world are thrust into the Root Center when disasters strike, such as hurricanes, floods, tornadoes, fires, plane crashes, epidemics. Warriors who go into the battle space enter by necessity into a Root Center focus.

A troubling Root Center expression these days are child soldiers thrust into drugs, killing, and cannibalism in war zones where there are no public services, education, medicine, or adult supervision. They wear sex organs as combat decorations and eat enemy hearts to protect themselves from bullets and danger.

On the positive side are people who do wilderness treks or go on retreats. As well, anyone who does Root Center jobs helps make an entire system work well, be it janitors or gravediggers. In the Hindu caste system the Untouchables who do the dirty work are at the very bottom, at the Root Center. Root Center work does not necessarily mean a Root Center life. In fact, many religious disciplines put people to work at Root Center activities such as scrubbing monastery floors or tending gardens to ground them and get them connected with those very basic realities of Life.

Post-Traumatic Stress Disorder can be seen as damage to the etheric network caused by extreme concentration of stress in the Root Center. Public health services worldwide are finally beginning to recognize PTSD with its concomitant depression and dissociation as a real problem. Treatment and acceptance is particularly vital for refugees and torture victims such as in sub-Saharan Africa, Bhutan, Cambodia, and trauma survivors worldwide.

A drop to the Root Center is observed in the phenomenon of "Suicide by Cop," where a disappointment in love drives frustrated men to force a police officer to put them out of their misery. It's estimated that as much as ten percent of the deaths caused by police may be due to "Suicide by Cop."

B. The Practice

Now that you have a familiarity with this Center, it's time to put your new knowledge into practice.

1. FOR YOUR CHARACTERS

- Build their Character Profiles based on the above information
- Find photos of actors or people who embody the character you want to create
- Construct a Character Profile Collage
- Write up their ID Statement
- Note card — make one from a piece of bark or a broad leaf, a torn paper bag, a scrap of fabric, a piece of metal. Scratch your character's name in a shard of glass or pottery. Write in red on black.
- Do the Wash — check the various aspects to be sure you have integrity of character every time they appear on the page or on screen: food, dialogue, actions, others' reactions to them, etc.

2. FOR YOURSELF

This is where you Walk the Walk and *Act As If*.

- Play tribal music, predominantly with strong repetitive drums and simple chants. Listen to sound tracks from Root Center films.
- Eat raw foods, including steak tartar if you're not a vegetarian. Just be sure you do it at a good restaurant to be sure it's safe. "Is sushi a Root Center food?", you might ask. Nope. Although the food itself is raw, the construction of it is very thoughtful and artistic. Sushi is Throat Center food.
- Work in a garden.
- Cook your meals out on your barbecue grill for a few days. No cheating with take-out or the microwave.

- Wear leather and fur.
- Go Goth.
- If you don't have tattoos, use the temporary ones. Or use self-tanning lotion and stencils, or your fingers, to paint on designs that'll last a week or so.
- Communist peasant pajamas carry a Root Center frequency.
- Depending on the laws in your area, carry a weapon. In Texas this is no problem, except that there are signs on the banks and many law offices reading, "Leave your weapons at the door."
- Go to a shooting range and learn to fire a gun, or refresh your marksman skills.
- Go to an archery range and see how difficult it is to pull a bow and actually hit a target.
- Go on a hunting trip (during season and following safety procedures). For those of you who are anti-hunting, remember that this exercise is not about you approving or signing on to an activity, it's about your getting a better understanding of those who do it.
- Go fishing, and if you get lucky, prepare and eat the fish.
- Gather up a bunch of old pottery or glass, find a good solid wall and a bunch of rocks or a baseball bat or club and break the glass. [Note: Do this with protective clothing and goggles so you don't become a wounded victim of your own research.]
- Ride a roller coaster or some other theme park thrill ride — the scariest one possible.
- Cut down on your dialogue and speak in monosyllables.
- Don't be terribly rude, but don't be your usual effusive or social self (if you are). People should say, "What's wrong with you?" Being in character you would simply growl and walk away, darkly, with great angst or anger.
- Watch the recommended movies.
- Read the recommended books.

3. EXERCISE

Complete your analysis from the "How To Use the Centers of Motivation" chapter on page 25.

C. Conclusion

A Root Center character will be in life-or-death dilemmas of their own creation or will be forced there by others or by circumstances. The answer to their question of "What's My Motivation?" will be simple — Sheer Survival.

If they're on the mayhem-dealing side of the equation, their motivation is about elimination of anything and anyone they want to, and can, eliminate.

On the softer side of it, a character might go "back to Nature" to reconnect with the life-giving force and find sustenance for survival there.

Because stories are metaphors for life, a character's death can also be metaphorical, as in *The Verdict*. Here Paul Newman's Frank Galvin is barely alive, an alcoholic lawyer without any business, his reputation in shreds and his self-respect non-existent. Not only is he driven from a Root Center at the opening of the story, but the case he takes on is Root Center: a young woman in a coma since negligence on the delivery table cost her her baby's life and, for all intents and purposes, her own.

For the most part, though, Root Center characters and stories will be physical life-or-death, particularly in the action film genre. Science is now proving what anyone in a darkened theatre has always known — images and story-telling give us an actual physical thrill. Through stories then, we can experience the scarier and more basic aspects of life without actually getting dirty or shedding blood ourselves. This very visceral nature of the Root Center is part of what makes it so powerful to storytellers and audiences alike.

So after all the blood and guts are shed and shredded and physical survival is secured, what's next on the rise through the Inner Drives? How about sex and money?

4.
Sacral Center

Why does Stanley Kowalski bellow "Stellaaaaaaaa!" in *A Streetcar Named Desire*?

Why did wife-beater undershirts become a sex symbol? Anyone who's ever been swept away by love, lust, or infatuation knows why: anything or anyone exuding such concentrated, smoldering desire is both seductive and a little scary... which can also be seductive. It's the moths-to-flame thing: the fires of passion draw in the lone individual from the cold of personal exile with the promise of intimacy and intensity.

Every character in *A Streetcar Named Desire* is on a Sacral focus, from the sensual predator Stanley to the passion-besotted Stella, to the fluttering over-the-hill nymphet Blanche. Their conflicts are all tied up with money, sex, jealousy, and fear. It's a real Sacral Center romp.

In the Sacral Center where sex and fear and money all meet, you find characters juggling them in varying degrees of expertise. To ensure dynamic complexity in your characters, add different aspects of this Center to their main goal. From *Othello* to *Unfaithful*, a little jealousy (fear of loss) mixed into the passion can take a story a long way towards high drama.

A. The Theory

MOTIVATION: UNCONSCIOUS CREATIVITY

- Sex
- Fear
- Money

In a seminar I once mentioned that the Sacral was the Center where sex, fear, and money all lived together. Someone raised their hand with a quizzical look and said they didn't see "how all those fit together?" Everyone else's head swiveled to look at him, astonished, and we all began to fill in the blanks: prostitution, alimony, jealousy, embezzlement, insurance, infidelity, the advertising industry. "Oh," the doubting fellow nodded, "I see what you mean."

Actually, advertising is the most fulsome example of the mixture of sex, fear, and money. The ad first makes you afraid that you're not going to get laid, because of bad breath or bad clothes or the wrong kind of car. Then it sells you something that'll supposedly guarantee that you will get laid: mouthwash, the latest fashion, the coolest wheels.

Another linking is Warren Beatty's portrayal of the supposedly impotent bank robber Clyde Barrow in *Bonnie and Clyde*. Or how about the sex-money-jealousy (fear) triangle among Robert Redford, Demi Moore, and Woody Harrelson in *Indecent Proposal*.

A lot of popular music is Sacral Centered. For instance, Elvis Presley's song "Suspicious Minds" and that line about being caught in a trap. Most love ballads are about loss, fear of loss, jealousy. Or how about Marvin Gaye's "Sexual Healing"? And then there are all the rock songs that are quite blatantly about sex. Notice that rap and hip-hop lyrics often link money (usually ill-gotten), guns (fear-inducing to say the least) and intimidation with sex, even to the point of rape.

Certainly not all Sacral Center activity carries distasteful or harmful connotations. A lot of it is quite lovely and enjoyable. In fact, a lot of it seems to be the driving engine for humanity. Certainly Sigmund Freud thought so. Many evolutionary psychologists and biologists point to the animal drives as explanations for a lot of human activity. Romance, lust, erotic love, sexuality, and sensuality undoubtedly play a major role in the motivations of many humans a great deal of the time.

Indeed the Sacral is one of the most active Centers for most of humanity. It is the site of procreation, of unconscious creativity. Besides reproduction, other examples of unconscious creativity in the animal kingdom are beehives, spider webs, elaborate bird's nests, etc. It's undeniably creative but it's instinctual. Creating is hard-wired into humanity but until it becomes a consciously thought-out procedure it's just procreation, simple reproduction.

Take having a baby: you don't have to even be conscious to do it. Women have become pregnant, carried to term, and delivered babies while in comas, as in the Pedro Almodóvar film *Talk to Her*. It's not like at eight weeks you have to think, "Ah, time to define those toes and fingers." And at four months, "Hmmm, best add some eyelashes right about now." It all happens without the mother's conscious involvement. She is the instrument for the creative expression, but has very little say-so about the process.

In that same vein, many people create their financial flow from a position of unconsciousness and/or fear. Too often, rather than carefully planning their finances, determining a market for their skills, researching best means and methods to increase their prosperity, and meticulously shepherding their resources, some people are happy just to have a job, to make ends meet, to get by. For the free-lance person, or for people caught in cycles of downsizing and restructuring, panic sets in and money is created out of desperation just a hair's breadth above the Root Center and Sheer Survival. "I must get a job today," they'll shriek. "I must sell X-many widgets. If I could only win the lottery. Maybe I'll rob a bank." Creating money from this Center is simply reacting to a need, usually out of fear.

Stanley Kowalski articulates a Sacral Center focus in *A Streetcar Named Desire* when he questions his sister-in-law, the ditsy nymphomaniac Blanche, about the Du Bois family estate, Belle Reve. After all, he notes, according to the Napoleonic Code, what belongs to the wife belongs to the husband, so show him the money.

Sex, too, is often unconscious. Haven't we all heard horror stories about the down side of that! Like waking up next to a stranger and going, "What was I thinking!?" (Obviously they weren't.) Granted there are varying levels of attraction between two people and that a physical, cellular attraction is quite valid, but it can also be much more interesting when it's coupled with and enhanced by attractions in the higher levels as well.

It's said that the higher you get in consciousness, the fewer people you can effectively interact with sexually. In simpler terms, you just get pickier because if you're only plugging in with someone on one level it feels rather shallow and unfulfilling. Remember that saying, "The best sex is of the mind"; we'll talk more about that when we're at the Throat Center, which is the seat of Conscious Creativity. Actually, Dr. Candace Pert in *Molecules of Emotion* notes that, just as common wisdom and the jokes have always observed, there actually are brain cells in the penis. Then the question is, which part of the brain has cells there, the old reptilian limbic system or the more rational cerebral cortex? More jokes abound.

There's also an interesting tenet in the Wisdom Teachings about sex, which relates to the ancient practice of temple prostitutes and the sacredness of the sexual act. To put it in more modern terms, "When you have sex with someone, you download their karma." That'll give one pause in choice of partners.

The ancient eastern practice of Tantric sex is growing in popularity among Westerners. Much of the philosophy behind it, often achieved by breathing exercises and designated postures, is about getting past fear and opening up to the powerful energies of sex. It is predominantly focused in the Sacral Center, though depending on the branch of Tantra being practiced, its ultimate goal may be to raise the consciousness to much higher Centers.

LOCATION

The Sacral Center is located about six inches below the navel, between the lumbar vertebrae #4 & #5.

ENDOCRINE GLANDS & HORMONES

Testes & Ovaries — These are the glands of procreation which allow the life-force its expression in physical bodies. It is the mechanism by which the form we know as "human" is made available for a life to be lived.

Most of us are governed in our daily lives by the dictates of these glands and their secretions. From a female's monthly menstrual cycle to a male's varying erection-ready cycle, and the approach to and decline from these fertility cycles, our bodies tend to tie us to these rhythms of the physical form.

Testosterone, Progesterone, Estrogen, Oxytocin — These hormones determine so much about us psychologically it is fair to say that we are the effect of their actions. Or as Dr. Sigmund Freud so aptly put it, "Anatomy is destiny."

The amount of these various hormones are seen to swing a person towards macho attitudes, ultra-femininity, homosexuality, bisexuality, and all the shades and permutations one can imagine.

Stories which illustrate the incredible tension and pull of physical attraction against all common sense or in the face of great danger illustrate the incredible power of this Center. Think of do-and/or-die romances such as Romeo and Juliet, Othello and Desdemona, Tristan and Isolde, or *Fatal Attraction* and *Damage*.

Nurturing and the maternal instinct are a byproduct of feminine hormones, which men also have in their bodies, just not to the same degree as women. Remember that during the early stages of fetal development all of us are female. It's not until the 8th week that the sex is evident, determined primarily by the XY genetic code but finessed with the hormonal soup of the mother's body, which is where science is increasingly showing that homosexuality is thought to click in, according to the ratio of hormones during that particular stage of development.

Oxytocin is a fascinating hormone in that it stimulates bonding. One of its most useful instances is during birth and nursing so the new mother won't kill the alien creature that has just caused her all that pain and now won't let her sleep.

It is also released by the brain during orgasm and during stimulation of the nipples in either men or women. Oxytocin-like compounds are found in chocolate, which goes a long way to explain why it's always been a lover's food and such a consolation to the love-lorn.

With the Baby Boom generation somewhat reluctantly yet somewhat adventurously venturing into middle age and the era of hormonal shifts, we're sure to see a lot more research and work in this area than ever before. When nature shifts our focus for us, the more information we have to understand what's going on, the better.

In some religions women are not allowed to participate in the spiritual rites because they are thought to be too closely tied to the rhythms of matter and the earth. This completely overlooks the fact that men are quite closely tied to their own rhythms as well as to those of women. A teacher of the female persuasion was once debating this with a professor of an Oriental religion who said women could not reach enlightenment because of their monthly cycles; they were too "earthbound." She countered with the observation that once past menopause then, there should be no problem? He did not reply.

Many Indian men leave their homes and families around age fifty to devote themselves to spiritual work after their obligations to career and posterity have been accomplished. Is it coincidence that this is the age around which the Sacral Center hormones are shifting, most often diminishing?

Mythic Meaning

The Sacral Center is the seat of unconscious creativity, as opposed to the Throat Center which is conscious creativity.

Societies and religions generally have two ways of dealing with this very powerful energy. One way is to Suppress it and the other is to Splatter it. Both manage to dilute the energy and keep people creatively impotent, as it were.

Repressive cultures and religions which cover the women from head to toe, only allow sex for making babies, practice female genital mutilation, only condone one sexual position and that one only between men and women who are married to each other at the time — that's controlling the sexual energy by Suppression. It's a really dangerous thing to do and once those extremely powerful energies find some other avenue of expression all heck usually breaks out in the form of rapes, stonings, riots, rebellions, and killings. Varun Khanna's film *Beyond Honor* deals with this situation in a contemporary setting.

Many of the old goddess religions used sexual activity timed with the seasons of the year to ensure crop fertility such as the Beltane Festivals on May 1st. Note the phallic symbolism of the maypole and the twining ribbons which resemble the spiral DNA, in one of those bemusing coincidences where myth presages fact. Or as discussed before perhaps, the myths embody facts that have gotten lost over time.

In a holdover from the days of pagan magic, priests would encourage their parishioners to have marital relations at a certain time once a week. Then the priest-magicians would appropriate all that energy for their own religious magic practices, unbeknownst to the people. It's rumoured that in some European villages, Catholic priests did this by suggesting that couples engage in marital relations every Saturday evening at ten p.m. and even rang the church bells to remind people and get everyone synchronized. In Kabalistic sexual practices people are encouraged to have sex at midnight on Shabbos (the Sabbath) to share those powerful energies for the quantum good and add more Light to the Universe.

Systems which use sex to sell things, or which have very profligate sexual practices, use the Splatter method of control. If an individual doesn't have the opportunity to marshal and control their own procreative energies they won't be able to build up the focus and tension necessary for real creativity and power. One really good way to keep a people controlled and ineffectual is to keep them crazed and distracted about sex. American media and marketing come to mind.

There are a lot of materials in the marketplace on creating better sexual relationships, prolonging pleasure, etc. And how many spam emails do we get every day offering to enlarge the size of the penis or breasts? Though the cycles of sexual revolution occur every forty years or so and though we have a consumer system permeated with sexual images and inferences, it also seems that most people are actually searching for that perfect mate, the soul mate, rather than an endless stream of random sexual encountres. Of course, one must also observe that there are ages and times dedicated to what used to be called "sowing wild oats" before a person settles down into marriage. It's almost as if the job of the late teens and early twenties is to do as much Sacral Center activity as possible.

Speaking of sex and fear together, stories about sexual infidelity have always been popular. Sometimes they're tragic, as in *Othello* or *Unfaithful*, and sometimes comedic, as in Mozart's opera *Cosi Fan Tutti* or the bedroom farces and screwball comedies. Perhaps they're popular because everyone can relate to them, either from personal experience or from fear or desire of having the personal experience.

Other than the obvious benefits of connection, warmth, and trust, there are some quite real creative benefits to sexual monogamy which relate directly to the physics of building up an electrical charge for specific use in specific creative procedures. You can find obscure references to the power of (at least serial) monogamy in the works of the medieval Alchemists. Dr. Carl Jung has commentary about this as well.

Activation of the Sacral Center often brings about mystic stimulation. Saint Theresa of Avila and her contemporary Saint John of the Cross both wrote about spirituality with exceptional sensuality and a famous marble carving of Saint Theresa by Bernini shows her ecstatically pierced by an arrow of divine love. If overdone, this can result in rabid spirituality, in styling oneself a bride or soldier of god, or in fear-based fundamentalism.

Sex and religion have been linked in rituals for aeons. Modern versions of the ancient Hindu Tantric sex practices are said to be about relaxation, opening to divine energy, and making powerful personal connections. However, some Tantric practices have a very, very ancient background. They were appropriate for the times and places in which they were developed back when humans, it is said, were more physically and emotionally based. They are considered rather outdated for where humanity is just now, purportedly developing our critical thinking skills and thus activating that mental part of our four-fold selves (physical, emotional, mental, spiritual).

One of the more questionable ancient sex-magic exercises positioned male and female sitting in the cross-legged yoga posture, sexually joined — a creative feat in itself. Sitting in the midst of a charnel house (a vault or tomb where dead and decaying bodies were put), at the moment of climax they'd roll their eyes clockwise then counter-clockwise and stick their tongues back down their own throats. This supposedly re-channeled the body's *chi* energy. No doubt. As the caveat from the TV commercials warns, "Trained professionals. Don't try this at home."

So though improving one's sexual abilities and sensitivities is a marvelous thing, you might just think twice about some of that really old Tantric sex-magic stuff and be mindful that the goal of an enlightened aware person is to operate all the Centers from an awareness focused at the highest Centers. Again, the best sex is of the mind.

In his *Dune* novels, author Frank Herbert calls fear the Little Killer and gives ways to guard against it and move beyond it. Fear can be life-preserving, such as in a Root Center fight-or-flight situation; but gnawing, nagging fear drains one's energy and makes one manipulable by others. Interestingly enough, one of the most frequent phrases in the Bible is "Fear not."

Cult followers will typically have their Sacral Centers controlled by the cult leader who instills in them some kind of fear: religious, political, societal, familial, personal. Note that cults often require devotees to give up all their money, leave family behind, and submit to the sexual dictates of the leader, be it suppression or splatter. Think how often we hear of cult members living in sex-separated dorms or on the other side of the spectrum, participating in group marriages or orgies.

In the Greco-Roman system the centaur Chiron (half-horse half-human) was mentor to Hercules, Jason, and many other heroes. Besides warrior skills, he also taught them the wisdom and nobility of nature, just as our own physical nature can teach us many valuable lessons. And, he taught the gods of medicines, which makes sense when you view medicine as dealing with the physical body. The young magician Harry Potter also has a centaur mentor.

The Greek witch Circe seduced sailors and turned them into animals. When Odysseus and his men landed on her island she turned his crew into swine. Interestingly enough, Circe fell in love with Odysseus when he didn't fall under her spell. It eventually turned out well for them, for a while anyway. One wonders whether this myth reflected or engendered those gender battle cries, "Men are pigs!" and "Women are witches!"

Some think of Aphrodite/Venus, the goddess of love, when they think of the Sacral Center. Actually though, it is her son Eros/Cupid who represents this Center. As we'll see later, Aphrodite is more about transformative love and Eros is about frivolous, sensual, Sacral "erotic" love. It's about obsession and possession.

Though at first glance the legends of the Holy Grail seem very aspirational and highly focused, they do express quite a bit of Sacral energy. Amfortas, king of the Grail Castle, is wounded in the thigh, symbolic of sexual malfunction, and his kingdom is plagued by famine and lack of fecundity until he is healed.

All the knights of the Round Table took off on the quest to find the Holy Grail. The only Grail knight able to find and see the Grail was Galahad, the pure of heart, the virgin. He was pure enough to be taken right up into the Light. Sir Parcival was quasi-pure so he got to see the Grail but did not get taken up into it. Sir Gawain, the ladies' man, didn't stand a chance.

Back to Homer's wandering Greek king Odysseus again. At one point in his travels home from the Trojan War he had to sail past the Sirens, females whose lovely voices lured sailors to their doom. Odysseus was determined to hear the Siren song without the danger of death so he had his men stop up their ears with wax and tie him tightly to the mast with strong ropes. As they rowed past the rocky shore the crew was oblivious to the singing but Odysseus heard every seductive note and struggled mightily against the ropes, determined to succumb to the Siren song. Fortunately the ropes held and the ship was soon past that danger and on to the next one. How often have you known someone freshly in love who disappears from their circle of friends, held captive in "love jail," victim of the Sacral Siren's song?

In a bit of myth-in-media, I was on a film set once where the producer was particularly enamored of the dancing girls in a musical number. The assistant director sidled over to him and teased, "What'll it be, Mister Jones, the ropes or the wax."

Most mythic systems exhibit a great respect and admiration for the Sacral Center when it's properly used in service to and under the conscious direction of the higher Centers. But mythology on the misuse of the Sacral is perhaps the biggest body of stories, along with misuse of the Solar Plexus. You can be assured of creating a fascinating story and compelling characters if you include some Sacral activity in your story line and character motivations.

Archetypes

Don Juans & Nymphomaniacs — The downside of sexuality. Not in the frequency or number of partners necessarily, but in the troublesome psycho-dynamics of compulsion, obsessions, and addictions.

Incubus & Succubus — Sexually demonic creatures, male and female respectively, who "lay with people as they sleep" and drain their energies. They tended to favor sexually repressed people and those sworn to chastity. Much medieval Church lore concerns mortification of the flesh and special prayers to ward off these sexual vampires.

Love Gods & Goddesses — Most cultures' pantheons have goddesses and gods specifically dedicated to eroticism.

In Hindu stories the playful blue-skinned god Krishna spends long nights dancing with the Gopis, or cow-girls.

The Hindu goddess Lakshmi is the ideal of feminine love and beauty. The wife of Vishnu is brilliant and perfumed, seated beside her husband on a white lotus flower. She is also the goddess of prosperity and good fortune, which ties in perfectly with the money aspect of the Sacral Center.

Eros/Cupid the Greco-Roman god of erotic love is usually depicted as a chubby cherub with a bow and arrow. Are we to understand that erotic love is infantile? Well, sometimes, yes. Think of Sugar Daddies, bimbos, and bimbeaux. And how about that tendency of new lovers to call each other pet names and speak in baby-talk?

Again, while you might consider Aphrodite to be in this category she is actually the goddess of transformative love and we find her at a higher Center (Aspirational Solar Plexus).

Lovers — There are hundreds of examples: Pyramus and Thisbe. Romeo and Juliet. David and Bathsheba. Guinevere and Lancelot. Tristan and Isolde. Rick and Ilsa. Note that a number of these stories involve infidelity and end badly for the lovers.

Monks & Nuns — What, you might say, would people who have taken vows of chastity and poverty be doing at this Center? There is a lot of power in denial, just try *not* to think about a pink elephant. As the sex scandals of the Catholic Church have shown, denial of the very strong Sacral Center is not always effective.

Pimps, Prostitutes, Panderers, Perverts & Paedophiles — More of the downside. And do notice the sex-fear-money connection. Interestingly enough, recent scientific work on the wiring of the brain has revealed that true sadists and masochists — people who claim they best experience sexual pleasure when it's connected with giving or receiving pain (as opposed to those indulging curiosity, playfulness, a tendency to meanness, or low self-esteem) — actually have an unusual wiring in the brain. Their pleasure and pain Centers are cross-wired, so to speak. Once again, modern science is "proving" people's accounts of their actual experiences.

Poltergeists — If you're doing a scary story, poltergeist activity is almost always caused by a repressed Sacral Center in a teenager entering puberty. They've got all this creative force surging through them, but it's got nowhere to go. If you've got a teenager who's beginning to be influenced by these hormonal creative urges you'd do well to be sure they have a healthy creative outlet like music, art or dance, chess, writing, or organized sports. They need something that's very structured so they can work on becoming more consciously creative. If the energy is really repressed, it's like trying to keep the lid on a boiling steam-kettle — it's going to break out somewhere and it's not going to be pretty. Doors start opening and closing, drawers start flying about, tables start following people across the room. Notice in most stories about this kind of activity there's usually a teenager at the Center of the problem, like in *The Exorcist*. If you don't have a sexually repressed teenager in your poltergeist story, you should.

Seducers/Seductresses — The most obvious example of a Sacral Center archetype is the siren seductress, a la Marilyn Monroe, Elizabeth Taylor, Sophia Loren, and the like. Their male counterparts are just as stunningly seductive: Errol

Flynn, Paul Newman, Antonio Banderas, Johnny Depp. Or just check out the check-out counter for the latest "Sexiest Man Alive" issue.

In older stories we find Delilah, Jezebel, and Salome from the Bible, Morgan le Fay and Gawain from the Arthurian tales.

Ariadne and Medea from Greek mythology both seduce heroes into taking them away from their homes in Crete and Colchis respectively. Usually seen as a good seductress, Ariadne helps Theseus defeat the Minotaur, her half-brother, but is later abandoned by him on their way back to Greece. Medea is a sorceress seductress and brings no amount of grief into Jason's life after she helps him get away with the Golden Fleece, also at the expense of her brother.

Modern versions of this archetype are the Glenn Close character in *Fatal Attraction*, Kathleen Turner's vamp in *Body Heat*, and those Sirens-in-the-Slammer in *Chicago*.

Wild & Crazy Partiers — The Greek god Pan rules music and merry parties and his compatriot Dionysus (Bacchus) is a complex god, some of whose domains include wine, drunkenness, and sexual frenzy. Women who ran through the wilds indulging in these revels were known as Bacchantes or Maenads and they had a nasty habit of tearing men apart when they were wild with wine.

SYMBOLS

Bow & Arrow — The bow and arrow, particularly in conjunction, are symbolic of the Sacral Center because of their obvious similarities to the sexual organs. Eros/Cupid carries a bow and arrow and sometimes his bow is shaped like lips.

Half-Human Half-Animal — Any half-human/half-animal creature, such as the centaur, faun, and satyr, is a perfect symbol of this Center. Usually the creature is known for its procreative powers and/or virility.

According to most religions, it is our animal nature we are striving so hard to overcome, to uplift, and redeem, as the missionary Katherine Hepburn preaches to dissolute Humphrey Bogart in *African Queen*. One of the longest speeches in *A Streetcar Named Desire* is when Blanche preaches to her sister Stella, who's sexually obsessed with her husband Stanley. The genteel Blanche sees Stanley as a crude creature who missed the evolution train and she urges Stella not to let animal attraction cause her to hang back with the brutes.

It's interesting to muse that perhaps the real meaning behind the symbols of the centaur, faun, etc. is that of genetic engineering. There are numerous legends about Atlantis that scientists were creating creatures made specifically for certain purposes such as six-armed miners, half-men half-horses, etc. So these symbols might actually be like trademarks such as we might today put on a tomato that has chicken genes, or a sheep with spider genes (which is actually being done to produce milk that can be spun out in webs). We might look at legends and myths as remnants of ancient advertising.

Rabbits & Pigs — Rabbits propagate often and prolifically. Before instant pregnancy tests, a doctor injected a rabbit with the woman's urine; if the rabbit died, she was pregnant. Some people infer that the White Rabbit in *Alice in Wonderland*, the one Alice followed down a hole and into a tunnel, was symbolic of sexual initiation. Some people say it was just a rabbit.

Pigs are frequently associated with fertility because of the frequency with which they breed and the number of piglets in a litter. Particularly in the old Celtic traditions of Europe the sow and the boar figured strongly in religious significance. In Egyptian mythology the goddess Isis favored the white sow. The evil Set, who slayed her husband and their brother Osiris, favored the black pig.

I know a guy who used to collect pigs: pig tea pots, pig pillows, pig salt and pepper shakers, pig hats. Eventually, he had to put a stop to it, but for a number of years he was defined as the pig-guy, who always made sure people heard how smart pigs are and how close they are genetically to humans. When using symbols like this, be creative. Certainly your characters can have pets or collections of the symbolic animals. You could also use these as clothes and accessories — a pig skin hand-bag or a rabbit coat, for instance.

Then too, think of the creative use of the pet rabbit in *Fatal Attraction*. It wouldn't have nearly the same resonance if she'd killed a gerbil. Not long after that movie came out I heard a girlfriend referring to an argument she had had with a soon-to-be-ex, "So I said to him, 'I decide when it's over, and hunny, it's not over 'til I boil your bunny.'" This is what you want from your use of symbols; you want them to be so strong and clever that they become part of people's everyday thinking.

Sex Organs — Psychologist Sigmund Freud saw most everything in sexual terms; so do teens going through puberty. So do lots of artists, such as Georgia O'Keefe and her exceptionally feminine flower paintings.

From the *lingam* and the *yoni* of Hindu iconography to the sex-sells advertisements such as a billboard featuring a certain "like a rock" pickup truck positioned between a man's legs, many large buildings and artwork are blatantly sexual in design. Some see the design of Gothic cathedrals as decidedly feminine with the arched entryways (vagina) topped by round windows (clitoris), and flanked with steeple towers (upraised legs).

Swords — Swords are phallic by their very shape, and are designed to cut and penetrate. If you have any doubt about this sexual symbolism, just watch that great scene in *The Mask of Zorro*, where Antonio Banderas undresses Catherine Zeta-Jones with his sword.

PLANETS

Jupiter — In Greek myths he represents lust and rampant fertility. Jupiter, or Jove as he's sometimes called, (and in the Roman pantheon his name is Zeus) has scores of children by many different goddesses and mortals. So intent is Jupiter/Zeus upon sexual congress that he turns himself into anything he can in order to score. He shows up variously as a bull, a swan, and even a shower of gold.

Jupiter is also the planet of good fortune and material wealth, but if those aspects are negative it can turn to greed.

Venus — The Roman name of the Greek goddess Aphrodite. Though it's more correctly allied with a higher Center, Venus is so often associated with romance and sex that it must be included here. The word *venereal*, as in disease, comes from Venus.

ASTROLOGICAL SIGNS

Capricorn — The Goat is often a symbol for sexuality. The Greek party god Pan is half-goat, half-man. In *A Streetcar Named Desire* Blanche DuBois notes that Stanley Kowalski's sign is Capricorn, the sexy goat.

Sagittarius — The centaur archer, the half-man, half-beast. Optimistic, adventurous, outgoing.

Scorpio — The sign of sex, secretive dealings, covert activities.

Taurus — The sensualist, ruled by Venus. (There'll be a higher counterpart of this sign at the Throat Center.)

COLORS, SHAPES, MATERIALS

- Greens and yellows — the fecund world of fertility, the bile of jealousy, the color of gold and money
- Money — currency, coins, ancient artifacts of same
- Red, orange, pink — the hues of blood-engorged organs, the tender color of seldom-exposed skin. Some primates display bright red in sexual areas during mating rituals.

- Furs
- Satins, silks, shiny slick fabrics like in *Chicago* and *Moulin Rouge* and on those classic movie sex symbols like Mae West, Carole Lombard, and Elizabeth Taylor
- Triangles — upright for male, inverted for female
- Panpipes — the instrument of the Greek sylvan god Pan, half-goat half-man; the modern-day version is the harmonica
- Hourglass — iconographic of the feminine form and, the soul enters the realm of time when born into a physical body
- Naked human forms — from elegant Greek statuary to porno

CLOTHING

- None. After all, it's about sex, right?
- Beautiful, sensual attire
- Sleazy, sluttish clothes
- Transparent, gauzy, see-through
- Spangles, sequins, and beads
- Tight, clingy clothes
- Outrageously expensive clothes
- Ragged clothes — the downside of money, as in not having any

STYLES OF SPEECH

One of the most Sacral speeches in films is in *Bull Durham* when Kevin Costner counters Susan Sarandon's quantum-physics-training-season-choosing-a-guy speech with his list of likes that includes long, slow, wet kisses. She responds with languid sighs over the thought of three days of that with him. Very Sacral. Watch it and see.

Styles of Speech will reflect the angst of lost love, the aching desire for money, the palpitation of fear, the breathlessness, the blindness, the surging compulsions of this Center. How about Ilsa's plea to Rick in *Casablanca*, when she's gone so girly she can no longer think and he'll have to do it for both of them. She's definitely in the Sacral Center and knows she's not going to be able to get up to the Throat Center with him around.

Another great Sacral speech is in *The Treasure of the Sierra Madre* when the old geezer tells Fred C. Dobbs (Humphrey Bogart) about how it is out there when the lure of gold gets to a man.

According to which aspect of this Center a character is playing out, their speech will be:

- Seductive, languid and slow
- Fast-paced and frenetic
- Tight, confined, short and clipped if the person is repressed
- Looking outside of self for satisfaction

A Sacral Center character would put a sexual spin on everything, would use innuendoes and double *entendres*. Freud would nod his head on this one for sure. Blanche DuBois sighs that the opposite of death is desire.

> "Saaaay, baby."
> "I have so much love to give, I just want to find someone to love."
> "How could they do that to me, after all the love I've given them."
> "Hell hath no fury like a woman (or man) scorned."
> "All she needs is a good love-session."

A Sacral Centered person might also be focused on money and profit.

> "It's all about sex or money. If I'm not getting laid or paid, why be there."
> "Yeah, I pulled in 120K last year, don't know where to put it, you know, stocks, bonds, parties..."

PHYSICAL ACTIONS

- Characters that operate from this Center will be gut-centered in their actions
- Their pain will be in this region
- Death-blows will come here
- The walk could be either a sexual swagger
- Or the walk could be a very tight, rigid step
- Flirtatious
- Belly-dancing, Salsa, the Tango
- Strip tease
- Violence, particularly sexual
- Sado-masochism
- Telekinesis, spoon-bending
- Poltergeist activities

FOIBLES, PHOBIAS, FOODS

- Sexual dysfunctions — from frigidity to nymphomania, from fetishes to so-called sexual addiction
- Actual physical dysfunctions of the sex organs: prostate problems, impotence, menstrual problems, ammenhorea (lack of menstruation, common in athletes and anorexics), infertility

- Venereal diseases, AIDS (when sexually transmitted)
- Though the wide spectrum of sexual expression is much more tolerated, and often celebrated, today, there are still many places where anything other than heterosexual missionary style sex is forbidden, denied, or both — even to the point of murder or execution

The film *A Streetcar Named Desire* glosses over two sexual aspects of Tennessee Williams's play: Blanche's young husband's homosexual behavior which had spurred her disgust, which had spurred his suicide; and her own nymphomania, which got her driven out of town.

- Depression
- Anhedonia — where nothing is pleasurable
- Poltergeist activity
- Anxiety attacks
- Shopaholics, compulsive shoppers
- Kleptomania
- Collectors

Addiction is a desire to feel and/or give pleasure, a desire for transformation whether it be through sex, drugs, rock-n-roll, or some other means.

Addicts on the Sacral level deal with pain by seeking a trance state where satiety and getting relaxed will get them beyond whatever pain it is that plagues them; which it may, for awhile.

When Sacral energy is locked in an obsessive swirl, nothing gets done, and the energy turns in on itself, creating even more obsession. The more conscious a person can become about their creative urges the better. Art therapy would be a good remedy for an obsessive character.

- Oysters — long considered an aphrodisiac
- Chocolate — stimulates oxytocin, that love-bonding hormone, but an overdose can cause over-stimulation and a drop into stress and a Root Center focus
- Champagne
- Finger foods
- Gooey, sugary, drippy foods

WOUNDS & DEATHS

Grail King Amfortas was wounded in the thigh (sex).

There's a wonderful scene in the BBC's made-for-TV movie of Joseph Conrad's novel *Nostromo*. The elder of two Italian daughters has been promised in marriage to Nostromo, the eponymous hero of the story, but he has fallen in love with the flirtatious younger daughter. When they're caught running off together the older sister stands screaming on the beach watching them row away, striking her fists against her lower belly (Sacral Center) again and again while crying his name in jealous agony.

In an episode of *Ally McBeal* when Ally learns that her rival is pregnant she "imagines" a cannon ball firing through her own belly and knocking a huge hole right in her sacral area.

Impotence or infertility.
Castration, genital mutilation.
Rape.
Disembowelment.
Dysentery.

EXAMPLES

Characters
One of the most Sacral characters in literature is the arrogant womanizing rake Don Juan from Mozart's opera of the same name. To keep the gender balance recall Bizet's *Carmen*, Nabokov's novel and the *Lolita* films, and Kathleen Turner in *Body Heat*.

The Marquis de Sade.

On the silly side, how about Steve Martin and Dan Akroyd as those "Wild and Crazy Czechoslovakian guys" from the old *Saturday Night Live* skits.

Some real life characters exhibiting Sacral Center qualities are Eva Peron and Mae West. The tabloids and paparazzi are always dragging celebrities down into compromising Sacral positions. Note the magazines and newspapers at the check-out stand next time you're in the market. Almost all the headlines have something to do with sex and jealousy and most of them concern people with lots of money wearing very little clothing.

The HBO TV series *Six Feet Under* has many characters struggling with their Sacral Center: the mom struggling out from her sexual repression; the gay son struggling to come out; the clingy, whiney dingy debutante of the first season who was trying to snag David, the gay son; the teen daughter exploring her sexuality, Brenda going over the edge with sex-addiction.

And then there's *Sex and the City* and now *The L Word*.

Most Tennessee Williams plays relish the Sacral with characters who either repress or overindulge their Sacral urges: Brick and Maggie in *Cat on a Hot Tin Roof,* Blanche and Stanley in *A Streetcar Named Desire.* The 1950s Hayes Code censored *Streetcar* the movie so not only weren't we sure that Stanley had actually raped Blanche rather than just slugged her, but Stella took the baby and ran away upstairs rather than being irresistibly drawn back to Stanley by passionate desire.

Films

American Gigolo

Beyond Honor

Body Heat

Bowling for Columbine — The Oscar-winning documentary posits that the fear-based consumer society of America spawns the obsessive gun culture and highest firearms murder rate on the planet.

Chicago

Chocolat

Cinema Paradiso

The Crying Game

Damage

Double Indemnity

Down and Out in Beverly Hills

Down With Love

Elmer Gantry

Evita — after the actual Eva Peron who Sacralled her way to fame and power

The Exorcist — repressed teenage Sacral Center = poltergeist phenomena

Eyes Wide Shut

Fatal Attraction — In a paean to Puccini, director Adrian Lyne even plays bits from the opera *Madame Butterfly* and used that story to foreshadow the plot, letting us know that in this story, like in Puccini's, an illicit love affair will come to no good end.

First Wives Club

The Full Monty

Glengarry Glen Ross

The Grifters

Hannah and Her Sisters

In the Realm of the Senses — an at the time scandalous Japanese film in which sexual obsession descends to the Root Center and death, based on a true story

Il Postino

Indecent Proposal

Jerry Maguire

LA Confidential
Last Tango in Paris
Like Water for Chocolate
Lolita
M. Butterfly
Midsummer Night's Dream
Mighty Aphrodite
Moulin Rouge
Poltergeist
Porno films
The Postman Always Rings Twice
Pretty Woman
Sex and the City
Shirley Valentine
Showgirls
Swept Away
Tartuffe
Titanic
The Treasure of the Sierra Madre
Unfaithful
War of the Roses

Musicals, Opera, Ballet & Theatre

I saw a poster once that read, "Men Cheat, Women Cry, People Die… It's Opera." Though there are often political backgrounds and plot points in operas, in the main they are about romantic and sexual love and jealousy. Death is often the result of that deadly mixture and the tales take a dive to the Root Center as various characters dive off balustrades or cliffs, kill each other, or dance into the arms of the enemy or the Nazis.

All That Jazz
Boy Gets Girl
Cabaret — and that wonderful song espousing the motto of the Sacral, "Money makes the world go round"
Carmen
Carousel
Cat on a Hot Tin Roof
Chicago
Cosi Fan Tutte
Equus
Giselle
Grease

Gypsy
La Boheme
Madame Butterfly
Miss Saigon
Much Ado About Nothing
Music Man
Otelo
Othello
The Pearl Fishers
Phantom of the Opera
Quills
Prélude à l'après-midi d'un Faune (Prelude to the Afternoon of a Faun)
Romeo and Juliet
Salome
Scheherazade
South Pacific
Suddenly Last Summer
La Sylphide
Taming of the Shrew
Tristan und Isolde
Turandot
Vagina Monologues
Who's Afraid of Virginia Wolf

Books

The Bible's Song of Solomon. "Thy two breasts are like two young roes that are twins, which feed among the lilies" and "Thy belly is like a heap of wheat set about with lilies."

John Updike, American novelist who chronicled middle-class adulteries of the 1950s and '60s, had a rather mechanistic accounting of Sacral Center activities. Phillip Roth, Henry Miller, and Norman Mailer also romp through America's Sacral Center.

The popularity of romance novels indicates the prevalence of the Sacral Focus in America, as well as a yearning to connect with something higher which cannot as yet, for some of the readers, be identified.

Tom Jones, Moll Flanders, and a great portion of Marcel Proust's *Remembrance of Things Past* are also Sacral focused stories.

Needless to say, pornographic books and comics are on the Sacral Center.

The Marquis de Sade's works.

Author Christopher Isherwood's account of decadence in Nazi Germany and the movie that came from it, *Cabaret*, are in the same frequency as the similarly set *All That Jazz* and *Chicago*.

The Bridges of Madison County is a Sacral Center book, albeit rather sappy.

Emma Bovary, Anna Karenina — two very Sacral chicks whose forays outside the bounds of matrimony come to no good end.

The Kama Sutra, Hindu love-making manual.

Gabriel Garcia Marquez's magical realism books are drenched in sensuality, from *One Hundred Years of Solitude* to *Love in the Time of Cholera*.

Pablo Neruda's poetry.

Shakespeare's sonnets to the Dark Lady.

Games

DopeWars — for the Palm Pilot and similar devices, there is Throat Center type strategy involved, but the motives are about amassing money through buying drugs in one city and selling them in another.

Grand Theft Auto — all the prostitutes, drugs, guns… and it's all about making enough money to be the main boss and have it all. It's also very Root Center with all the killing.

Max Payne — Rockstar games are SO good at Sacral!!

Music

Sacral music is, as you might well suppose, sensual. Saxophones come to mind. Have you ever noted that whenever the composer or film scorer wants to denote sensuality, particularly sleazy sensuality, they bring out the saxophone?

Country-Western music, particularly before it began to cross over, was predominantly about loss: loss of your lover, your spouse, your job, your best huntin' dawg, your best shotgun, your pickup truck, your trailer house.

Most pop songs are about finding and losing love, getting or not getting sex, and paying people back for the way they broke your heart.

Ditto the Blues.

When it was first introduced, the waltz was condemned as being way too sexual because the couples actually touched. It was surely a corruptor of morals and no "good" person would be caught dead doing the waltz. Needless to say, this proscription increased its popularity. The tango was viewed similarly and even today is still referred to as "sex standing up."

When Igor Stravinsky's *Rite of Spring* debuted in 1913 the compelling Sacral rhythms and blatantly sensual music created a scandal.

Jazz is thought by some to be very mental (i.e. Throat Centered) and some of it undoubtedly is. But most jazz, by its very origins, surroundings, and nature, is Sacral.

Belly-dancing music, lots of pop dance music.

Also on a Sacral frequency, at the more spiritual end of the scale, are flowery love songs to god or to the divine mother.

Historical

History has plenty of examples of Sacral Center madness, from the Roman Emperor Claudius's teenage trollop wife Messalina to the recruitment tactics of the Crusade era Hassassins, who used contrived "visits to Moslem Paradise and the company of sloe-eyed *houris*" to enlist young suicide assassins. *Houris* are those virgins said to flock around martyrs in groups of seventy-two. Actually, the number seventy-two has to do with degrees of the circumference of the earth rather than the number of hot dates in heaven. That's bound to be a disappointment to those boys who martyr themselves with hopes of *houris*.

There is an unfortunate history of sexual repression in the Inquisition and the burning of millions of so-called witches, a peculiarly twisted phenomenon not limited to Europe and America.

In the popular novel *The Da Vinci Code*, an important aspect of the plot is the centuries-long suppression of the Goddess religion by the Christian and Catholic Churches.

Mata Hari and other spies who use seduction to steal state secrets. Spies in training are warned against such "honey traps," male or female.

Current Events

In current events we find the Catholic Church of the early 2000s going through a major Sacral cleanup from incorrect use of those energies.

The growing movement against female genital mutilation is beginning to address another distortion of control of Sacral energy. In modern times we still have two million women who've undergone this horrifying cultural (not religious) rite. The independent film *Beyond Honor* shows the tragedy of this practice which is meant to control female sexuality and "protect" males from temptation by females.

In a reprise of the witch burnings of old there are many cases in the news these days of demonic possession, stealing of genitals, and witchery of sexual potency in sub-Saharan Africa. Those accused are often summarily tried and executed. One wonders if the introduction of Viagra might save more than face and relationships in those situations.

A number of animals are facing extinction because their various body parts are popular aphrodisiacs. Here, too, modern medicine might help save some endangered species.

So-called honor killings in the Middle East have gotten press lately, as women are slain by their families if they're thought to have stepped outside the strict sexual dictates of the society. Or recall the two women in sub-Saharan Africa condemned to stoning for having committed adultery. Interesting enough, the men involved were not punished. One detects a slight Sacral Center imbalance there.

Gay rights issues are a swirl of Sacral energies, including a large dollop of the fear bit on all sides. The gay marriage debate in America has stirred up a Sacral swirl of federal proportions.

Just turn back the pages of politics a few years and recall how the entire world was subjected to a shaking down of the President of the United States over Sacral Center activity. This is not a new phenomenon; the pages of every country's history fairly sizzle with sex scandals in high places.

B. The Practice

Now that you have a familiarity with this Center, it's time to put your new knowledge into practice.

1. FOR YOUR CHARACTERS

- Build their Character Profiles based on the above information
- Find photos of actors or people who embody the character you want to create
- Construct a Character Profile Collage
- Write up their ID Statement
- Note card — Currency. Use paper money as the base, or trim the card with coins. If your character is seductive, use sequins and satin on the card. Hearts and flowers would work for a softer Sacral character. Spray the card with

cologne: Obsession or Poison would be perfect. Depending on which end of the spectrum your character inhabits, add bits of lacy hearts and flowers or black leather, chains and studs.
- Do the Wash — check the various aspects to be sure you have integrity of character every time they appear on the page or on screen: food, dialogue, actions, others' reactions to them, etc.

Another thing to remember is that generally speaking (and there are always exceptions), men process sensuality visually and women process it verbally. In other words, give your male character something to "see" that will stimulate him Sacrally and give your female character something to "hear." Just think of the difference between "girly magazines" and romance novels. The former is mainly images (though of course lots of guys buy them "for the articles") and the latter mainly words. This is also a bit of explanation as to why a woman wants to hear a man say sweet nothings, or declare his love in actual words, regardless of how well he treats her. Visual cues for men, verbal cues for women. Practically speaking, you could make one of these events a turning point in a character's arc when the girl finally dresses sexy again for her guy, or when the guy finally says those three-little-words.

2. FOR YOURSELF

This is where you Walk the Walk and *Act As If.*

- Play that jazz, blues, the soundtracks of the musicals and/or movies, some Patsy Cline or Hank Williams albums, sexy dance music
- Wear silk, spangles, fringes. Something sensual, very tactile
- Put exotic artwork or statues near your creative space
- Eat luxurious foods: oysters and caviar
- Drink champagne
- Go to a strip club or exotic dancer bar (only for the research, of course)
- Take a course in Tantric Sex (but see provisos above)
- Go to a skid row area to see how the downside of the money aspect of the Sacral Center manifests
- Watch the movies
- Peruse TV for ads that use sex to sell. Keep a tally of how many you can spot in one day's watching
- Read the books
- Look for magazines and billboards that use Sacral Center motivation. Any time you see something rather sexual or sensual used to sell something seemingly not sexual, like clothes or cars, you can bet the advertisers are using the Sacral Center energies to lure you into spending your money.

- Call up someone you know who tends to be Sacral Centered and engage in a conversation of at least ten minutes. Keep a tally of how many times they make sexual references or innuendoes. Use that dialogue as a guide for your Sacral Centered character.

3. EXERCISE

Complete your analysis from the "How To Use the Centers of Motivation" chapter on page 25.

C. Conclusion

Your Sacral Center characters will be focused on sex and sensuality, on money, or on fear. Sometimes it's a fear of losing money or sex. Everything they do, remember, will have as its ultimate goal the acquisition of money, indulgence in something sexual, or the alleviation of fear.

Jealousy, a fear-based emotion, can also play a huge part in Sacral Center living.

The answer to their question of "What's My Motivation?" can run the gamut of Sacral aspects: "To get laid," "To get paid," "To win the lottery," "To enjoy life and love," "To seek and give pleasure," "To party down, dude," "To wallow in my misery 'cause I done lost my love," "To get my love back."

The tone of expression of a Sacral Center focus can run the gamut as well, from vicious mad sex and jealous frenzies to luxurious enjoyment of the physical pleasures. It can run from poverty and "ain't gettin' any" to prosperity and indulgence of the senses.

Since most of humanity still has a very active Sacral Center and is motivated in great part by the Inner Drives of Sex-Fear-Money, it's no surprise that this type of story and character appeals to a large audience.

Some characters are always going to be motivated by money and sex, regardless of how much of either they get, how old they get, or how the circumstances of their life change. But many individuals move upwards in consciousness and begin to expand the parameters of what's important to them. As a character begins to rise above these more tribal and animal motivations of the Sacral Center, what's next? Me. I. Me, me, me. Mine, mine, all mine.

5.

*L*ower Solar Plexus

The Solar Plexus is the home of emotional polarity, the home of opposites. It is divided into two Centers:

    a) the Lower Solar Plexus

    b) the Aspirational Solar Plexus

We'll explore the motivations of each as we look further into the two separate aspects of this Center, which often play off each other.

Location

The Solar Plexus is about six inches above the navel between the Thoracic Vertebrae #11 & #12. Put your little finger over your navel, spread your fingers up and out, and your thumb will fall pretty much over your Solar Plexus.

Endocrine Glands & Hormones

Spleen & Pancreas — These glands supply and control the source of energy for the human body, in particular through our insulin/sugar system. It's said that the life force of the planet streams from the sun, comes into our bodies through the Solar Plexus chakra and is processed by the spleen. This *prana* is then distributed throughout the body according to the health and needs of the individual's system. Someone with a malfunction in either spleen or pancreas will have energy imbalances and will suffer in vitality. The processing of carbohydrates, proteins, sugars, and fats all plays into this energy level, too.

In Oriental medicine it is observed that excessive intellectual activity puts a strain on the spleen and depletes one's energy. This explains why after working hard on a script (a seemingly effortless activity to anyone who's never done it) you can be totally exhausted even if you've lifted nothing heavier than a coffee mug or a martini glass.

An overabundance of this energy isn't pleasant either. Outbursts of anger or pique are often called "venting your spleen."

The influence of this Center on our Inner Drives also explains how some people can seem so very strong in their rather unsavory aspects and actions. Remember that the life force enters at the Solar Plexus. One often wonders why good does not always prevail, how the selfish overwhelms the selfless. Persons operating from the Lower Solar Plexus have an awfully lot of sheer energy at their disposal, while someone operating from the higher Centers, if not yet fully grounded in their shift of focus, will not hold up against the onslaught of this powerful concentration of raw power. A tenet of the Wisdom Teachings is that "A higher focus is not necessarily a stronger focus," as the world has often seen to its woe.

Liver — In Oriental medicine the liver is the commander of all the *chi* in the body. In Western traditions the liver is ruled by Mars, the god of war. The emotion of the liver is anger. If anger is not expressed it becomes frustration and/or depression and causes ever so many problems — many of which can be fascinating for your characters to exhibit.

The liver is also home to decision-making and purpose. On the down side you have wishy-washy people unable to decide anything. On the other extreme you have the stubborn people who, once they have made up their so-called mind (once they have settled on a fixed emotion), cannot be moved, no matter what. Bringing a character into moderation from either of those extremes offers great opportunities for drama: watch the Jack Nicholson character in *As Good As It Gets*, who starts out an opinionated, spiteful, old grouch and ends up being kind and considerate to others.

DYNAMICS BETWEEN LOWER AND ASPIRATIONAL SOLAR PLEXUS CENTERS

The Solar Plexus Center has two points of light, as you would expect for the Center of polarity, conflict, and emotions. Basically the Lower Solar Plexus is about the individual and is separatist and exclusive and the Aspirational Solar Plexus is about the group and is expansive and inclusive. Inner Drives from the Aspirational Solar Plexus are often mistaken for Heart Center actions but we'll see later on why and how they are different.

Since most humans process *prana* (life energy) through this dual Center, everything going through the Solar Plexus becomes a duality. This can explain how you get religious people preaching love being quite willing to slay the infidel or burn heretics at the stake. It could also explain Love-Hate relationships. It's the conceptual cause behind the effect of groups warring within themselves, internecine strife, civil wars, two party politics, familial splits, and idealism flip-flopping into fanaticism. It's the cartoon illustration of the devil on one shoulder and the angel on the other.

Certainly much of our reality is based on duality. Male-Female. On-Off. Day-Night. Black-White. Dark-Light. Good-Evil. Will-Love. Love-Hate. Selfish-Unselfish. The 1-0 binary code of computers.

Duality seems to be reflected as well in some aspects of theoretical cosmology: the Big Bang and the Big Crunch (or the Big Fade, depending on which theory holds at the time) where the universe explodes out of nothing, expands for billions of years, then runs out of energy and collapses back in on itself or drifts further apart into utter darkness. Ancient Hindu writings call this process the Days and Nights of Brahma. They see this particular cosmos as only one of many in a long chain of *manvantaras* (a manifestation of energy into matter) and *pralayas* (the quiescent resting stage before big bangs and after big crunches or fades). The new String Theory posits multiple dimensions called Branes crashing together periodically to create universes anew; similar again to the Hindu *manvantaras* and *pralayas*.

On a personal level, most humans are well aware of the emotional ups and downs of this polarity. At the higher Ajna Center one begins to work with these opposites and to transform conflicting concepts into powerful paradoxes. But for anyone focused in the Solar Plexus, the world of emotions, life is a duality and one is often rather troubled by that. For story-tellers, that's good news since drama is conflict. Stories and/or characters moving between these two Centers will be discussed at length in the section on "Mythic Structure." For now let's explore each of the Solar Plexus Centers.

3a. Lower Solar Plexus

Why does Rocky Balboa train and fight against all odds in *Rocky?*

He is motivated by his Lower Solar Plexus Center and is acting out the Wakeup Call Mythic Theme.

Say you want to craft a story based on the Wakeup Call, a coming-of-age story, a fallen warrior redeemed, or a rise of the individual story. What is a good place to start your character's journey; where do you put them, psychologically speaking? And then where do you take them? One very effective position from which to begin is a Lower Solar Plexus focus. As you can see from the listing of attributes below, most of them are at least slightly unattractive and could well do with a wakeup. Chapters in "Mythic Structure" will explain further how to make those changes, once you are familiar with the Centers.

You also might want to bring a character from the sometimes mindless robotic nature of the Root Center or the tossed-by-hormones Sacral Center to a position of actually thinking for themselves. In that case your Wakeup Call character would begin focused on one of the lower Centers and would move up to the Lower Solar Plexus and begin to exhibit independent thinking and grow in confidence.

Rocky Balboa starts at the Root Center in a nowhere job beating up other people and living in a junky room. He even admits to Adrian that he is nobody. Pursuing the shy Adrian, he rises to the Sacral Center and makes a solid connection with her. Once challenged by Apollo Creed (a very Lower Solar Plexus character) Rocky determines to just go the distance. He applies personal willpower, gains self-confidence, and ultimately reaps the recognition and rewards of having made the shift from a lower Center to a higher one.

A. The Theory

MOTIVATION: PERSONAL POSITION, POWER, POSSESSIONS

- Appetites
- Arrogance
- Boundaries
- Competition
- Greed
- Humility
- Individuality
- Loyalty
- Perfectionism
- Respect for power
- Self-confidence
- Separatism
- Will power

The Lower Solar Plexus is all about personal self-is-ness, personal power. It's individualization and self-identity. It's separative. It's turf wars, one-upsmanship. It's about conflict, conquest. Possession. Acquisition. Its motto is, "Me, mine, I want, I want, I want!" It is insatiable.

This focus exhibits as self-centeredness, myopic vision, self-obsession. Close-knit tribal loyalties lead to the vehement exclusion of all others. Think of gangs and cliques, tribes and terrorist cells. Think ethnic cleansing. Chauvinism in all its forms is generated from an LSP Inner Drive. An agitator is usually a Lower Solar Plexus person.

Boundaries and territories are extremely important to someone on a Lower Solar Plexus focus. One end of the scale of the hormonal effect of pancreas/gall bladder connection is that a person will express frustration rather than anger. Keep in mind that anger is sometimes righteous and necessary to correct wrongs.

An aspect of character change could be your character having a real problem with boundaries at the beginning of the story. They would begin by letting people run over them, never expressing an opinion, and cowering at the mere thought of confrontation. Through experience, observation, advice, trial-and-error, and possibly therapy they learn to set appropriate boundaries and take their rightful balanced position in the Lower Solar Plexus Center. At the end of your story they would now stand up for themselves, they would be willing to take on conflict in the interest of correctness and self defense. They would gain greatly in self-esteem and self-confidence.

There are also many positive aspects of this Lower Solar Plexus Center. After all, if an individual didn't go through this phase they'd always be like simple-minded children without a separate sense of self. Without the self confidence to step out on their own and explore new ways, humans would not have made much progress beyond simple animal survival and reproduction. In this sense the Lower Solar Plexus is the crux of individuality and personality diversity.

It has also been the spur for much of the seeming progress in human social evolution: from the individualism of Greek democracy to today's forms thereof and from the independent thinking pursued by the Protestant Revolution against a hierarchical Catholic Church where dogma ruled. The movie *Luther* starring Joseph Fiennes deals with this particular shift in focus among the religious of Europe at a time when pretty much everyone was either religious or greatly influenced by religion.

LOCATION/HORMONES

See the introduction to the Solar Plexus.

MYTHIC MEANING

Average humanity is said to be currently focused below the diaphragm, subject to the ravages of emotions and duality. Most of humanity sees the world as duality. Within those dualities, an individual will usually find themselves at the center of their world.

The saying I saw on a T-shirt said it well: I am the center of my universe. Everyone else is either a star, a black hole, or an insignificant speck of useless matter.

A sense of being in exile is unique to humanity, as far as we know. Some anthropologists define being human as being able to remember the past and imagine the future, as opposed to animal nature which supposedly is mostly focused in the "now." Once we learn to really communicate with animals this uniqueness may be challenged.

In some cosmologies the reason the universe exists at all is because god was lonely and wanted someone to converse with and something to do. Or as the novelist Joseph Conrad (*Lord Jim, Nostromo, Heart of Darkness*) so eloquently put it, "We live, as we dream, alone." Yes, we do, if we're in a Lower Solar Plexus focus. That loneliness can eventually drive a character up towards the Aspirational Solar Plexus.

In Aesop's Fables a cocky little dog is trotting across a bridge with a nice juicy bone clasped firmly in his mouth. He happens to glance over the edge of the bridge down at the stream and sees a dog with an even bigger bone in its mouth. Water distorts the size and location of objects, remember. Torn between the right-now-okay taste in his mouth and the even-better-bigger imagined taste, he growls at the other dog — who growls back. Greed and pride triumph; the dog drops his bone and leaps into the water after that other dog with the bigger bone. Both dog and bone are swept away and drown.

In Greco-Roman mythology the beautiful youth Narcissus also suffered from a raging case of arrogance. He spurned the affections and attentions of all the fluttering maidens, mortal and immortal alike. But one of the rejected girls convinced Nemesis, the goddess of righteous anger, to deal with the cruel boy. She devised a clever curse for the self-absorbed youth. Bending over a clear pool of water for a drink, Narcissus caught sight of his reflection and fell instantly, irretrievably in love with himself. Pining away with unrequited love, he finally understood the pain he had caused others; but there was no help for it. Never taking his eyes from his own reflection, Narcissus fell into it and drowned.

Another mythic meaning is the challenge of balancing opposites. Since this is the home of emotions and duality, we must to learn to juggle, to find that middle path. In the case of anger, for instance, there's too much force swirling around the Solar Plexus Center; in the case of depression, too little. One of the most dramatic things your story characters can do is to struggle for balance, to work on controlling their dark sides, to have the courage to change for the good. Their vacillation is fascinating.

One of the best examples of this is Bud Fox in *Wall Street*, where he battles his good upbringing against his acquisitiveness and the mentoring of "Greed is Good!" Gordon Gekko. Others examples are discussed in the "Mythic Structure" chapters.

Since most humans are attempting (consciously or by the sheer force of evolution) to rise out of this Center a lot of our stories are focused here. The well-told, mythically-aligned story will show both the down side and the up side of this particular Inner Drive. It will show us how to uplift our focus of consciousness and not to suppress these energies but to control and properly use them.

As we see again and again, Lord Acton (1834-1902) was right when he observed that power tends to corrupt and absolute power corrupts absolutely.

ARCHETYPES

Bully & Bullied — Both are on an LSP focus, at opposite ends. The bully crosses boundaries; the bullied have very weak boundaries. Ralphie Parker in *A Christmas Story* is a bullied little boy whose Christmas gift of the BB gun begins to give him a new sense of boundaries and a new perspective on the bullies in his life.

Cabal or Cartel — Usually secretive, usually powerful, and usually manipulative to their own separatist ends, cartels apply force in order to control their special interest. Usually they use economic rather than physical force, like OPEC or the diamond cartels. Sometimes they keep information from the people, like the government of the People's Republic of China still tries to do and before that the very suppressive media of Pravda, the Communist-controlled Soviet news outlet. In the city-state of Singapore, satellite dishes were not allowed until during the first Gulf War when local bankers and money markets started losing millions because they were caught behind the curve of information. The law changed a bit to accommodate that cartel but they still don't allow x-rated movies into the country. Not legally anyway.

Conspiracy theorists see this intense and usually secretive Lower Solar Plexus activity and perceive danger. Sometimes, they just might be right. The very successful TV series *X-Files* was based on the existence of a Cabal that was working with the aliens to subvert and take over the earth. *Three Days of the Condor* and a lot of Tom Clancy movies deal with conspiracies. And how about *Conspiracy Theory*, starring Mel Gibson?

Cowboy — An action version of the Loner. Particularly in the mythology of America, which is founded on the ideal of the individual and his (and now also her) rights, the lone individual who takes action is practically apotheosized.

There's a term in international affairs called "Cowboy Diplomacy." Guess which country is usually doing it? Yup, ma'am, that'd be the U.S. of A.

The Cowboy is a pioneer, a go-getter, a take-names-later-kick-hiney-now, actions-speak-louder-than-words character. They may occasionally dip into the comforts of civilization but they're much more at ease out on the fringes where they can make up their own rules. Think John Wayne. Think recent American military policy.

In the fine BBC Masterpiece Theatre mini-series *Jewel in the Crown* based on Paul Scott's four novels of *The Raj Quartet*, one of the characters expresses glee (as much as a proper British officer would ever express something so effusive as glee) at being assigned to the Kashmir region because out there away from the central bureaucracy there are no hard and fast rules, you get to think on your feet, and make things up as you go along. Rather like Indiana Jones.

Cult Leader, Godfather, Big Man — Though the members of a cult, gang, or tribe are usually on a Sacral or Root Center focus, the leader will usually be on Lower Solar Plexus. They will be the controllers, the manipulators, of others. It's about them, them, and only them. Everything they do is calculated to keep them in power, and that often includes mob wars, military coups, and genocide.

Some cult leaders will order their followers to think of them while they're having sex. Others will even have sex with their followers, appropriating the Sacral energies for their own Lower Solar Plexus use. Think Charles Manson, Jim Jones, and David Koresh, all of whom were working to promote themselves at the expense of their followers. The TV movie *Guyana Tragedy: The Story of Jim Jones* shows Powers Boothe accurately portraying this type of person.

Fundamentalists — I'm right. You're wrong. God said so. End of story.

Hate Groups, Racist Groups — We're chosen. You're not. God said so. End of you.

A great number of creation myths, crafted in those isolated times before sailing ships and air ships, often supposed that "the people," as people often named themselves, were the only ones around. Made sense to think of themselves as special, as chosen. Some SETI advocates and sci-fi fans think earthlings suffer from the same short-sightedness. The Krikkit in *The Hitchhiker's Guide to the Galaxy* suffer from this delusion and with their high-tech abilities attempt to rid the universe of anything not-Krikkit.

Lobbyists — Do the words "special interest" have a ring here? Indeed they do. But if you promise to vote our way, we'll donate lots of money to your campaign. Just as not all LSP activities are negative, neither is all lobbying, just the kind that brings harm to others in order to benefit an exclusive group.

Loner — Because a person on this focus is beginning to step outside the Tribal mentality and think for themselves, they will often be ostracized from their larger unit or simply not fit in any more, not feel comfortable. The mechanics of this frequency are easily seen in the dynamics of developmental psychology with both the "terrible twos" and the typical teenager's repulsion from their parents and family.

The Loner will often express disdain for the mindless herd-like actions of those on lower Centers and will strive mightily to stand out from the crowd. Watch James Dean in *Rebel Without a Cause*.

The Loner tends to sulk.

Politician — Keep in mind the difference between a statesman and a politician. The statesman acts with higher motives in mind, the greater good for the greater number. The politician acts with self-interest in mind. This is a telling distinction and you can see it at work in any government situation, from your local school board to the U.S. Congress to the United Nations. Or just watch CSPAN for a couple of hours.

The movie *Power* features Richard Gere as a political consultant who gets embroiled in dangerous LSP machinations. *Dave*, starring Kevin Kline, dramatically illustrates the differences between the politician and the statesman. *The West Wing* TV series delineates dramatically between politicians and statesmen and *My Fellow Americans* shows two ex-presidents making shifts between LSP and ASP.

Servant — The archetype of the servant falls in the Lower Solar Plexus focus. Regardless of why they are there, the very actions of being a servant imply a lack of personal boundaries, a frustration of individual will.

Your characters need not be actual servants, like Anthony Hopkins's Stevens in *Remains of the Day* or in a humorous vein, like Jeeves in the *Bertie Wooster* series. Actually, Jeeves is on the Throat Center, but Bertie is oblivious to that and treats him like he's LSP. For a wild spectrum of characters in this position see *Gosford Park*.

A character on this Center could perfect their role and find personal meaning and self-confidence in it, like Morgan Freeman's Hoke Colburn in *Driving Miss Daisy*. Or they could strive to move beyond this position like Melanie Griffith's Tess McGill in *Working Girl* who moved up from Sacral, through LSP on her way to Throat and then Ajna.

Small Tribe or Gang — Out for itself, with no illusions about that. Separatism and exclusivity are the watch-words for these groups. It can even be those deadly cliques of the school years. Interesting enough, many situations thrive on dividing up people into small groups, tribes, or gangs. Think of the houses in British public school systems, most recently popularized in the *Harry Potter* series, like that ongoing rivalry between houses Griffendor and Slytherin.

The "gang-related" genre is evident in most media. Rap music is the holy liturgy of this Center focus. Though many gang members would probably claim to be warriors, they do not fit the mythic profile of the Warrior: To protect the weak and the innocent; to defend and uphold the Good, the True, and the Beautiful. Without those two ideals they are simply gangsters or mercenaries like in *Gangs of New York*.

Just as Prohibition of alcohol and tobacco in the 1920s and '30s produced tommy-gun toting gangs of Al Capone and Baby-Face-This and Big-Guy-That, with the Feds led by Eliot Ness and *The Untouchables*, so has the Drug War of the 1990s produced the Medillin Cartel and the DEA, a la *Traffic*.

A positive side to cliquishness occurs when a small group of people band together to accomplish something for themselves, such as a sports team. And just think of the fervent fan rivalry! Having gone to high school in a small town in Texas, I am here to tell you that football is taken very, very, very seriously in the Midwest. On football Friday the team all wore their gold and white football jackets, white shirts, black slacks and ties, and carried their golden helmets under their arms all day... to English class, to Algebra class.... And, they were not allowed to speak. They were required to be "thinking about the game." Yep, we do take our Lower Solar Plexus high school football seriously.

A drama troupe, though they may be in Throat Center focus when performing, will usually be personally on a Lower Solar Plexus focus. Watch Christopher Guest's charming film *Waiting for Guffman* for excellent examples of this.

Warriors, Groups of Warriors, Warlords, 2nd Stage Revolutionaries & Mercenaries — Myths are replete with these Lower Solar Plexus heroes. Though the differences of opinion about motives and means are rife and rampant, to illustrate this point we would place the Palestine Liberation Army and the combating Zionists, the Irish Republican Army, the Muslim Brotherhood, and al Qaeda in this group. Say what you will about methodologies, their motives are Lower Solar Plexus and very very separatist. Remember in the introduction to this section we talked about the duality of this Center and how you'd find the religious adherent willing to slay the infidel in defense of their religion of peace?

In the second stage of a revolution you can no longer reach the revolutionaries through the original slogans because they are no longer fighting for the original cause — now they're just fighting because fighting defines them and gives their lives purpose. They have moved from ASP to LSP.

On the positive side is Warrior Bonding — where people who share life-threatening experiences bond in ways no other people can. Just ask anyone who's shared a fox-hole or a front line.

SYMBOLS

Fire & Water — Fire and water are considered opposites, and the Solar Plexus is the home of opposites. Water is always, always, always symbolic of the emotions and its various states represent various emotional states:

- Solid water, ice = blocked or frozen emotions
- Liquid water = free-flowing emotions. But are they contained? Calm? Turbulent?
- Gaseous water, steam = stirred up, pent-up, dangerously hot emotions

An interesting story point from physics is a state of change called "vaporization." This is when a solid is subjected to intense heat and goes directly to a gaseous state without passing through the liquid stage. When a character explodes under pressure they can be said to vaporize. They "go postal," to use a tragically applicable term. Some of the characters in David Mamet's *Glengarry Glen Ross* exhibit this quality.

If the steam is then converted from a gas back into a solid without going through the liquid phase that's called "sublimation" and is a process for purification. In a character or a situation, the intense propulsion of the emotions or the story into a highly volatile state and then resolving it back down to calmness, but with a lesson learned, a purification, would be sublimation. Examples would be:

- An explosion of temper that resolves a long-suppressed issue: relationship conflicts (*The Long Kiss Goodnight*)
- The blatant exposure of a wrong so that it can be righted: political, economic, social scandals (*Norma Rae*)
- A violent social upheaval that quickly dies down: riots, uprisings (*Network*)

Ram — The Ram is the symbol for the astrological sign of Aries (March 21 – April 21) and if you look back historically the Age of Aries (2000 B.C. to 1 B.C.) was the Heroic Age. Warriors were *It*. It was the time of the individual hero conquering the multitudes, that individualism thing again in great heroes such as Perseus, Theseus, Hercules, most of the guys in the Trojan War, Achilles, Aeneas, Cuchulain, Bran the Blessed, Rama, Hanuman the Monkey King, etc.

Salamanders — These creatures are like lizards, only made of fire. Both nymphs and salamanders are pairs of opposites that make the Solar Plexus Center so dramatic.

Sea Serpents — Serpents are symbolic of that kundalini energy winding its twining way from the Root Center up the spinal column. Water is always symbolic of the emotions so the serpent (rising energy) immersed in water (emotions) is a perfect symbol of the Lower Solar Plexus.

Water Nymphs, Mermaids, Selkies — The water spirits, female and gorgeous, seductive, and ultimately deadly. There's a marvelous painting by James Waterhouse titled "Hylas and the Nymphs" which shows Hercules' young squire (and some say boyfriend) Hylas on the trip with the Argonauts to get the Golden Fleece being lured into a sylvan stream by beautiful water nymphs. Hylas never returned from the stream and the desperate Hercules searched for him so long that the other Argonauts eventually had to leave him there and continue their journey without him. *The Secret of Roan Innish* is about selkies, seals which can become human.

Yin-Yang — The Oriental sign of equally matched pairs of opposites is a perfect display of the dynamics of the Solar Plexus Center.

PLANET

Mars — The red planet. The God of War. Impetuousness.

ASTROLOGICAL SIGNS

Aries — A very individualistic sign. Explorer, warrior, innovator. Very independent, freethinker, loathe to take orders.

Leo — Though often quite attractive and outgoing, the lower-level Leo person is also very self-promoting and self-centered; how could they be anything but Lower Solar Plexus?

Pisces — Two fish swimming in water: duality in the emotional state. Intuitive, perceptive, emotional.

COLORS, SHAPES, MATERIALS

- Reds — dark, brilliant, fire red, blood red
- Blacks — glossy blacks, matte blacks
- Blues — solid bright blue, navy blue, cop uniform blue
- Fire — running the gamut from smoldering to blazing
- Water — in all its forms: gaseous, liquid, solid
- Sharp weapons — swords, spears, knives

CLOTHING

- Emphasis on the waist
- Heavy belts and belt-buckles — Rocky's boxing belt
- Knotted sashes, belts
- Vests that draw attention to the Solar Plexus
- Warrior outfits

If your character is moving from another Center to a Solar Plexus focus you can have them put on heavy belts, begin knotting sashes, etc. As they move out of Lower Solar Plexus you can have them remove these heavy, emphatic, constricting objects.

Conversely, if a character has had trouble becoming independent, then putting on such a significant belt will be a sign of victory for them.

STYLES OF SPEECH

- Self-oriented
- Me, mine, I want, I need
- Get, acquire, possess
- "What's in it for me?"
- Hateful, separate
- Us against them
- Combative — and they're always sure they're right
- Opposition — you say white, they say black; you say up, they say down; always opposites and polarities

Recall that Brad Pitt's Achilles in *Troy* admitted that he wanted what all men want; he just wanted it more.

A Lower Solar Plexus person will always turn every conversation back to themselves and they'll always be thinking of what they're going to say next rather than listening to the other person. A perfect example is the vain person who asks after a discussion about more important issues, "Does this look good on me?" Or as in *Galaxy Quest*, when Dr. Lazarus (Alan Rickman) scorns Captain Peter Quincy Taggart (Tim Allen), "It's always about *you*, isn't it."

PHYSICAL ACTIONS

- Forceful
- Fighting, combative stances
- Demanding
- Centered
- Fists to the waist

- Hands on hips
- Putting themselves outside the crowd, holding themselves apart
- If in a small tribe or group, clinging to the significant others

FOIBLES, PHOBIAS, FOODS

- Abdominal and intestinal troubles
- Spleen and pancreas imbalances
- Diabetes
- Insatiable appetites — the stereotypical psychic who puts on weight for protection against all the odd energies
- Compulsive-obsessive
- Clean-freaks — Howard Hughes in his later years
- Control-freaks
- Gambling — seeking personal power over Fate and over other people
- Fatigue due to stress
- Obsessive thinking, worry
- Rage
- Revenge
- Tuberculosis, asthma, lung problems
- Emotional separateness diseases: skin diseases, leprosy, eczema, psoriasis

The spleen filters old blood cells and foreign organisms from the blood and produces white blood cells; functions that are about separatism and deciding what's "alien."

- Predator mentality
- Low self-esteem
- Indecisive
- Poor impulse control
- Rebelliousness
- Manipulative
- Seeing auras

Addictions — People on an LSP focus deal with pain through arousal, which gives a sense of power, a feeling that they can overcome the pain.

A character attempting to overcome their addictions would try for a regular, balanced diet with lots of fiber and water, since the Lower Solar Plexus affects digestion and elimination.

- Sweet foods
- Ethnic foods, emphasize separateness, tribal thinking. Will eat this, will not eat that because it's "their" food

- Detox foods like teas, carrot juice, broccoli and cauliflower, since an LSP person is likely to indulge

The spleen processes the vitality from sunlight. When that's lacking, eucalyptus and pine offer pre-digested prana; the oils of both are said to be good for nerve damage. You could have a character burning incense of either of those essences. Or you could put them in a pine or eucalyptus grove. "Sheesh," you might say, "How's that going to tie into a story?" In D.H. Lawrence's novel and the movie made from it by Ken Russell, *Women In Love*, there's a great scene where Alan Bates' Rupert Birkin, having had a serious tiff with his ex-sweetie Hermione, strips naked and runs out into the forest. He tree-hugs. We are to understand that he is reconnecting with nature and obtaining the strength to go on.

WOUNDS & DEATHS

A wound in the gut from a knife, gun, fist, or kick could work.

Sepuku or hari-kari.

Cut in half, like in the old melodramas with the giant saws or trains about to do in the heroine.

Fire.

Another very good death for a Solar Plexus character would be drowning, being overwhelmed by the emotions, which are always symbolized by water, remember.

EXAMPLES

Characters
From the age of the Warrior there is an abundance of stories about Lower Solar Plexus types: lone fighters, rugged individuals who took on demons, gods, goddesses, and other warriors. For the most part they tended to be a bit arrogant and cocky.

One of the most complex mythic characters who was probably a real person is the Assyro-Babylonian king Gilgamesh. His mythic tale is a classic example of someone solidly on a Lower Solar Plexus focus who by the end of the tale has risen to the Aspirational Solar Plexus. This Mesopotamian story of arrogant, sophisticated, womanizing Gilgamesh, King of Uruk (or Erech) and Enkidu, the gentle, naive animal-loving man of the wilderness is also one of the oldest "buddy stories." It pits the city against the countryside, the vain against the humble, worldly versus innocent, the outgoing versus the introvert. It coalesces them into a true friendship that battles petty gods, scorned goddesses, scorpion men, fickle fate, helpful strangers, and the ultimate tragedy of separation by death. In the end, Gilgamesh has made that transformation from me-me-me to us-and-all and becomes a wise king.

The Greek hero Odysseus spends most of the Trojan War as told in Homer's *Iliad* and a goodly portion of the ten-year return to his kingdom of Ithaca as told in the *Odyssey* at a Lower Solar Plexus focus. He's the feisty, arrogant, crafty warrior king who's eventually transformed by his experiences.

A fellow Greek warrior who doesn't quite make that change is the great Achilles. This is a guy who almost throws the entire Trojan War because he's pouting in his tent for three days over Briseis, a war-prize babe. It was more about competitiveness with the General King Agamemnon than it was about love for the girl Briseis. Though the filmmakers play havoc with Homer's story, Brad Pitt in *Troy* plays this insolent, arrogant, spoiled, and self-indulgent LSP character to the hilt.

An interesting small group from myth is Jason and the Argonauts, a bunch of combative and competitive Greek heroes and demigods who set off with the prince Jason to get back the Golden Fleece so he could take his rightful place on the Grecian throne.

The real-life person Heinrich Harrer was quite LSP, as you can tell by reading his book or seeing the movie *Seven Years in Tibet*. No matter what was going on in the world around him, Harrer seemed to make all decisions based on his own selfish interests, even if it meant betraying or slighting friends or innocent others.

Or how about everyone's favorite self-centered heroine, Scarlett O'Hara from *Gone With the Wind*. And then there's the troubled James Dean in *Rebel Without a Cause*. He had a cause all right, to express his Lower Solar Plexus focus, but nobody quite got that.

Most of Ernest Hemingway's stories featured heroes on an LSP focus. Tragedies usually ensued when they were seduced down into the Sacral or attempted to rise up, prematurely and unprepared, to higher Centers.

A large group on a Lower Solar Plexus is the Borg collective from *Star Trek*.

Michael Douglas in *Fatal Attraction* is at a Lower Solar Plexus focus. Notice that he falls into the Sacral (Sex-Fear-Jealousy), then tries to get out; but most of his actions are very selfish and about him-him-him.

In *American Beauty* most of the characters are on this focus. The hero has such a difficult time because he is attempting to rise above that and is meeting great resistance from all the others.

Other characters are Cal the power-strutting fiancé in *Titanic*, Claude Rains' power-broker Louis in *Casablanca*, Powers Booth's power-mongering Colonel in *Blue Sky* and Linda Hamilton's character in *Terminator II*. Sarah Connor should have been an Aspirational Solar Plexus and sometimes Heart Center character in *T-II*, working to save her son and hence the world. Perhaps what happened was that Linda Hamilton had worked out and buffed up for the film so her performance actually came across as LSP, though the role and the dialogue was ASP. Watch *T-II* with this in mind and see just how powerful a personal focus can be, inappropriately so in this case.

Jack Nicholson's portrayal of Melvin Udall in *As Good As It Gets* is a perfect example of a Lower Solar Plexus focus at the beginning, then throughout the film he moves up to Aspirational Solar Plexus focus.

Films

A Christmas Story
American Beauty
Anger Management
As Good As It Gets
Conspiracy Theory
Fight Club
Gangs of New York
Godfather(s)
Gone With the Wind
Goodfellas
Karate Kid
Lion King — see in *Musicals* below
Martial arts movies
Power
Raging Bull
Reality TV shows — especially the ultra-competitive ones
Rebel Without a Cause
Rocky(s)
Seven Years in Tibet
Soap Dish
Terms of Endearment
Three Days of the Condor
Traffic
Troy
Waiting for Guffman
Wall Street

Warriors — the competition between street gangs
X-Files
The Year of Living Dangerously

Musicals, Opera, Ballet & Theatre
A Doll's House
Annie — orphan girl searches for identity, a family, and a home
Fiddler on the Roof — about the effects of a separatist mentality on individuals and small villages
Gypsy — Though ultimately daughter Louise does strip-tease (Sacral), she does it from a Throat Center focus. The main character is the self-centered stage mother Momma Rose and show biz, which is usually LSP for the performers.
Hedda Gabler
Jesus Christ Superstar — You'd think a musical about Jesus would be Heart Centered, but it's all about Judas's disillusionment that Jesus has started to believe the press about him and is drawing too much personal attention, has gone too Lower Solar Plexus. There's nary a line in there about the higher ideals of Christianity; it's all about Jesus the man and his close companions and how they approve or not of what he's doing.
King Lear
The Lion King — To be mythically complete Simba should have risen higher while in exile; but the music was great.
Mame — As with lots of those larger-than-life characters who suck all the oxygen out of the room when they enter it, her motto is "Me, me, me the really fabulous, aren't I wonderful, Me!"
Petrushka — This tragic ballet character didn't have enough personal identity to survive the rough-and-tumble Russian circus world.
West Side Story — All about gangs, separatist rivalry. Some love, yes: Maria is Sacral, and see the chapter on "Center Arcing" for Tony's character arc.

Operas seem to find good use for LSP characters, usually as the villains. Baron Scarpia in *Tosca*, Doctor Bartolo in *The Barber of Seville*, and the Egyptian princess Amneris in *Aida* come to mind, selfish cruel creatures all. In *The Pearl Fishers* a great friendship between two men is tested by a Sacral drop, yes, a woman.

Books
The Count of Monte Cristo
Gone with the Wind
The Great Gatsby

Ernst Hemingway wrote mostly from an LSP perspective and mostly about LSP people.

Henry Miller's books, though often about sex, are all about him. Open one up at random and count how many I's there are on the page.

Many characters in many books are LSP; this Center of duality and polarity offers fantastic opportunity for dramatic conflict.

Games
Alias (game based on the TV series), though her methods and motives often switch between LSP and ASP.

Arc the Lad

Wizardry: Tale of the Forsaken Land

Tekken, Black & Bruised, Bloody Roar, and other head-to-head fighting games (these games seem to be more about yelling at the person you're playing with than actually playing the game).

Most sports games, especially football and 'Extreme' (read: violent or life-threatening) sports fall under this category.

Most first- and third-person shooter games are LSP with 'heroes' who do anything to 'win' whether it's treasure or power at the end of the game e.g. *Doom, Quake, Armed & Dangerous,* etc.; also, the characters in these games often dip down to Sacral, then back up to LSP.

Music
Though lots of rock-and-roll is Sacral Center music, a lot of the more powerful, driving, violent, hostile pieces are pure Lower Solar Plexus. If it's forceful, angry, cocky, and loud, good bet it's LSP.

Historical
History is written by the winners, and the winners are usually those with the strongest Lower Solar Plexus focus and abilities. Though many times the ideals for which warriors go to battle are lofty, the actual waging of the battles is, by the very nature of fighting, a duality. And by the nature of that duality, it's us-against-them. In the moment of fighting, in that battle space, recall, one is plunged into the Root Center.

One theory of history is that an era extrudes a personality: that if the particular Napoleon Bonaparte or the Julius Caesar that we have come to know and love or loathe had not been born, some other individual would have filled that role in that time and place. Perhaps. Under that theory we could then suppose that these individuals are the manifestation of a culture's Lower Solar Plexus. It would be interesting to do an historical investigation along these lines.

Suffice to say, plenty of go-it-alone rogue types have turned the tides of time, from the aforesaid Roman and French dictators to Genghis Khan, Atilla the Hun, many of the New World conquistadors, and the list goes on.

Current Events

Current events, unfortunately, show us many examples of a Lower Solar Plexus focus in warring street gangs, tribal conflicts, ethnic cleansing, cult leaders, and the leaders of terrorist cells.

For a while in the 1970s and '80s some of the self-help movements promoted very Lower Solar Plexus attitudes as exemplified in the cocky mantras of their graduates: "What's in it for me?," "I'm not responsible for your feelings," "No one can really help anyone else," etc. While these things are true, they are not the whole truth. Granted, a person must want help (i.e. the AA concept that you can't start back up until you've hit bottom), but encompassing that can be the broader impersonal Buddhist dictum to "Relieve suffering," and also the Hippocratic oath of Western medicine, "First, do no harm." Someone on a Lower Solar Plexus would be able to hone even those two dicta down to apply only to themselves and their own exclusive little cadre.

If you have kids or ever were a kid, you can recognize a Lower Solar Plexus flexing in the Terrible Twos and in the troubled teens.

In California in the mid-1970s a grass-roots voters' proposition lowered and fixed homeowner taxes. Certainly rampant taxation is undesirable, but it's a very Lower Solar Plexus attitude to deny any connection between oneself and the community and to refuse to participate in and support the community through taxation for social services that benefit all: schools, police forces, fire departments, roads, etc.

Whether it's a caste system, an imbalanced let-them-eat-cake aristocracy, or digital age haves and have-nots, this LSP split has been seen to engender either torpor and decay or resistance and revolution. Demonstrations at World Trade Organizations aren't quite guillotines in the plazas, but they are symptomatic of similar LSP separatist situations.

Much international policy must deal with LSP dictators and warlords with lots of weapons and a fervent following.

How often in war or conquest do you find the propaganda machine turning the enemy into "other," often demoting them to the level of sub-human? Unsettling examples of this LSP tactic abound on every side of all conflicts.

Cowboy diplomacy (or the lack thereof) is also an example of LSP focus. It is seldom well received by its targets or the world at large: witness the growing general disapproval of and resistance to American cowboy-actions in Iraq in 2003.

B. The Practice

Now that you have a familiarity with this Center, it's time to put your new knowledge into practice.

1. FOR YOUR CHARACTERS

- Build their Character Profiles based on the above information
- Find photos of actors or people who embody the character you want to create
- Construct a Character Profile Collage
- Write up their ID Statement
- Note card — Metallic. Aluminum foil even. Or camouflage colors. Jagged edges.
- Do the Wash — check the various aspects to be sure you have integrity of character every time they appear on the page or on screen: food, dialogue, actions, others' reactions to them, etc.

If you want to teach someone who's obsessing in a Lower Solar Plexus tailspin a lesson about kindness, you can design a secondary character operating from the Aspirational Solar Plexus to shame him, and/or a Sacral person who can make him feel needed and responsible. To an extent that happens to Jack Nicholson in both *As Good As It Gets* and *Terms of Endearment*.

2. FOR YOURSELF

This is where you Walk the Walk and *Act As If*.

- Play heavy metal, furious rock and roll. Strident music
- Marching songs. Get some collections of Marine or Navy Seal marching songs, guaranteed to put you in a warrior mood
- Wear show-off clothes: a uniform, casual camo, big belts
- Bare your midriff, but no girly frillies
- Eat and drink the most ethnically pure cuisine you can find for the background of the character you're creating. Keep each type of food on your plate separate from the others
- Go shopping in an ethnic market
- Do stomp about a bit
- Have a friend agree not to get offended and then ring up and be rude to them
- Go to a boxing match or a gym or martial arts studio to observe
- Take a couple of boxing or martial arts or sword fighting lessons
- Watch the movies

- Read some Hemingway. Or stories about big game hunters. Or war stories
- Go play a paintball war game
- Get into a game of touch football or pickup basketball

3. EXERCISE

Complete your analysis from the "How To Use the Centers of Motivation" chapter on page 25.

C. Conclusion

As the actress said at the Hollywood cocktail party, "Enough of me talking about me, why don't you talk about me for awhile."

A Lower Solar Plexus character will be centrally focused on themselves or their tight little group and will run the gamut of self-centered aspects.

The tone of the expression of a Lower Solar Plexus Center can run the gamut as well, from utter selfishness to learning to stand up for one's self.

Because so many of the world's problems today are centered around some people oppressing other people, stories about the acquisition of a strong sense of individuality resonate with real-world situations.

The move from states and tribes where people are ruled by oppressive dictators to states where every individual person has a voice and vote follows the same pattern as the individual's rise through the Centers of Motivation. As we can observe from current events, however, it's difficult to impose individual consciousness on people who aren't ready for it. Democracy and representative republics, like good character development and good acting, must come from within.

Perhaps the fact that so many humans today are struggling with this particular Center is part of what makes it so fascinating to storytellers and audiences alike, whether it's stories about South Africa's freedom and leap to higher consciousness (*In My Country*), tales of the fall back into tribalism and oppression (*The Year of Living Dangerously*), or the movies that are sure to come from the opening up of Eastern European countries and their inclusion in the European Union.

So what's next after an individual has grasped and mastered their own self? How about expanding out from "me" to "we"?

6.
*A*spirational Solar Plexus Center

Why does Norma Rae climb up on that factory table and take a stand for her fellow workers in *Norma Rae*?

By the very nature of the Aspirational Solar Plexus a person will aspire to something higher than themselves. To actually show these Inner Drives through physical action is a powerful story device. Besides Norma Rae's "stand," watch Robert De Niro the warrior (Lower Solar Plexus) struggling up that cliffside with all his armor to try and become a monk (Aspirational Solar Plexus) in *The Mission*. Try to work an actual shift of physical position for your character into the story line.

A. The Theory

MOTIVATION: ASPIRATION, ALTRUISM

- Brotherhood, sisterhood
- Greatest good for the greatest number
- Service to others
- Spiritual growth for self and others

A person in this state of awareness will be group oriented, inclusive, caring for others, driven by spiritual awareness and striving. They thirst for meaning in their life. They want to give back to the community, to the world.

LOCATION/HORMONES

See the introduction to the Solar Plexus Center.

MYTHIC MEANING

When a person finally realizes, usually through inordinate suffering, that what they're doing isn't working, they begin to look around them and open up to the possibility of a brotherhood of man and of the One Life encompassing every-thing that is, from snails to stars. They begin to soften, to consider other points of view. They begin to see other people as individuals, as worthy beings, as bits of a greater intelligence. They begin to care about something other than their own immediate comforts and pleasures. It is said that "Humans learn through suffering; the angels learn through joy." Not that you won't ever suffer after you start the rise up from the lower Centers, but spiritual teachings promise incredible joy to help lead you through the parlous times.

As a person raises their consciousness from one Center to the next they still have access to and use of the lower Centers. It's not about leaving the lower ones and moving to the higher, but rather about incorporating the lower ones into an expanded consciousness.

Many of the ancient and traditional initiation ceremonies are designed to help effect this change from a Lower Solar Plexus focus to an Aspirational Solar Plexus focus. Many people who've experienced an epiphany, a "religious experience," a near-death or abduction experience will come through it a changed person, suddenly having shed their more self-centered egotism and embracing a new connecting, sharing, generous, open framing of reality and the world around and within them. Many people call this the opening of the Heart chakra, but for most of humanity it is the development of the Aspirational Solar Plexus. (We'll examine the Heart Center in the next section and you'll see why that distinction is made.)

The Christian story of Saul on the road to Damascus illustrates this switch in Solar Plexus frequencies. According to the New Testament story, Saul had been vehemently persecuting Jesus and his followers and was on his way to Damascus to lead a hate rally. Striding purposefully down the dusty road and mumbling spitefully to himself, he was suddenly blinded by a brilliant light and heard Jesus' rather disappointed voice emanating from the sky, "Saul, Saul, why persecutest thou me?" Talk about your epiphany. After that experience, Saul changed his name to Paul, became one of Jesus the Christ's most devoted followers, and the rest is Church history.

When gang leaders and members call a truce and begin to collaborate for the betterment of themselves and their community, that's Aspirational Solar Plexus at work. When the three American soldiers in *Three Kings* expanded their awareness beyond Saddam Hussein's hidden treasure and dedicated their efforts to helping the Iraqi refugees, they went from their initial Lower Solar Plexus greed-based motivation to Aspirational Solar Plexus motivations.

Some of the steps in 12-step programs are specifically about ASP work: mending old hurts, forgiving others, appropriately asking forgiveness. It's about expanding the formerly confining boundaries of the self to include others in love and kindness.

In the film *The Mission*, the Jesuit priest played by Jeremy Irons operates from an ASP awareness and strives to redeem Robert De Niro, a warrior focused in the Lower Solar Plexus. Having fallen into the dark side of the Sacral, the conquistador soldier de Niro had slain his own brother in a fit of sexual jealousy. After paying penance and doing service among the local Indians, by the end of the film De Niro, guided by Irons, has made the transfer in consciousness from LSP to ASP and redeems himself in the fatal, heroic protection of innocent native people. Interestingly enough, he does a combination ASP/LSP at the end because he uses his LSP Warrior skills to accomplish those higher goals. We'll explore this more in the Mythic Structure chapter on "Pairs of Centers."

In his famous painting "The Birth of Venus," artist Sandro Botticelli depicts the goddess of love floating above the waters on a seashell, symbolic of the Self rising up out of the swells of uncontrolled emotions.

Aphrodite/Venus is the goddess of transformative love, as opposed to her son Eros who is the immature god of flirtation, infatuation, and lust. Nothing wrong with the latter, but they pale in comparison to the magnificent life-changing affects of Romantic love with a capital "R." That's Aphrodite love. It's the kind of love that leads a man to say to his Muse, "I have decided to become the kind of man you think I am."

In the chivalric lore of medieval Europe the fervent poetic love of the unattainable Lady was meant to civilize those rambunctious Knights and bring a sense of greater love and beauty to the individual and society.

During the Romantic era of English poets Byron, Keats, Shelley, and their buddies, the idea of chivalric love evolved into a rich, refined, indulgent devotion to a Love so perfect it was simply better to die than to watch it fade or be despoiled by ordinary life. This concept of *liebestot* or love-death is reflected in many stories, sometimes comedicly, sometimes tragically. "'Tis better to have loved and lost, than never to have loved at all," wrote Tennyson.

Those marvelous yearnings for a love you can't quite reach have created beautiful art and music, such as the love poetry of the Provencal minstrels and the Arthurian cycle of stories about Camelot and the Knights of the Round Table. Ever notice how when people fall in love they begin to write poetry, to paint, to sing, to love everyone. "Everybody loves a lover.".. unless they're going waaaay over the edge and become treacley and nauseous about it.

The negative side of the Aspirational Solar Plexus would be using this expansive style as a deceptive device to get followers. There are extremely charismatic people who use this inclusive magnetic charm of the ASP to draw in converts, followers, and devotees for their own selfish ends, but by the time they're acting selfishly they have "fallen" to Lower Solar Plexus or below.

The determining factor between the Inner Drive of this Center and the Heart Center is the payoff. Some cynics say there's no real altruism because even if a person's motives are fairly clean, there's still a personal payoff in ASP actions. You get to feel holy. You get to think you are doing the correct thing. You are rewarded by the inflow of love and appreciation from others. You are open to spirit and your life is full of synchronicities that seem to lead you to the right place and the right people at the right time. You get to be the good guy. But hey, that's okay for a while, and we certainly could use a lot more ASP in the world right now, couldn't we?

ARCHETYPES

Devotees — Devotion to an Ideal is the motivation for many spiritually and religiously inclined people. The extreme yearning for the highest expression of that Ideal is behind much great art and music. The downside of this expression is the fanaticism that can evolve from such extremes and devolve a character down to LSP. Another down-side is that Devotees can become mindless in their desire to truly experience the Ideal and then they are fair game for manipulation. When this occurs they are often pulled down to the Sacral Center by an unscrupulous leader.

Diplomats, Arbitrators — They also appear at the Throat Center. Here it's about their bridging and conciliatory abilities.

Freedom Fighters — The ones who only fight the bad guys and try hard not to hurt civilians in collateral damage. After the battle is done, these guys and girls turn their swords into plowshares, as opposed to Lower SP fighters who are in it just for the fight, and who keep prolonging a conflict in order to maintain their identity as warriors, and often to do some raping and pillaging as well.

Gracious Hosts/Hostesses — If even only for the duration of a dinner party, the act of hospitality and caring for others' needs can place one in an ASP focus.

Healers, Doctors, Nurses — They also appear at the Throat Center. Here the Inner Drive is about compassion rather than science.

Knights — Particularly of the Chivalric Age; particularly the more spiritually advanced, gentle, yet brave Knights of the Round Table. They were all devotion to the Ideal, whether it was the Ideal of unity, service to the feminine, protection of the weak and the innocent, the search for the Holy Grail, etc. But those are difficult Ideals to sustain and the lore is littered with tales of fallen knights, including the famous Lancelot, felled by a Sacral drop-and-wallow with Queen Guinevere. The Hindu Kshatriya Warriors also fall into this Knights category.

Mentors — Though it's often a one-on-one situation, the frequency is about lifting others up by including them in a body of knowledge or a profession in order to help better that larger group, as well as the individual protégé.

Mother Goddesses & New Age Sensitive Guys — You know the type: all-embracing, given to large, long hugs. A person on this Archetype will express a soft idealism, as opposed to the fierce idealism of the Freedom Fighter or Terrorist. They might feel the burden of *weltschmertz*, "the sorrow of the world," and will be determined to heal as much of it as they possibly can. Their openness will often be expressed sexually.

Relief Workers, Volunteers — Peace Corps, NGOs (non-government organizations), Red Cross, Doctors Without Borders. When disaster strikes, many regular people experience a rise to the Aspirational Solar Plexus as they donate to victims or go help out themselves. The exhilaration of people aiding the 9/11 event was in part due to their plugging straight into the power center of the ASP (and often, the Heart Center).

Spiritual Leaders, Priests, Nuns, Pastors, Rabbis, Gurus — But only when they are manifesting the Ideal. Needless to say, just holding the title of a spiritual leader does not automatically place one in an ASP focus. Would that it did, we might have far fewer sex and power scandals in religious organizations. Though they wore the religious vestments and spoke supposedly holy words, most of those doing the witch burnings and the Inquisition were probably not motivated by an ASP focus. Far from it.

Regardless of the downside of people in religious systems, a great number of those in any clergy are motivated by an Inner Drive to serve a greater good, to minister to others, to align with the highest principles, and to improve themselves and the world.

Teachers — They also appear at the Throat Center but here it is about their Inner Drives to share with others rather than about the knowledge. Though we met him in the Sacral Center, the centaur Chiron also fits here. Physically he symbolizes the half-man half-beast aspect of the Sacral Center but by what he did in teaching honor, valor, and warrior skills to the local Greek heroes he exemplifies the Aspirational Solar Plexus.

Unions, Union Leaders — Remember our icon for this Center, Norma Rae.

SYMBOLS

Crosses — Regardless of where the cross-arm meets the vertical arm, or even if it's a T-tau or the Vedic swastika (hijacked by the Nazis), the cross is about the meeting of two diverse things to form one unit.

God-ess/Heroes with Water — Water is always symbolic of the emotions and it's quite interesting how mythic imagery and stories reflect different emotional states. In the Judeo-Christian system you've got the Old Testament hero Moses parting the waters of the Red Sea to walk through a corridor of water in order to save his compatriots. Later in the New Testament there's Jesus actually walking across the surface of the waters to make a philosophical point to his apostles. The former system takes one through the emotions, the latter system shows how to rise above them.

Venus on the half-shell. In this painting by the fifteenth-century century Italian artist Sandro Botticelli the goddess of Love is borne up out of the foaming surf. Symbolically speaking it is about Love which rises above sentiment, rivalry, and conflict. It is about transformative Love, Love that brings out the very best in one, that sacrifices the individual happiness for the greater good. It is also the Love which worships the feminine principle as embodied in the Queen Consort or Princess Lover.

Knots — Again, it's about conjoining, about creating a unit from diverse parts.

Mother Goddesses — The archetype of the compassionate mother symbolizes that protective and supportive quality of the Aspirational Solar Plexus which cares for others, holds a higher focus within the self, and serves as an example to the individual yearning and striving to improve the world. Note that this is different from the impersonal Earth Goddess at the Root Center.

The Greco-Roman Hera/Juno belongs here on her good days when she wasn't off on a jealous frenzy, having dropped into the Sacral over yet another marital indiscretion by her errant husband Zeus/Jupiter. So does her fellow Olympian goddess Demeter/Ceres, the goddess of corn. When her beloved daughter Persephone was abducted into the underworld, Demeter's sorrow brought famine. When reunited with her child, the earth was fruitful again. Until, that is, Persephone returned to the underworld for three months out of every year, thus explaining the changing seasons.

Superheroes — Hercules, Xena, Superman and Spiderman, Wonder Woman, X Men, etc.

Webs, Nets — Interconnectedness is very Aspirational Solar Plexus. Many Native American tribes honor Spider Woman as the weaver and originator of a world. In Hindu iconography there is Indra's Net of Gems which encompasses every individual in an interconnected web.

PLANET

Venus — In esoteric lore this planet supplied earth with some of its spiritual guides in distant times. In contrast to the hot life-negative surface of the planet we can see, in legends the planet is said to be very much alive, in another dimension.

ASTROLOGICAL SIGNS

Aquarius — Quintessential New Age, all-for-one-one-for-all, human potential movement, genteel, caring, giving, loving, visionary

Cancer — The homemaker, the nester, the caregiver

Pisces — Duality and sensitivity

COLORS, SHAPES, MATERIALS

- Purples, violets
- Virgin Mary blue
- Goldens
- Iridescents
- Pastels
- Hazy borders, colors and designs blending into each other
- Celtic knots
- Webs and nets
- Soft materials such as down comforters, mohair, cashmere
- Encompassing materials like plushes, velvets, thick furs

Though ASP people are usually against hunting and wearing furs they will usually wear leather and silk. This disconnect in logic as to which sorts of animals are worth protecting could provide dramatic conflict.

CLOTHING

- Clean, neat
- Flowing
- Complex
- Encompassing, in a comforting supportive way
- Knots
- Mesh, net-like fabrics
- Feature point around the lower sternum area
- Uplifting between the breasts (but that Wonder Bra belongs in the Sacral)

STYLES OF SPEECH

- Your Aspirational character will use inclusive words: we, us, let's, together, all, join, group, synergy, bridge, link, join, meet.
- Their sentence structure would be compound: lots of clauses, lots of prepositional phrases.
- In *A Beautiful Mind* John Nash paraphrases economist and philosopher Adam Smith figuring out formulae that are good for self and good for the group.
- Their enthusiasm for inclusion might also produce a grab-bag of thoughts: they start out telling you about the freeway traffic on the way to the meeting and end up on the outer rings of Saturn… but somehow it all fits.
- They'll have some of those soft-fuzzy words and if they're bent towards religion or spirituality will be doing a lot of "surrendering to spirit," "going with the flow," "letting god guide us," "what would Jesus do?", etc.
- An Aspirational Solar Plexus character will exhibit that rare quality that gets the other person to talk about themselves and to seem truly interested in what they say. It's an ability (and a developable skill) called Charm.

PHYSICAL ACTIONS

- Gentle
- Graceful
- Hugging
- Smiling
- Nodding knowingly
- Kindly petting
- Stroking
- Very enthusiastic, outgoing, wanting everyone to join in the party or the event
- Sweeping gestures, hugging (especially group hugs), arms around shoulders, big handshakes
- Protective of others, placing self in front of others when they're in danger: "Taking the bullet" a la the special guardians and secret services for popes and presidents

They'll often have that dazed glow of the devotee, the maddeningly beatific smile, the strangulation-inducing good nature gone over the edge that is so often suspect among other folk.

FOIBLES, PHOBIAS, FOODS

- People-pleasing to the point of nauseous niceness, forced bonhomie
- Interfering do-gooders

- Bleeding Heart Liberals (in the worst sense, where you waive responsibility and simply try to "fix" a person or situation)
- Enablers
- The Martyr Complex — but with a heavy dollop of guilt for those supposedly benefiting from the sacrifice. "After all I've done for you…"
- Fear of being alone and all the stupid mistakes one makes trying to remedy that, such as hooking up with inappropriate people
- Match-making, whether others want it or not
- Indecisive, wishy-washy
- Bossy; they think they know best what's best for all

Like the LSP this Center is subject to an overload of what the Vedas call *siddhi* powers. As a person rises out of the self-centeredness of the LSP to the expansiveness of the ASP they become more receptive to other people's emotions and to the frequencies of place and situation. Certainly this makes them more sensitive. However, too much sensitivity can be an uncomfortable and scary thing.

- Psychic phenomena
- People making this shift often get very involved in things like Ouija boards, automatic writing, aura reading, and such
- Hearing voices and seeing things that others cannot
- Uncontrolled paranormal episodes
- Rampant synchronicities
- Prolonged incidences of *déjà vu* as the etheric network rewires itself
- If not guided by a knowledgeable mentor these episodes can frighten a person right back into their insular shell, and no wonder.

Many social events begin with a ceremony of the attendees imbibing the same drink or food. This similar consumption is meant to produce similar states of mind and feeling. Think how unsettling it is when someone passes up what everyone else is taking — they immediately become an outsider and therefore suspect.

- Chocolate (for that bonding chemical oxytocin)
- Alcohol
- Smorgasbord
- Fusion cuisine
- Always more than one food or type of food
- Movable feasts with appetizers in one place, entrees in the next locale, dessert somewhere else

WOUNDS & DEATHS
- Similar to LSP.

- Spleen, pancreas, and liver problems.
- Broken or wounded arms, since their tendency is to encompass and embrace.
- A good Aspirational Solar Plexus death would be off a bridge into water.
- Captured and cocooned in a net or web would be a symbolic ASP death.

EXAMPLES

Characters

The Greek heroes Theseus, Perseus, and Odysseus have many adventures, sometimes solitary and sometimes in teams. Some of their exploits are rather self-serving but at times, because they are princes and kings, they are operating from that higher focus for the greater good.

For instance, when Theseus puts himself among the fourteen Athenian youths and maidens to travel to Crete as part of the tribute sacrifice to King Minos, his intent is to end this oppressive rule. It works. He slays the Minotaur and the young people all go back to Athens, where Theseus establishes a prosperous commonwealth of self-governing citizens.

Tennyson's *Idylls of the King* are replete with stories of Chivalric Knights performing brave and glorious deeds for the sake of Love, Loyalty, God, the Lady. Stories centered around the Camelot legends feature that yearning aspiration to the greater good, sometimes at great personal sacrifice. *Camelot, Excalibur* and *The Sword in the Stone* are good examples. In the Hindu system there are the Kshatriya Warriors of Justice.

Heroes who stand in the line of fire for the good of more than just their own close little circle are exhibiting Aspirational Solar Plexus qualities. Examples from legend and history are *Ben-Hur, Spartacus, Robin Hood* — though in *Prince of Thieves* I was rooting for Alan Rickman's delightfully wicked Sheriff rather than Costner's bland Robin.

A smaller but just as meaningful version of this type of tale is *The Little Princess*. A comic version is Whoopie Goldberg's Oda Mae Brown in *Ghost*. In *Galaxy Quest* a group of LSP actors make a transition up to ASP as they help the Thermians defeat the evil Sauron.

Jimmy Stewart in *It's A Wonderful Life*, T.E. Lawrence in *Lawrence Of Arabia*, *Norma Rae*, and William Wallace of *Braveheart* all operate from the Aspirational Solar Plexus, putting their own happiness and their very lives on the line to help others. Some of them make an occasional foray up into the Heart Center, as we'll see in that section.

Jack Nicholson's portrayal of Melvin Udall in *As Good As It Gets* moves from a perfect example of LSP to a neophyte ASP.

In many films it is the rise of a character from LSP to ASP that comprises that "character arc." Because there is such a contrast between the exclusive, selfish, power-grabbing LSP and the expansive and generous ASP, your audience easily feels the frequency shift... they feel moved.

Films
As Good As It Gets
Ben Hur
Braveheart
Camelot
Dave
Erin Brockovich
Excalibur
Field of Dreams
Galaxy Quest
In My Country
It's A Wonderful Life
Lawrence of Arabia
The Little Princess
The Mission
Norma Rae
Prince of Thieves
Robin Hood
Schindler's List
The Secret Garden
The Sound of Music
Spartacus
Sword in the Stone
The Three Kingdoms (Chinese epics, Camelot similarities)
Three Kings
We're No Angels (1955)

Musicals, Opera, Ballet & Theatre
In the world of musicals, opera, and ballet there are plenty of heroes and heroines who rise to the occasion and help save the day for their family, their tribe, their people, their country.

Aida
Camelot (moves to Heart at times)
The Valkyrie (Die Walküre)
Evita (she moved up from the Sacral)
Man of La Mancha (moves to Heart at times)
The Sound of Music

Swan Lake
Tristan and Isolde

Books

Literature has often featured heroes and heroines with an Aspirational Solar Plexus focus. They're the inspiring ones who rise above their own wants and needs and come to the aid of others. Just a few of the many examples are:

The Color Purple
The Magnificent Obsession
A Man Called Peter
The Scarlet Pimpernel
Scarlett — Miss O'Hara actually moves from selfish LSP to generous and thoughtful ASP in this sequel to *Gone with the Wind*. A colorful read; and of course you want to find out if she and Rhett get back together, don't you?
The Three Musketeers

Games

Superhero games and many role-playing games have heroes and heroines who help others.

.hack — about a kid saving his best friend
Alias — based on the TV series; though her methods and motives often switch between LSP and ASP
Baldur's Gate
Banjo-Tooie — In these "critter and pal" games a critter and an assistant, often another, smaller critter, work together to save the countryside.
Buffy the Vampire Slayer
The Clock Tower
Dr. Muto
Drakan
Final Fantasy — especially because it's group focused
Freedom Fighters — Need I say more? It takes place in N.Y. against "The Red Army"; the tagline is "Only you can give a war-torn Manhattan its freedom!"
Halo
Jak & Daxter
Mario Brothers
Pirates: The Legend of Black Kat
Ratchet & Clank
Rygar
Sphinx and the Cursed Mummy
Super Hero games: Batman, Superman, Spiderman, Hulk

Music

Music on this Center will be inspirational and aspirational. Think harps. Think New Age. Think Yanni.

Historical

Historically, the bright spots in the march of time are lit by the radiance of people and groups who've stood up to evil and separatism. Spartacus stood up for Roman slaves and ultimately, in a Heart Centered sacrifice, gave his very life for their freedom.

The Briton queen Boedica, the Spanish El Cid, the Zulus fighting back the British invaders, Chinese Mao leading the Communist Great March... all were acting for their larger group and often verged on a Heart Center focus, acting for all of humanity.

Schindler and others like him who helped rescue Jews from the Nazis were ASP. As was Confucius and his philosophical system that favored "human-heartedness" and a social system that respected individuals while promoting a Benthamesque "greatest good for the greatest number." The hippie Love-Peace movement of the 1960s and '70s.

Current Events

In these times of instantaneous interconnectivity it's easier for us to see the activities of Aspirational Solar Plexus people around the world. Jimmy Carter, Mother Theresa, Lech Walesa, Kofi Annan, Nelson Mandela, Burma's Aung San Su Kyi... fortunately for the world, the list is long. And as you might suppose, since the ASP is about group activity, we would place a number of organizations in this category: Habitat for Humanity, Grameen Bank (making micro-loans to individuals, usually women), the USO, Red Cross, the Peace Corps, Americorps, Doctors Without Borders, and the like.

A great example is the Truth and Reconciliation Commission of South Africa, which successfully rose above the Lower Solar Plexus greed, separatism, and oppression and is still bringing about healing and optimism in that beautiful country. Although it was limited to South Africa in scope, the TRC was often operating from the Heart Center in its principles and methods. See the film *In My Country*.

B. The Practice

Now that you have a familiarity with this Center, it's time to put your new knowledge into practice.

1. FOR YOUR CHARACTERS

- Build their Character Profiles based on the above information
- Find photos of actors or people who embody the character you want to create
- Construct a Character Profile Collage
- Write up their ID Statement
- Note card — Iridescent. Scavenge some Halloween toy cobwebs, color them and glue them to the card. Or glue on multi-colored cord, fringe, or tassels.
- Do the Wash — check the various aspects to be sure you have integrity of character every time they appear on the page or on screen: food, dialogue, actions, others' reactions to them, etc.

2. FOR YOURSELF

This is where you Walk the Walk and *Act As If.*

- Play the uplifting music listed above
- Wear a cross medallion
- Wear mesh or knots
- Wear clothes and accessories in the ASP colors, shapes, and materials
- Braid your hair and/or weave ribbons (or even hippie-style flowers) in it
- Glide when you walk. Push off from your toes rather than landing on your heels; it's a subtle difference from the outside but makes a huge difference in how you move, feel, and look to others
- Eat your own fusion cuisine invention: Swiss-Mexican or Thai-German, etc. Have a parfait or a layer cake. Drink layered or multi-mix drinks
- Throw a pot-luck party and request that everyone bring a special dish from their land of origin or from their favorite vacation locale
- Host a party and invite the most diverse people you know; then help them all mingle and meld
- If you're out at an event, be very host-like and help at least five strangers there meet each other
- Visit some elaborate places of worship and participate appropriately
- Go to some local civic organization events
- Visit a professional mixed group like Rotary or your Chamber of Commerce. Closely observe the ways they bond over issues, ideals and traditions
- Watch the movies, including documentaries about freedom fighters and people who make differences within communities
- Read biographies of people like Albert Schweitzer, Florence Nightingale, the barefoot doctors in China, financier-philanthropist George Soros
- Volunteer at a charity organization, help feed the homeless at your local church or mission

- Carry easily accessible money (as opposed to opening your wallet out on the street) and give some to every person who asks you for "spare change." The next day, give money to people who do not ask. And when you hand them the money, look them in the eye, acknowledge their presence on the planet, and nod respectfully to that spark of the One Life that is in us all, like the Buddhists do the Namaste greeting. Sometimes it seems hard to find the spark of the One Life in some people, but as a teacher once said, "You think you've got problems with that personality, think what problems their own soul is going through trying to work with such a faulty tool."
- Volunteer to help schoolchildren in sports, music, or class work
- Interview a pastor or a health care worker, a firefighter, or a teacher for character research. Ask about their motives, their struggles, their rewards

3. EXERCISE

Complete your analysis from the "How To Use the Centers of Motivation" chapter on page 25.

C. Conclusion

An Aspirational Solar Plexus character will often be quite likable and admirable, as opposed to characters on the lower Centers, who may be quite interesting, but not always admirable or likable. Because an ASP Inner Drive is about self-sacrifice and nobility, these characters embody the better human qualities and can inspire the audience to similar noble acts.

If you have a political or religious agenda you'll surely have characters on this Center; just be careful not to have them too nice, or too namby-pamby touchie-feelie, lest they begin to seem unreal and you lose touch with the audience you wish to reach.

This Center is often the goal of a character's arc and the uplifting and heartwarming aspect of this Inner Drive, coupled with its frustrating and sometimes freaky downside, make it relevant and compelling to storytellers and audiences alike.

At the beginning of this Chapter it was noted that the Aspirational Solar Plexus focus can at first glance seem like a Heart Center focus and many people mistakenly give themselves or others credit for Heart Center actions and motivations. But here we've seen that though an ASP character works for the greater good, there's still something in it for them. What about pure unconditional love, then? That is Heart Center, a rarely expressed Inner Drive with often dire consequences, as we shall see in the next chapter.

7.
$\mathcal{H}$eart Center

Why does William Wallace sacrifice his very life for freedom in *Braveheart*?

Because that's what real heroes do.

"Greater love hath no man than this, that he lay down his life for his friends," or her country, or his species, or her planet, we might add to Jesus' words in John 15:13.

Too often Hollywood movies wimp out and save the heroine at the end, whereas the real integrity of a Heart Center character is their willingness to die for something greater than themselves. *The Last Samurai* would have been even more dramatically effective if Tom Cruise's redeemed warrior had died in battle, as he had been willing to do, rather than going on to a pleasant little domestic life. That's hardly heroic.

If you're creating a Heart Center character, please allow them the dignity of completing their sacrifice.

A. The Theory

MOTIVATION: PURE ULTIMATE SELFLESS LOVE

- Impersonal brotherhood/sisterhood/humanhood
- Love of all humanity, without exception
- Unconditional love
- Selfless sacrifice for the good of all humanity

This is different from the Aspirational Solar Plexus wherein the actor will likely receive some benefit from their actions. Heart Center actions have no hidden agendas. They too often get you dead, usually in a most unsavory fashion.

LOCATION

At the physical heart, between Thoracic Vertebrae #5 and #6.

ENDOCRINE GLANDS & HORMONES

Thymus Gland & the Immune System — The thymus gland lies beneath the breastbone and is directly linked with the immune system. It processes lymphocytes, the white blood cells which attack alien bodies, and stimulates antibody production. The thymus grows from before birth through to puberty and then it gradually decreases. This may have something to do with Jesus' admonition to "become as little children" who by nature have a more active Heart Center.

An interesting aspect of this Center is that when a person "opens their Heart" in loving sympathy and positive action, it has a positive affect on their immune system so they are able to serve in situations that might otherwise cause them illness. A Father Damien of the Lepers, a Mother Theresa, Dr. Albert Schweitzer, missionary doctors, *Médicins Sans Frontières* (Doctors Without Borders), Red Cross workers, healers of this ilk — the Mystery Schools teach that these people can do the work they do because they have strengthened immune systems.

Medical science has now identified part of how this so-called Helper's High works. An antibody in saliva, s-IgA, is the first line of defense against germs entering through nose and mouth and is an integral part of the body's defense against infectious disease. This Immuno globulin-A is also produced by laughter, which has been called "the best medicine."

MYTHIC MEANING

In the early stages of the developing embryo the heart is topmost on the little form. Only later as the spinal column unfolds more completely do the Throat, Ajna, and Head Centers unfurl and rise above it. Esoterically the Heart Center is not considered a Center of the personality but rather a Center of the soul. It, like the Crown Center, is of a higher frequency than the other Centers and is considered a gateway to the higher energies of life, consciousness, and creativity.

In many religions the Heart is a very central theme in their symbolism; most conspicuous are the Sacred Hearts of Mary and Jesus and the heart sacrifices of some ancient Meso- and South American Indian cultures. I once heard an esoteric explanation for the heart-ripping sacrifices performed by the thousands atop the stepped pyramids of the so-called New World. According to this version, the priests had misinterpreted their gods' command to "lift up your hearts" and took it literally. The lesson here is to read the directions very carefully and get a second opinion.

Two minor Centers in the palms of hands get activated along with the Heart Center, which is why icons often show streams of light coming from saints' hands. Christ's wounds and devotees' stigmata echo these secondary Centers.

Just as in the human body the heart provides life, so in any group or organization one person will usually hold the Heart Center focus and provide the life of the group. It won't always be the acknowledged leader, like the CEO or president;

it could be someone behind the scenes. Think of your own family, close peer group, or work situation. There's usually one person who tends to "process" the emotions of the group, to whom the others all go for advice and comfort, who makes peace, who holds the group together. If the group has a Vision or Mission Statement, that individual will seem to embody it. That person is the Heart Center of the group.

Some say you can die of a broken heart and there may be something to that. Spouses often die soon after losing their mates, such as singer Johnny Cash following his beloved wife June Carter by just a few months. The Heart Center's gland is the thymus, which regulates the immune system. A deeply emotional blow there has systemic effects on the body.

In the New Age world many people mistake the awakening of the Aspirational Solar Plexus for the awakening of the Heart Center. A quick and easy way to delineate between the two is to apply the mantram, "What's in it for me?" If the person gets any personal gain from the actions, then it's ASP. If not, if it's totally impersonal and they might even actually suffer for their actions, then it is probably Heart Center. Not to decry the value and beauty of the ASP at all, but just to keep in mind that point of discrimination between the human and the so-called divine. In *The Fisher King*, for example, Jeff Bridges' Jack Lucas begins as a very Lower Solar Plexus schlock-jock DJ and makes a move, eventually, to Aspirational Solar Plexus. He is changing to alleviate his own pain and guilt, rather than in service to all of humanity. That's how you differentiate ASP from Heart: the character's motivation.

Certainly if you are doing a story about a god or a saint they will probably be working from the Heart Center; that is expected. What is more dramatic and interesting is for ordinary people to take a Heart Center position.

It takes an act of conscious will to move up to a Heart Center focus. Once there, a character's effect on the environment will have a different tonal quality and will have a wider effect than before. Basically, it is a recognition of our identification with the divine.

In *The Thin Red Line*, Witt muses that perhaps everyone is part of one big soul. That sounds a lot like John Donne's observation that: No man is an island, entire of itself; every man is a piece of the continent, a part of the main… any man's death diminishes me, because I am involved in mankind; and therefore never send to know for whom the bell tolls; it tolls for thee.

Needless to say, most of us don't spend much time up in the Heart Center but we do occasionally have moments up there. Having seen the need and agreed to pay the cost for their actions, your story character could rise to the Heart Center and do some great act of beauty, chivalry, and sacrifice with no thought for reward or safety.

There's a wonderful scene in *The Shawshank Redemption* when Andy Dufresne (Tim Robbins) has received books and phonograph records for the prison library after years of requesting same. He puts a record on the public address system and a gorgeous, plaintive duet from Mozart's *Marriage of Figaro* wafts out across the entire prison. Everyone hears it. Everyone responds; including the Warden and the nasty guard, both of whom want to beat up Andy and have just found a perfect excuse to do so. Andy doesn't give in when they order him to turn off the music. Rather, he turns the music up and at that moment has a sacrificial-lamb expression on his face. Morgan Freeman's character tells us why this particular action rates as a Heart Center action. He recalls that the music was so beautiful that it made your heart ache and that for a brief moment, everyone who heard it felt free. Watch this scene and feel how it affects you.

An acknowledgement of this ultimate sacrifice was voiced by President Clinton at the fiftieth anniversary of D-Day on the beaches of Normandy. Looking out over the rows of seventy-year old veterans of World War II, he said, "When these men were young, they saved the world."

These types of actions in your characters will move and inspire your audience, because just as with all this seemingly esoteric stuff, it's hard-wired into us and it is in our nature to respond if you use the tools well.

ARCHETYPES

Demigod / Child of God — Humanity seems to be comprised of both an instinctive, non-thinking animal nature and an inspired, reasoning, higher nature; the conflict between the two has always been a rich source of story.

Most cultures have at least one myth about interbreeding between immortals and mortals. Genesis talks about the sons of God looking upon the daughters of men and finding them to be quite fair. Greco-Roman myths are rife with stories of Jupiter/Zeus' amorous exploits with mortal women.

So prevalent is this concept that one could consider it an explanation of the dual nature of humanity. It's a spiritual version of the Dr. Jekyll and Mr. Hyde story. In the *Matrix* films, Neo is considered a type of god, but he spends most of his time being very human and kicking lots of non-god, non-human hiney.

For more examples of these divine half-breeds, see my article "Dysfunctional Families, Doomed or Divine?" on the MYTHWORKS website.

Gods / Goddesses / Angels / Spirits — Needless to say you would find the positive gods, goddesses, angels, and spirits coming from the higher Centers. But not all of these beings are coming from such a highly motivated place; in the TV series *Xena: Warrior Princess* and *Hercules*, the gods were often petty and cruel. Fallen angels and demon spirits also come to mind. When these so-called higher beings are expressing love, mercy, and compassion they would be on the Heart Center. When operating from a position of authority they'd be more on the Crown Center.

The Virgin Mary, Mother of Christ, is a Heart Center character. The Buddhist Kwan Yin, goddess of mercy and compassion, also holds a Heart Center focus.

Saint, Martyr — When a human takes a stand for some principle that affects all other humans, and risks their life to do it, they are taking a Heart Center position. The hagiographies (stories about saints) are a good source of story lines.

Savior Gods — The Norse Balder, Judeo-Christian Jesus, and Persian Mithras are all young gods who die in service to humanity, and are often reborn.

SYMBOLS

Heart

Lion — The lion is the king of the jungle. Why? Certainly not because he's the smartest, or the strongest, or the wiliest. If anything, the lion is a lazy lay-about letting the lionesses go out and hunt and then strolling in for dinner. The lion is the symbol of the Heart Center because its mane is like the corona of the sun.

Sun — The sun gives life to the solar system and to everything on earth. The physical heart gives life to the physical body.

PLANET & ASTROLOGICAL SIGNS

The Heart Center is not related to the personality, but is an aspect of the Soul. Therefore it is not affected by the astrological signs, which have to do with an individual lifetime.

However, some systems that do not recognize the Solar Plexus split will ascribe the qualities of the Aspirational Solar Plexus to the Heart and you'll see Venus and Leo aligned with the Heart Center.

COLORS, SHAPES, MATERIALS
- Gold
- Tawny yellow
- Brilliant white and/or golden light

- Orbs
- Hearts

CLOTHING

Again, since most humans don't spend much time here the typical Heart Center garb would be saintly robes or godly garments. However, what usually happens is that in a story a character is going along doing their heroic thing and then they make that personal sacrifice and rise up into the Heart Center — without stopping to change into their super-hero outfit in most cases. So you've got them in their work clothes a la *Norma Rae*, their prison garb a la *Shawshank Redemption* or their battle gear a la *Braveheart*.

- Simple, pure
- Humble, like Gandhi's home-spun white cotton *dhoti*
- The white priestess robes in tales of bygone temples
- The whiter-than-snow raiment of angels

STYLES OF SPEECH

- Very gracious
- Valiant
- Chivalrous
- Inclusive
- Generous
- Merciful and forgiving

PHYSICAL ACTIONS

- Composed
- Gracious
- Gliding; almost seeming not to have feet
- Focused yet inclusive
- Arms outstretched to embrace all humanity
- Eyes turned up to the heavens
- Head bowed in humility or reverence
- For a human on this Center, a glowing, angelic, open expression that can border on simpleness or madness

FOIBLES, PHOBIAS, FOODS

- Foibles? None while in this Center focus, which is another reason we foible-filled humans don't spend much time here.
- Thymus problems would occur when the Heart Center isn't working fully.

- Heart hormones effectively inhibit the growth of cancer cells. You could have a character ill with cancer make a recovery after they open their hearts and perform some self-sacrifice for the greater good of all.
- If your character has been in a Heart Center focus and then falls or is tempted down, you could give them heart palpitations or congestive heart failure.
- Compassion Fatigue. People, organizations, and countries who "process" the emotions of others in their group tend to have heart problems. You'd see this in refugee workers or people doing Mother Theresa-like work.
- Food? None. Except maybe manna or ambrosia or some other divine food. But remember that this Center is not about being human, it's about a direct connection to the source of life.

Wounds & Deaths

Heart attacks.

AIDS, because it's about the immune system and recall that the thymus which regulates immunity is the endocine gland associated with the Heart Center.

A gory but symbolic death is to rip someone's heart out, still beating if possible. (Eeewwwww.) Some of the old Meso- and South American civilizations even constructed special ritual tools to do just this. Some martial arts experts can do this with their bare hands — so it is said.

Jesus' wounds in the palms of the hands and the tops of his feet are iconographic, since both those places have mini-centers related to the Heart Center.

Savior gods tend to get slain, and often end up strung up on trees like the Norse Odin and the Christian Jesus. In another tree metaphor, Dionysius the Greek god of the vine and wine was torn to pieces. But like many gods who bring enlightenment and the encouragement that death is not the end, he too was resurrected, just as the vines flourish again each year.

Examples

Characters

As you might suppose, there are not many characters or stories on a Heart Center focus since it is about the higher self or soul, as opposed to the lower self or personality.

That said, a few come to mind, at least for a goodly amount of story time. Joan of Arc falls into this category during much of her life, though no doubt the English would not agree. And indeed, many of her actions were political. Here was a girl who heard the voice of god and changed the map of Europe.

In the TV series *Babylon 5*, there's an episode titled "The Apotheosis" wherein Captain John Sheridan (Bruce Boxleitner) is returned to life after having made a sacrifice to the death for the good of the universe as he knew it. Subsequently, rather than staying on the pedestal and being worshipped, he works very hard to stay out of the Heart Center and be just a regular guy, captain of a space station, and leader of the free world in space.

In *Braveheart*, the historical figure William Wallace (Mel Gibson) spends most of the movie in the Solar Plexus, both Lower and Aspirational. At the end however, he pays the ultimate price for Freedom — which is something that ideally all humans should have, not just the Scots.

Films
Bible Epics — at least some parts of them
Braveheart
Close Encounters of the Third Kind
Dead Man Walking
Gandhi
The Inn of the Sixth Happiness
The Insider — Because of the reach of the tobacco industry, it's about protecting the health of all humans everywhere
Kundun
Joan of Arc
Life is Beautiful — parts. Most of it belongs in the ASP category since it's about family love, but the sacrificial aspects for freedom and idealism are very Heart Center
Lost Horizon
Rosewood —at the moments of personal sacrifice to save innocents from a race mob and make a stand against racism
Schindler's List
Spartacus — note Spartacus was crucified at the end
The Song of Bernadette
The Thin Red Line — the narration is very Heart Center

Musicals, Opera, Ballet & Theatre
1776 — about the signing of the Declaration of Independence
Angels in America
Camelot — the concepts of unity, equality, chivalry

Books
Holy writings of all spiritual traditions
The Robe

The Rubaiyat of Omar Khayyam
Rumi's mystic Sufi writings

Games

It's hard to find Heart Center games because the protagonist's motives don't tend to be pure or self-sacrificing: he/she usually wants to get something out of it, even if it's just revenge.

Kingdom Hearts — This is *all* about heart: losing your heart, getting it back, the meaning of friendship and self-sacrifice.

Legend of Zelda — In all its incarnations, it's about a boy who wants to save his princess and his land with no thought for his own safety or well-being.

Music

Some might say that the only real Heart Center music is the "music of the spheres," the vibrations of the cosmos inaudible to the human ear, audible only to the human soul.

Others find that some religious music resonates with such a Heart Center focus that it affects atheist, agnostic, and aspirant alike. Handel's *Messiah* is given as an example, as is a lot of Mozart's music. Watch again that wonderful scene in *Amadeus* where Salieri is reading the sheet music and goes off into jealous raptures, certain that Mozart was simply taking dictation from God. Gregorian chant, "Amazing Grace" (even on bagpipes), and many spirituals also carry this frequency of divine, unconditional love.

Because of the associations with worship services and media imagery, harp and organ music might seem Heart Center to some people. By that same reasoning, the long horns and two-tone throat chants of Tibetan monks might call up that frequency for Buddhists.

Historical

Though people working from this Inner Drive are relatively rare, there are a number of historical figures who operated at times from the Heart Center. Some of them are Richard the Lion-Heart, twelfth-century King of England; gladiator and slave rebellion leader Spartacus; and according to romanticized accounts, the eighth-century French king Charlemagne.

At the Battle of Thermopylae in 480 B.C.E. a few hundred Spartans held back a gigantic Persian invading force. They lost the battle but their sacrifice helped save their city-state. Their valiant example was a motivating story point in *The Last Samurai*.

Mahatma Gandhi in his latter years was operating from a Heart Center focus as he put his life on the line for the sake of nonviolent resistance to British rule in India. He won independence for India but at the eventual cost of his own life.

Others who reach that elite aerie of the Heart Center are the medical workers of the Nobel Peace Prize-winning *Médicins Sans Frontières*. Also from real life are Mother Theresa, Father Damien of the Lepers, Dr. Martin Luther King, and Joan of Arc — all of whom lived a Heart Center focus in their finest moments of standing up for the good of all humanity at real danger to themselves.

Current Events
In current events there are fortunately a number of people who've moved at times into a Heart Center focus, unfortunately because the times require it.

Burmese freedom leader Aung San Su Kyi has suffered greatly for her stand for democracy: she was not able to be with her husband at the end of his life, she is separated from her sons, and has been under house arrest in Rangoon for years.

The Dalai Lama continues to advocate for peace and reconciliation regardless of the cost of exile from his homeland.

Nelson Mandela has consistently held up the ideals of freedom, even at the cost of spending twenty-seven years in prison for his convictions. His former wife was revealed to be rather LSP in scandals over power and violence. The Truth and Reconciliation Commission of South Africa was certainly ASP and often Heart Center as it successfully rose above the Lower Solar Plexus greed, separatism, and oppression and is still bringing about healing and optimism in that country. Even the name of the Commission resonates with these elevated frequencies.

Kofi Annan, Secretary General of the United Nations, also seems to embody Heart Center characteristics. The concept of the United Nations and the League of Nations before it, is Heart Center in motivation and for the most part, in methods. The blue-hat troops of the U.N. are peace-keepers, not peace-makers.

Aung San Su Kyi, Nelson Mandela, Jimmy Carter, Kofi Annan, the Dalai Lama have all been awarded the Nobel Peace Prize. This is not a sure sign of a Heart Center focus, however. Henry Kissinger also won it.

B. The Practice
Now that you have a familiarity with this Center, it's time to put your new knowledge into practice.

1. For Your Characters

- Build their Character Profiles based on the above information
- Find photos of actors or people who embody the character you want to create
- Construct a Character Profile Collage
- Write up their ID Statement
- Note card — Red velvet covered. Or gold foil covered. Heart-shaped. Or a circular shape. The symbol of the Sacred Heart with swords through it, or the Three of Swords card from the Tarot deck, where three swords pierce a heart.
- Do the Wash — check the various aspects to be sure you have integrity of character every time they appear on the page or on screen: food, dialogue, actions, others' reactions to them, etc.

2. For Yourself

This is where you Walk the Walk and *Act As If.*

- Play no music at all. Experience silence and solitude. Learn to listen to the inner voice that only becomes audible when your chattering monkey-mind is stilled.
- Actually, if you could find an isolation tank, so popular in the '60s and '70s, that would be a great experience to tune into that impersonal Heart space deep within us all.
- Wear the simplest clothes possible. Recall Gandhi in that homespun cotton *dhoti.*
- Clothes made of hemp would work well.
- You might even try giving a homeless person the shirt off your back, literally.
- Eat — nothing. It's about self-sacrifice after all.
- If you can fast, do it with the motive of expanding your Heart Center awareness, particularly on the third day when the light-headedness begins. Donate the money you didn't spend on food to people who you deem need it.
- If fasting doesn't work for you, cut out something you really like, such as coffee, martinis, or chocolate and again, donate the money you'd have spent on that.
- Go to High Mass at a Catholic or Episcopal/Anglican cathedral. Note the effect on your physical body of the architecture, the music, the incense, the colors — the so-called "smells and bells." Choose one of the high holidays for this as you want to experience the most pageantry and the highest aspiration possible. Modern or simpler places of worship, though they certainly may be about Heart Center activities, simply won't have the same effect on your senses as a place like Chartres Cathedral or an Easter Mass at the Vatican.
- Visit a hospital maternity ward, but only the new baby part, not the actual

delivery rooms. Observe the unconditional outpouring of love towards the new arrivals and consider the exceptional sacrifice most women make in giving birth. (A normal birth should be easy, but misinformed traditions and modern medicine conspire against this and too many women still perish in childbirth.)

- Attend a planetarium show.
- Visit the NASA website and ponder the photos from the Hubble telescope of star nurseries and distant galaxies.
- Put a photograph of the earth from space or the moon up near your desk and contemplate the wholeness and unity of Life.
- Read hagiographies, the stories of saints. Boy howdy, there are some examples of Heart Center sacrifice. Whether you believe them or not, the incidences are great examples of what people think sacrifice should be all about.
- Read biographies of the Nobel Peace Prize winners.
- Read biographies or watch documentaries on the Congressional Medal of Honor winners.
- Visit the website of The Carter Center, former President Jimmy Carter's organization to monitor and deal with conflicts and problems around the world.
- Live your side of an O. Henry short story and give up something you treasure in order to gift a loved one with something they greatly desire. Choose an exchange that actually "hurts" you in some way.
- Interview a hospice worker, someone who helps people die.
- Interview veterans who've seen combat (if you don't know any, you can visit a VA hospital) and respectfully ask them about sacrifices made on the battlefield.
- Make a list of 1) what you would be willing to die for and 2) who you would be willing to die for. Seriously.
- List three changes you would make in the world, if you could wave your magic wand and make them happen, that would benefit *each and every* human now or forevermore to live on the planet.

3. EXERCISE

Complete your analysis from the "How To Use the Centers of Motivation" chapter on page 25.

C. Conclusion

A Heart Centered character is a rare occurrence. It is more of a temporary position that will have a huge effect on the environment around that character. It will also have a huge effect — usually detrimental, often fatal — to the character herself.

Unlike the other Centers there is not a great deal of range here between extremes. Because a Heart Center action must be a conscious action, the person needs to know full well what may befall them if they perform it. You might have a character surprised at herself by her own actions, but it will be an almost "holy and humble" surprise… they didn't know if they really had it in them. Mostly though, the character will have known that it might come to this but they slogged on in spite of that dire prediction, focused on that Greater Good.

The tone of the expression of a Heart Center focus, as we've seen in the examples above, is usually that of a dire conflict which can only be resolved or addressed by great personal sacrifice.

The rarity and sanctity of these actions make this Center compelling and inspiring to storytellers and audiences alike. These will be those times when a character exhibits what Abraham Lincoln called "the better angels of our nature."

So how can you go up from the rarified heights of the Heart Center? Recall that this Center, along with the Crown Center, are considered to be spiritual rather than personality aspects. The next center up our spinal column is the Throat Center and it's one that will really interest all you creative types.

8.
Throat Center

Why is John Nash so obsessed with mathematics in *A Beautiful Mind*?

The stereotype of the absent-minded professor became a stereotype by being kind of true. How often have you gotten so absorbed in a creative project that you lost track of time?

Your Throat Center characters need not be as far out as Nash, but you will want to show their innate aloofness from the concerns of lower Centers, whether it's Ralph Feinnes' Charles Van Doren ignoring professional ethics in *Quiz Show* or Gene Hackman's photojournalist Alex Graziere ignoring personal danger in *Under Fire*.

In these days of the short attention span, a Throat Centered character has the ability to focus, concentrate, and see things through to completion.

A. The Theory

MOTIVATION: CONSCIOUS CREATIVITY

- Advertising
- Art
- Architecture
- Choreography
- Computers
- Finance
- Media
- Music
- Science
- Statecraft
- Technology
- Writing

LOCATION

Between the Cervical Vertebrae #6 and #7 at the pharyngeal plexus.

ENDOCRINE GLANDS & HORMONES

Thyroid & Para-Thyroid — The thyroid gland affects metabolism, weight loss or gain, memory loss, hair growth, depression, and lack of concentration.

The parathyroid controls calcium and phosphorous metabolism: high levels of its hormone bring on bone degeneration and low levels lead to muscle spasms and convulsions.

MYTHIC MEANING

Recall that the Sacral Center is the home of Unconscious Creativity? The Throat Center is its higher correspondent, the home of Conscious Creativity. This is the channel through which our great creations originating in those higher realms of imagination and inspiration get funneled down into reality. The Sacral is an animal center expressing some of our lower, but not necessarily negative, aspects. The Throat is a human center expressing some of our higher, but not necessarily always positive, aspects.

Anything that requires logic, precision thinking, plotting, an overview as well as details, or a grasp of consequences falls into a Throat Center focus. It is usually an unemotional frequency, ruled by the head rather than the heart. This does not mean it does not take emotion into consideration but rather that it is not unduly swayed by sentiments.

There's a helpful distinction to make between emotions and sentiments. Sentiments are those easy-to-pull heartstrings that get tugged with paintings of big-eyed kids and kittens, the sloppy sentimentality of some soap operas or romance novels, the manipulations of some filmmakers: the violins begin to quiver and your throat tightens as tears spring to your eyes. Just think how some people are labeled "sentimental" and you'll get the idea. Sentiment is usually personal, confined, and fleeting. The emotions then, in this distinction, are connected with higher, greater values and ideals. They're more linked with concepts like loyalty, love, sacrifice, etc. They last.

Advertising and propaganda are perfect Throat Center examples. Throat Center people plan a series of words and images to affect other people on the lower Centers in specific ways, to influence them through their emotions (or usually through their sentiments) to perform certain actions. In military or political psy-ops (psychological operations) the goal is not to get people to *think* a certain way but rather to influence them to *act* a certain way.

Myth systems that have an ultra long view of human evolution often give it a retrospective similar to the development of the human brain. A lot of mainstream academic evolutionary biology and psychology also follows this train of thought. The narrow brain stem is the most primitive (akin to tubeworms), the limbic system is often called our reptilian brain (dinosaurs and serpents), the cortex layered on over that gives us more complexity in conscious choice and the beginnings of socialization (larger herd animals and primates), and the pre-frontal cortex gives us the sophistication of modern humanity.

A number of mythic systems bespeak this development pattern. The Maori of New Zealand call the primitive brain the Ancestor, the mid-brain is the Parent, and the forebrain is the Child. How did they know this, one wonders? Possibly warriors bashing open heads of the enemy stopped to ponder the functional anatomy; possibly there was a tradition of knowledge passed down from very ancient times.

The Hindu *Vedas* also have a go at this system. The broad strokes go like this: The Lemurian humans were learning how to use the Physical Body; the Atlanteans were learning to master the Emotional Body; and this current root race, the Aryan, is supposedly learning to use the Mental Body. The next one will be the race of Conscious Souls, people who are aware of their spiritual heritage and their capabilities and who have a continuously active Creative Body. The so-called Indigo Children are said to be the first of this Kingdom of Conscious Souls. Needless to say, no matter where we as individuals may find our current focus, we still have glitches and challenges in the other bodies as well and all of us are working in varying degrees of success to best manifest the ideals of each of these.

Greek philosopher Plato calls the Throat Center the "isthmus or boundary" between the higher and lower selves, keeping one from polluting the other.

So how do we get from Sacral Center unconscious creativity to Throat Center conscious creativity? In the myths of many cultures you find the appearance of a Teacher God who brings the arts of civilization to humankind. The presumption is that humans were at first rather primitive and then by the grace of the gods were given the gifts of fire, domestication of animals, agriculture, brewing, architecture, speech, writing, music, makeup, and government. It's interesting that these stories presume humans are unable to invent these things on our own. Just look at modern technology and think if we perpetuated this same type of mythologizing. People like Edison, Watt, Einstein, Bell, and Gates would be considered gods, because mere humans certainly could not have come up with electricity, the steam engine, atomic energy, the telephone, and computer software. Okay, so maybe some of those guys considered themselves gods, but that's not the same thing.

Some of the more prominent Teacher Gods include the Egyptians Hermes Trismegistus and Thoth, the Greek Hermes and Roman Mercury, the Greek sun god Apollo who was a musician, an archer, and taught mankind the healing arts. The dark-featured Indians of the Americas credited the pale-skinned, blond-haired, blue-eyed god Quetzalcoatl and his companion Viracochas with having brought the arts of civilization to them long before the conquering and colonizing sixteenth-century Europeans arrived to destroy so much of it in their own misguided religious fervor.

Other famous Throat Center icons from myth and legend include the Greek Daedalus, creator of wax-wing flying machines and architect of the Cretan labyrinth, built to hold the half-man half-bull minotaur, and Hiram Abiff, the architect hero of Masonic legend credited with building Solomon's Temple. Greek Orpheus was a great musician, and the Celtic bards were both accomplished musicians and poets, able to memorize entire libraries. These *merlins*, or bards, also had a complex sign language for passing secrets among themselves; it made them look ever so psychic in royal courts and out on the battlefields.

The Wisdom teaches that the next great battle between Darkness and Light will be the Battle on the Mental Planes. Now you might think that would be decidedly better than battles on the physical plane, which tend to smash things and kill people, or battles on the emotional plane, which tend to repress and control people, often through religion (just look at all the religious wars currently raging across the planet). But this isn't just a bunch of folks sitting around scowling at each other and thinking foul thoughts. It's the use of the mind to think up new ways to control each other; it's the very real use of consciousness to create reality (think *Matrix*, *Harry Potter*, or *Wizard of Oz*); it's about deception and perversions of perception. Mostly it's about those who are focused on a Throat Center using thought to control others for their own purposes. "Pay no attention to the man behind the curtain...."

Another thing about the Throat Center — when it's active you tend to want to eat, drink, smoke. Writers, have you ever noticed that as soon as you sit down to write you crave something to put in your mouth — Cheetos, martinis, cigars? It's an unfortunate side-effect of having an active Throat Center. Some would say that explains the tendency of lots of creative types to overindulge their senses; but what about scientists, who generally speaking, don't? Perhaps it's a difference in temperament related to how accessible the other Centers are to the personality. It'd certainly be worth a study, but you'd probably burn out the artists and freak out the scientists before you reached any conclusions. Ah, well....

ARCHETYPES

Artists — Particularly the modern artists. Two-dimensional representational art is called "primitive"; up to the point when perspective appears, then it becomes "modern." Yet the use of symbols and stylized representation are at least seventy thousand years old, as recently found in Australia.

Pointillism and impressionism are more mental art forms, as is Modern and/or Abstract Art. Modern artist Wassily Kandinsky wrote some very good books explaining the creative process of modern art, including analyses of the various planes of abstract ideals, conceptual thoughts, and concrete expression.

Even when the artwork itself is emotional, the artist who creates it uses the craft of color, composition, perspective, etc. to evoke those emotions in the viewers.

Artists in particular are good story fodder because they tend to bounce back and forth between Centers. To be artistic they must have an active Throat Center, but to be effective they must also have access to their emotions, so you will often see them vacillating between being extremely creative and being distressed because they can't be creative, for whatever reasons. Watch the early scenes of *Shakespeare in Love*, when Will had writer's block. The chapter on "Center Transfers" explores this further.

Bureaucrats — regulation-bound micro-managers, like in a Dilbert cartoon.

Choreographers — The designers of dance are using spatial-relation skills, sequence analysis skills, and synergetic skills. Most dancers themselves will be coming from a Solar Plexus focus, usually the Lower.

Composers, Musicians — Brain studies now show how the formal study of music, particularly complex classical music, enhances the neural connections and creates pathways in the brain that enhance both creative and analytical thinking. Even just a year or two of formal music studies at a young age makes a great positive difference in a person's subsequent scholastic performance.

Detectives — From Miss Marple to Inspector Morse, from Columbo to Nick and Nora Charles of *Thin Man* fame, detectives must use their intellectual analytical skills to be successful.

Doctors & Dentists — The scientist aspect. They make for interesting story characters because you can create such a vivid change for them, going from all scientific to more emotional.

Educators

Journalists — Both for observing and analyzing events and for being the mouthpiece of public awareness.

Intelligence Analysts

Lawyers, Judges — Think of all the law and order shows on TV these days, including the rabbit-replicating *Law and Order.*

Mathematicians, Cryptologists

Philosophers

Psychologists

Promoters, Publicists, Marketers — They serve as mouthpieces for other people's creativity, often in very creative and clever ways. As any artist knows, often to their great chagrin, without marketing your work is just self-entertainment or self-enlightenment. Nothing wrong with that, but it doesn't pay your rent or get you that Oscar.

Scientists — Both the hard and soft sciences: engineering, medicine, astronomy, botany, etc. as well as anthropology, archaeology, sociology, etc.

Statesmen — Not politicians, who are very Lower Solar Plexus figures. Statesmen care about all the constituents, the future, and the greater good, not just about getting elected or re-elected. Plato's *Republic* describes the perfect leader. America's founding fathers were attempting to be perfect statesmen, though they all certainly had personal faults and foibles.

Teacher Gods — Often shown with the item they invented or gave to humans: Apollo with his lyre, Ariadne with her spinning wheel and web. The Sumerian teacher-god Oannes is shown as a combination of merman and deep sea diver. Some legends speculate this stranger from afar was an alien, or a submariner from Atlantis. The Egyptian gods Osiris and Thoth are both teachers, as was the Greek Hermes. A majority of pre-Columbian American legends refer to bearded blonde teacher gods...Vikings perhaps?

Writers — Words are the form thought takes in the physical dense world. Some say the first writing was created for accountants and royal messengers, yet even ancient Egyptian writings include love poems and tales of the goddesses and gods.

Though writers often feel our initial inspiration comes straight in through the Crown or Heart Centers, the art of writing and the craft of rewriting are both very Throat Center.

Writers use words to change hearts and minds. They create new worlds by giving voice to imagination, by grounding abstract concepts such as space travel into concrete forms that can be accessed by minds of more scientific bent.

Also note how much the Religions of the Book (Judaism, Christianity, and Islam) honor those humans who transcribed the sacred messages. Also note how many wars and how much persecution has ensued from zealously guarding and interpreting the words. Throat Center gone radical.

SYMBOLS

Bull — A solid, grounded, strong animal, just as words are the solid, grounded manifestation of thoughts. And as we're told, the pen is mightier than the sword. A Papal Bull is a letter issued by the Pope containing important information. And then there's the word *bullshit* to denote words that aren't true.

In the Mithraic religion of ancient Persia (modern Iran) the bull was often shown being slain by a man pulling back its head and slashing its throat; all sorts of esoteric symbolism there.

Eagle — The eagle represents the Throat Center because though it is an animal it is free of the earth, just as with the use of the mind the human animal rises above the dictates of instinct and evolution and can make free-will decisions. The eagle also has a higher vision than earth-bound or water-bound creatures.

Mouth — In hieroglyphs and other symbolic systems, the mouth is usually about speaking rather than eating. It's the output, not the input. Egyptian, Hindu, and Tibetan iconography all show lots of mouths.

PLANET

Mercury — The planet of the messenger, communication, movement.

ASTROLOGICAL SIGNS

Gemini — Communications, particularly verbal

Libra — Logical balance, often to the point of obsessive-compulsive

Taurus — The bull symbolism again

COLOR, SHAPES, MATERIALS

- Orange
- Sterile, flat white (think hospitals, lab coats, etc.)
- Multi-colors in complex precise patterns
- Plaids, checks, stripes
- Rigidity and order, precision patterns
- Geometrics

- Wires
- Metallics a la technology
- Silicones, plastics, vinyls
- Man-made materials
- Wiring diagrams, silicon chip designs

CLOTHING

- Plaids
- Stripes
- Checks
- Geometrics
- Polyesters, vinyls
- Fake furs
- White lab coats
- Thick glasses
- Bow-ties
- Button-down collars
- Sweaters tied around the shoulders
- Cardigan sweaters
- Elbow patches a la professors
- Argyles
- Scarves and mufflers wound around the neck
- Choker necklaces
- Coordinated outfits

STYLES OF SPEECH

- Articulate, intellectual, complex, cryptic
- Exaggeration
- Lying
- Gossip
- Compound sentences, long sentences, really long sentences whose complex construction leads the reader or listener, whichever it might be at the time, into a veritable labyrinth of imagination and evocation of the sorts of things that would otherwise not even appear on the horizon of a person's world, were they even to consider the possibility of such an occurrence.
- Multi-syllabic words, unusual or arcane words
- Professional jargon, techno- or psycho-babble
- Accents of the elite and upper classes
- The sexy voice — using the Throat to affect the Sacral
- Argumentative, in a logical, ordered, almost impersonal way

- Legalese — bearing in mind the heretofore alluded to considerations of the aforesaid nature of the alleged character....
- Specific words: logic, reason, sure, scientific, analysis, debate, critical thinking
- Foreign words and phrases peppered in *quid pro quo, a la, mélange, n'est-ce pas? Ciao, bella!*

Usually the Throat Center person will not bother to translate, figuring others are either smart enough to know what they're saying or not worthy enough to know. People other than Americans will do this easily since most other cultures are multilingual; few Americans are.

Also, making up words as did author James Joyce in *Ulysses* and *Finnegan's Wake*, and *Alice in Wonderland* author Lewis Carroll in his poem, "Jabberwocky":

> 'Twas brillig and the slithy toves
> Did gyre and gimble in the wabe:
> All mimsy were the borogoves,
> And the mome raths outgrabe.

In a seeming reversal, a Throat Center character could make very effective use of silence, whether in holding secrets or in prompting others to speak as they become uncomfortable with silence.

PHYSICAL ACTIONS
- Playing at the throat, pulling at the tie, toying with the necklace
- Coughing
- Clearing the throat, for a slightly repressed person
- If a person becomes more adept at communication throughout the story-line, you could have them progressively loosen the constrictions at the throat: ties, collars, scarves, etc.
- Rubbing the back of the neck
- Shrugging the shoulders, rolling the head, jutting and stretching the chin
- Counting things
- Arranging and rearranging things, absently or obsessively

FOIBLES, PHOBIAS, FOODS

As creative individuals, most of you reading this book probably have a very active Throat Center. When you sit down to write, do you suddenly crave something for your mouth? Smoking, drinking, and eating excessively is very common among creative types. Knowing this is a natural occurrence can alleviate guilt and help you make a more conscious expression of this Center stimulation. Since you probably will be driven to consume, perhaps it could be water instead of martinis, carrots instead of cigarettes? A bit boring, perhaps, but healthier overall.

- Laryngitis, asthma, pneumonia — for more repressed or distressed people
- Chancre sores
- Sore throat
- Congestion
- Mute
- Teeth and mouth problems for the inarticulate
- Thyroid imbalance — goiter
- Hyperthyroidism — hair loss, fast heart rate, nervousness, shaking hands, protruding eyes, increased perspiration
- Parathyroid imbalance: twitches, muscle spasms, convulsions
- Turret's Syndrome — uncontrollable inappropriate speech
- Being over-talkative, a blabber mouth, a tattletale
- All brains, no mind. Lots of details and information but no common sense, much less wisdom
- Poor circulation, cold extremities — symbolically cold and cut off from the emotions

Addictions — In dealing with pain, a Throat Center character will strive for perfection, often expressing as obsessive-compulsive behavior.

In any group, from a house party to a lecture, there will always-always-always be at least one person who will be the Throat Center of the group. They seldom simply ask a question, but will ask show-off questions or make show-off comments designed to illustrate their own great knowledge. These people are often a source of great annoyance to everyone else in the group. One good thing they do, however, is to raise questions that more shy people might not voice. It is up to the group leader to appropriately control this Throat Center person(s).

Chastity (related to the Sacral which is the lower counterpart of the Throat) exacerbates throat problems. Just look at the scandals of sexual abuse in the Catholic clergy of the early 2000s and the concomitant cover-ups. What happened was an overabundance in one area (Sacral) and suppression in the other (Throat), when the system was supposed to suppress the Sacral to enhance the creative Throat Center. Debate still rages over whether or not sexual repression may be one direct cause of sexual abuse, but we can certainly observe some "mythic" correlation.

- Eating disorders. Overeating, anorexia, bulimia, etc.
- Milk, cheeses and other calcium foods

- Salt with iodine, because of the thyroid and goiter
- Bananas, for the potassium

Wounds & Deaths

- Beheading comes to mind
- Brain tumors
- Throat problems
- Hacking cough
- Getting one's teeth knocked out or tongue ripped out would be Throat Center woundings
- Tracheotomy, particularly a non-professional one. In Oliver Stone's *Salvador*, photojournalist Jack Cassady gets strafed by a low-flying plane and dies of bullet wounds in the throat despite Richard Boyle's (James Woods) emergency tracheotomy with a switchblade and a ball-point pen. It's a perfect Throat Center death for a Throat Center character.
- Garroting or strangling would be appropriate, as would the guillotine

Examples

Characters

Though most of humanity is usually operating from the Solar Plexus, Sacral, and Root Centers, there is a significant minority working from the higher Centers. They include artists, scientists, doctors, statesmen (politicians are LSP), and the marketers and advertisers who are using their mental aspects to affect the emotional aspects of the audience and bring about a physical action such as a purchase of toothpaste, clothes, a car, or a burger.

Some characters who exemplify the Throat Center are the Vulcans and the robot Data in the *Star Trek* series. The ultimate Throat Center types are the organic thinking machine Mentats in Frank Herbert's *Dune* novels.

Tim Robbins' Andy Dufresne in *The Shawshank Redemption* is a Throat Center character; his profession is finance and he campaigns to get books and records into the prison library. Jeff Goldblum played Throat Center characters in *The Fly, Independence Day*, and *Jurassic Park*. Scully in *X-Files* was very throat-centered. Ewan McGregor's Christian in *Moulin Rouge* is a Throat Center character in a Sacral Center film.

A good example of Throat Center activity is when John Nash in *A Beautiful Mind* figures out that economist Adam Smith was wrong, using the blonde in the bar as his thought experiment. Note that he didn't approach the girl, it was all done in his head.

Speaking of girls, how about Ariel in *The Little Mermaid*, who gave up her voice for a boy?! Talk about denying your Throat Center.

Three people across the Throat Center spectrum appear in *Under Fire*, where Gene Hackman, Nick Nolte, and Joanna Cassidy are all war correspondents in the 1979 Nicaraguan revolution.

A classic contrast of Throat to other Centers is the Robert Louis Stevenson story *Dr. Jekyll and Mr. Hyde*. In the Spencer Tracy-Ingrid Bergman version it's a very blatant Throat-Sacral conflict.

Terminator(s) and all the technology run-amok-stories have strong Throat Center aspects. *Terminator II* has the scientist as a pivotal character, though on the whole the first two *Terminator* films are very much Root Center.

Films
A Beautiful Mind
A Brief History of Time
Adam's Rib
A Few Good Men
The Agony and the Ecstasy
Altered States
Amadeus
Apollo 13
Back to the Future(s)
Being There
The Client
The Conversation
Dr. Jekyl and Mr. Hyde
Dying To Tell The Story — documentary about war correspondents
Educating Rita
Faust
The Fly
Gattaca
Good Will Hunting
The Insider — in Russell Crowe's Dr. Jeff Wygant, a scientist whose enthusiasm
    for the magic of chemistry runs through paranoia and stress of his situation
LA Confidential
Law and Order TV series
Matrix
My Fair Lady
My Left Foot

Network
Pollock
Renaissance Man
Quiz Show
Shakespeare in Love
Shine
Stand and Deliver
Technology-run-amok stories
Terminator(s)
Thin Man series
Time-travel stories, at least that aspect of them
Twelve Angry Men
Under Fire

Musicals, Opera, Ballet & Theatre

Copellia
Die Meistersinger von Nurnberg (Richard Wagner) — The trial for this story's hero to win his love is to compose and sing a song according to the rigid rules of the Mastersinger's guild.
The Knot Garden (Michael Tippet) — An English country house gathering swirls around a labyrinth of psychological intrigue.
Proof
Sunday in the Park with George (Stephen Sondheim) — This musical features impressionist artist George Seurat and his sculptor grandson, both working from a Throat Center.
Witness for the Prosecution

Books

Altered States — Paddy Chayefsky
Ayn Rand's novels
Dune series and all other Frank Herbert novels — The movie and TV series play more on the power struggles and love affairs, but the novels are very heavy on the logic and mental machinations.
Foucault's Pendulum — Umberto Eco
The Neuromancer — William Gibson
A Portrait of the Artist as a Young Man — James Joyce
Red Mars, Green Mars, Blue Mars — Kim Stanley Robinson's trilogy on the colonization of the red planet. Scientifically fascinating, emotionally dry.
Snow Crash — Neal Stephenson's fascinating speculations about the origins and effects of the ancient Sumerian language on the brain and on computers. Plus there's lots of skateboarding, raves, and fundamentalists.
The Trial — Franz Kafka

Games

Age of Mythology — Align with the ancient Greeks, Egyptians, or Norse, build and defend villages and cities, strategize warriors and gods, learn about mythology and bygone cultures.

Bejeweled/Bedazzled — strategy-based

Civilization

Monster Rancher, Pokemon, etc. — kids' games based upon creating creatures, raising them, then fighting them gladiator style

SimCity — the predecessor to The Sims, in which the player builds cities rather than controlling characters' lives

SoCom, Halo — and other "authentic" military games that require tactics and strategy

Solitaire, Free Cell — and other computer card games; there's even bridge online!

Sphynx

Tetris

Tomb Raider — although it revolves around the Root Center issue of survival, it's based around archaeological themes

Zoo Tycoon — in the same vein as *SimCity*, but building zoos, determining size and content, and dealing with the results of your decisions

Music

Bach

Samuel Barber

John Cage

Handel

Indian ragas

Organ music

Stravinsky

Synthesizer music

Historical

Jesuits, the scholar missionaries of the Catholic Church, are disciplined, highly educated, and dedicated to the Pope. In the era of European colonization the Jesuits often went in first to "New World" lands, before the soldiers or settlers.

Theologian and paleontologist Teilhard de Chardin was a Jesuit who fell out with the Catholic establishment and made some futuristic speculations about evolution and consciousness.

Great philosophers from all cultures help ground the major questions of humanity: who are we, why are we here, where are we going? Disagreements ensue over the answers.

Long-lasting turning points in human history are usually precipitated by a Throat Centered activity. The inventions of agriculture, brewing, gunpowder, rifling, paper, the longbow (pivotal in the *Henry V* story of the English victory over the French at Agincourt, with that marvelous ASP Saint Crispin's Day speech), the printing press, telephone, flight, and internet have all changed the world.

We still don't know exactly how such great monuments as the pyramids and Angkor Wat were constructed, but they were obviously designed with intricate skill by people with very active Throat Centers.

Fourth-century B.C.E. Greek philosopher and natural scientist Aristotle analyzed and categorized everything he could think of. Most Greek and Roman philosophy was solidly Throat Centered. At the height of Islam's flowering Muslim scholars not only preserved the works of the classics but also contributed greatly to the arts and sciences, including mathematics and ophthalmology.

After huddling in mud huts through the Dark Ages and knocking about during the age of chivalry, Europe's Renaissance was built in part on the Throat Center work of Islam, which had preserved Greek and Roman intellectual treasures and done an awful lot of innovation on their own in medicine, science, architecture, art, poetry, genetics, and navigation. Leonardo da Vinci's fertile mind was active Throat Center extraordinaire. Robert Downey, Jr. in *Restoration* offers a personal look at this era. Europe's Age of Reason or Enlightenment in the eighteenth century was another resurgence of Throat Center activity. Out of this came the U.S. Constitution as well as the Industrial Revolution and modern science.

One of the biggest changes, often bemoaned by New Agers, was the supposed separation of science and spirituality headed by French philosopher and scientist Rene Descartes. The Cartesian split (named after Descartes) didn't do away with God, though; Descartes, Isaac Newton, and other famous scientists were also rather spiritual, sometimes even mystical.

The Throat-Center science of psychology analyzes the motives of others and even deals with the Inner Drives, though it uses different terms. Sigmund Freud and Carl Jung are prime examples in this discipline.

Beginning in the late 1800s theoretical physicists explored incredible new frontiers in Throat Center activities, taking us into the depths of physical reality with quantum mechanics and string theory, and out to the far reaches of the cosmos.

Literacy has often been a thing of awe, almost magical. The mental skills conferred by the ability to read and write are so powerful that they are often used as a political tool. In ancient Egypt there were three languages and only the priestly caste was allowed to use the most complex one. Chinese village women had a secret written language called *nushu*. A UN report notes that females with at least an eighth grade education have one third the babies as those without. Educating women and second-class citizens is seen by despots or repressive cultures as so dangerous as to need control. On a lesser scale, think of the cultural barriers that had to be broken in the movie *Stand and Deliver*.

The late philosopher and author Ayn Rand is exceptionally Throat Centered, as are all her works.

Current Events

There is a crisis in education in America. Social passing of unqualified kids to the next grade levels means colleges and businesses are saddled with remedial training. Money for education is continually cut. To conspiracy theorists it appears that somebody wants all Americans to be dumb, vapid couch potatoes who don't think, don't vote, don't resist, and simply consume, consume, consume.

Yet despite this overall decline in the intellectual prowess of the average American, there are incredible minds at work here and around the world. The intellectual advances of mathematicians and scientists often echo with the tenets of ancient philosophy (*The Tao of Physics* and *Dancing Wu Li Masters*). Physicist Stephen Hawking has become a media darling, narrating his own bio-pic of the universe, *A Brief History of Time*.

No look at Throat Center activity would be complete without a nod to computers. Bill Gates is today's popular icon of this Center, along with Steve Jobs and legions of other hardware and software innovators (some obscure).

Popular "baby genius" products promise to give your infant a head start through exposure to classical music, which research has shown helps enhance mental skills.

Finance runs most of the world these days. The World Trade Organization (WTO) and the International Monetary Fund (IMF) impose monetary order on many countries. Sometimes it takes, sometimes it does not. Read up on Argentina and on popular resistance to globalization and the WTO for insights into the down side of this Throat Center activity.

The military-industrial-entertainment complex is pure Throat Center. See some of their work at USC's Institute for Creative Technologies where the Army, Silicon Valley, and Hollywood merge.

Much modern commercial technology has come from DARPA, the Defense Advanced Research Projects Agency, including the internet itself. Eighty percent of scientific work is done under the auspices of the military. The *X-Files* TV series made great play of DARPA's work.

The U.S. has Battle Labs where the defense industry and war-fighters work together perfecting technology. At the end of each day of war gaming at the National Training Center in Fort Irwin, California, officers gather for an After Action Review (AAR) and analyze every action, cause and effect, lessons learned, and future policies. All very Throat Center with lots of interactive media.

The Army Academy at West Point has a new class, "Mental Skills for the New American Warrior" at their Center for Enhanced Performance. Check out their website at *http://www.dean.usma.edu/CEP/*

For a look at some really fantastic Throat Center activity check out the Massachusetts Institute of Technology's Media Lab.

If you're writing something science based or simply wish to keep up on what's happening, a great source is *Science Week*, which offers brief overviews of advances in all scientific fields: chemistry, psychology, astronomy, genetics, physics, etc.

And in something that particularly affects us creative types, how about the crisis in intellectual property rights? How can society ensure that the artist is adequately recognized and rewarded for creativity in order to ensure their ability to keep creating? What about the middleman, be it media company or retailer? The many juries, including that of public opinion, are still out on this one.

B. The Practice

Now that you have a familiarity with this Center, it's time to put your new knowledge into practice.

1. FOR YOUR CHARACTERS

- Build their Character Profiles based on the above information
- Find photos of actors or people who embody the character you want to create. Ralph Fiennes in *Quiz Show*, Tim Robbins in *I.Q.*, Russell Crowe in *A Beautiful Mind*, etc. Or a person from a magazine who resembles your character. Draw it if you must. But draw it neatly; remember, this is the Throat Center — conscious and controlled creativity.
- Construct a Character Profile Collage
- Write up their ID Statement
- Note card — A computer card. A musical score. A lined green accounting ledger. Type it up. Remember, it's about neatness, order, and control.

- Do the Wash — check the various aspects to be sure you have integrity of character every time they appear on the page or on screen: food, dialogue, actions, others' reactions to them, etc.

2. For Yourself

This is where you Walk the Walk and *Act As If*.

- Play Mozart, Handel, Bach, Beethoven, Stravinsky or one of the other intricate, polyrhythmic, complex composers
- Go to a symphony
- If you can read music, obtain the full score for a complex piece of music and play it in your mind. Conduct it. Do that "air musician" thing
- If you can play an instrument, even if you haven't done it since high school, pick it up again and play
- Compose a piece of music, play it exactly (improvisation is more Lower Solar Plexus)
- Wear plaids, stripes, checks
- If you usually do that rumpled bed-head look, go ultra neat instead
- Do a button-down, conservative, corporate look. Include panty-hose and heels or lace-up hard-sole "daddy" shoes and a tie. Wear this to work in. If you dress like this most of the time, you might try something more costumey like surgery scrubs or a lab coat to stay in the Center yet be different from your norm. Notice how different you feel than in low-slung jeans or your sweats
- Be really meticulously neat in your garb and your immediate environment
- Clean your desk and put things in order. You don't have to clean or sort everything, just line it all up, make the edges straight. When things are rectilinear (straight lines and right angles) it looks and feels orderly, regardless of what is actually in those piles
- Clean out your closets and put things you have not used and will not use back out into circulation by giving them to friends, having a garage sale, or donating them to charity
- Organize your photos, with labels on the back noting the time, place, and people. Your heirs and the researchers writing your biography will heartily thank you
- Eat sushi. It's a very artistic, carefully crafted food made with precision, and the art takes years to learn
- Research spin-off technologies from space exploration and try to find samples of food first invented for space: Tang, liquid turkey, etc.
- Do a comparison test between genetically modified food and organic food. What's the difference?

- Remember that being creative stimulates your Throat Center so as you sit down before your computer to compose, have snacks and drinks readily available. And as the old Army saying goes, "Smoke 'em if you got 'em." If you don't smoke cigarettes and don't want to, a visit to a good cigar shop might be in order for your experiment
- Play chess. My 3-D *Star Trek* chess game came with directions but they must be written in some obscure dialect of Romulan as none of us have yet figured out the rules
- Play Throat Center computer games (see list above)
- Do crossword puzzles — in ink
- Play solitaire and computer card games — fast, faster
- Learn to use an abacus
- Help an eighth grader do math homework
- Balance your checkbook — without a calculator or computer
- Memorize tables of numbers and work at being able to repeat them at faster and faster speeds
- Say the multiplication tables at least once a day
- Do jigsaw puzzles, the kind with just a few colors
- The more adept you become at holding a lot of ideas in your mind at one time, the better you'll become at writing complex yet vivid characters and scenes
- Brush up on foreign language skills and/or learn up to tourist level of a new language. I've found Klingon a very handy language to use in foreign travel as it deflects a lot of unwanted sales hype
- Write or find a poem or speech to memorize and find ways to work it in to your social or professional life — impress and/or astonish others
- Watch scary or weepy movies and be analytical; feel yourself rising out of the gut reaction of such as *The Ring* or *Steel Magnolias* and observe how they are crafted, what reactions they are designed to elicit
- Watch other movies in this section
- Read about science; read science texts. Visit the Science News website *http://www.sciencenews.org*
- Hang up the periodic chart of elements
- Get a science kit and do the experiments yourself
- Help a young person with their Science Fair project

3. EXERCISE

Complete your analysis from the "How To Use the Centers of Motivation" chapter on page 25.

C. Conclusion

As a creative type you can probably identify a lot with the Throat Center. There are so very many problems inherent in the free expression of creativity that this Center affords a vast realm of stories and characters. Particularly in today's world where communications and creativity are vitally important for the entire species to survive and to thrive, it behooves us to learn as much as we can about how best to utilize our Throat Center capabilities.

These challenges, whether it's suppression of free speech and action, the misuse of technology, or the dire results of that misuse a la *Terminator* or *The Day After Tomorrow*, are Throat Center themes that give us the opportunity to explore the consequences of our actions in imagination and then, hopefully, avoid those consequences in reality.

Many mythologists, poets, musicians, and artists of all sorts proclaim that the creation of beauty is the closest humans come to the divine. Think of that telling scene in *Amadeus* when Solieri's heart is breaking with jealousy as he reads Mozart's compositions and says it was like he was "taking dictation" from God.

As storytellers we create entire worlds and people them with creatures of our own crafting, becoming almost god-like in the process. No doubt you've worked with a few partners here and there who behaved like petulant gods. Regardless, Throat Center activity is exceptionally rewarding because it is so very creative and plugs one right into the main power source of Life.

Coupled with the rich complexity and productivity of this Center are its frustrating and often repressive downsides of rigid bureaucracy, demagoguery, and those other unattractive aspects. All in all, a very rich mine for conflict and drama.

So after this marvelously creative Center, what more could a character possibly desire? How about vision? How about balance? How about an integration of the many aspects of the other Centers? Well, that's just what the next center is all about.

9.
$\mathcal{A}$jna Center

What keeps Frodo Baggins on the road to the volcano in *The Lord of the Rings*?

One thing is that Frodo develops an Ajna Focus as the trilogy progresses, learning through trial and error to balance and integrate his mind, his emotions, and his body.

Like any Ajna Center character, Frodo can see the big picture. Aided by Bilbo, Gandalf, the Fellowship of the Ring, and the other characters he meets along his quest, he has a growing sense of the past and how it creates the present, as well as a sense of how the present creates the future.

He is also willing to balance his own needs with those of the group, to use all the resources available, to remain compassionate in the face of betrayal, and to hold the ultimate goal always in mind, regardless of seeming setbacks and distractions.

Your Ajna Center characters always need to have vision, a sense of balance, and the ability to synergize people, events, and things to accomplish that vision.

A. The Theory

MOTIVATION: SYNTHESIS

- Balance all the other Centers
- Integrate all the other Centers
- Receptive to higher energies
- Seemingly magical effectiveness
- Visionary

LOCATION

Three inches in front of the forehead, often depicted as a small golden sun. This is not the "third eye" per se but rather a function of the third eye, which is itself deep inside the brain. The Ajna is like a lens through which the focused consciousness of the individual is beamed out to the world, rather like the concentrated and focused light of a laser. The Hindu *bindi* mark — sometimes red pigment, sometimes jeweled bits — signifies the development of this esoteric function.

ENDOCRINE GLANDS & HORMONES

Pituitary — The pituitary, located in the center of the brain, is the control center for all the other glands and hormones. Esoterically the pituitary gland is considered feminine and its actual appearance includes what look like perfectly formed little breasts and buttocks. According to Manly P. Hall in his anatomy overview *Man, Grand Symbol of the Mysteries*, the pituitary has long been called "the gland of persistent effort."

Pituitrin — This substance extruded by the pituitary is referred to as "brain dew" and the "water of life." Spiritual practices which work with stimulating and altering this substance believe that the distribution of this dew or brain fluid down the spinal column can affect change on the other Centers and bring about transformation of the individual.

MYTHIC MEANING

The Ajna Center is named after the Hindu warrior-prince Arjuna. The story goes like this:

Arjuna was in a dilemma. As a royal prince, his duty was to defend his kingdom. So far, no problem. However, across the battlefield waiting to whomp on him and his troops and take over the kingdom was his enemy, which coincidentally also happened to be his traitorous and ambitious uncle and cousins. Therein lay the crux of his problem: in their culture it was taboo to shed familial blood. What was the Prince to do?!

Fortunately for Prince Arjuna he had a very wise charioteer, the blue-skinned god Krishna. (You should always request a god for your chauffeur.) Krishna observed Arjuna pacing back and forth before his tent the night before the battle. He approached the Prince and asked what was troubling him. Arjuna spilled his guts and limned the dilemma: he had to defend his country but the enemy army was led by his relatives.

Krishna said something to the effect of, "Dude, let's walk and talk." The god then explained to the human the difference between greater and smaller duties, between ethics and morals. Basically what Krishna showed him was that Arjuna's greater duty was to defend his country, even if it meant breaking the local taboo of shedding familial blood. Thus straightened out on his priorities, Prince Arjuna went into battle the next day and handily won.

The iconography about this incident shows the regal Prince with his bow and arrows in his royal chariot, a fabulous golden bejeweled conveyance. Arjuna is symbolic of the personality, our individual identity in the physical world. His driver is the blue-skinned god Krishna, symbolic of the higher energies, god, spirit, inspiration. Pulling the chariot are horses symbolizing our bodies. Sometimes it's three horses representing the Physical, Emotional, and Mental bodies. Sometimes it's four horses representing the four elements of the physical world: earth, air, fire, water. Sometimes it's five horses representing our five senses.

It's all about the ideal of our individual personality (Arjuna) being able to balance and integrate our various bodies/senses (the horses) and use them under the direction and inspiration of higher energies (the god Krishna).

The pituitary is often seen as feminine as it greatly resembles those lush, rotund goddess fertility figures and is partnered with the masculine pineal gland, which we'll explore more under the Crown Center. In this goddess aspect the Hindu Radha, the Egyptian Isis, and many other queen goddesses serve as pituitary symbols.

Medieval alchemists concentrated much of their efforts on balancing the pituitary and its essences with the pineal gland and its essences. This was often referred to as the Royal Marriage where the Pituitary is female-red-blood and the Pineal is male-white-semen. The place where the pituitary and pineal reside in the head is called the thalamus, which is Greek for "bridal chamber."

The pituitary is often referred to as the Holy Grail since it collects a fluid from the third ventricle of the brain and then redistributes it out to the rest of the body, just as the Grail chalice is thought to hold the blood of the Christ, gathered by Joseph of Arimethea during the crucifixion, or some other magical substance granted from higher realms and then redistributed out to the Knights of the Round Table. You can see direct influences here in the Christian ceremony of Holy Communion. References are replete in the Vine and Branches symbolism of the New Testament.

The pituitary is about accessing and controlling time — past, present, and future.

In the Wisdom Teachings the pituitary gland, as the central directing force of the physical realm, imbues the individual who attains its mastery with almost paranormal qualities and an almost omniscient sense of awareness. It is reminiscent of the mystical heroes of the Frank Herbert *Dune* novels, the Kwisatch Haderach, he who can be in all places at once, and of Neo in *The Matrix*.

The interesting thing about this particular Center is that although it is a Center of the personality, unlike the Heart and Crown Centers which are of the higher energies, this one has to be consciously developed. You don't just wake up one morning with an active Ajna. If only that were so. Rather, it takes lots and lots of dedicated effort, attention, practice, more dedication, more effort, more practice. The process is like becoming adept in martial arts or the cello, a long and arduous but ultimately rewarding journey.

One of the most dangerous, hence most interesting, characters is one with a fallen Ajna Center. If an individual who has obtained the powerful coordination of their own self and Centers has learned to affect the selves and Centers of others, and has learned to manipulate time and perception, drops their focus or chooses the dark side — look out. Examples such as Hitler, Jim Jones, David Koresh, Hannibal Lecter, and Darth Vader come to mind.

The ideal stance of an active Ajna Center is Harmlessness and Detachment. There's a lot of both Buddhist and Christian aspects here, as well as the physician's rule of *primum non nocere*, or "First, do no harm," and the sole dictum of Wicca, "Do what thou wilt, an' it harm no one." That last one gets really tricky, though, because you have to count yourself in the "no one" equation, so even if you think you're committing a victimless crime, are you harming yourself physically, emotionally, mentally, or spiritually?

Detachment comes about when you have no emotional ties to the outcome of a situation, kind of like Rhett's give-a-damn speech to Scarlett. But detachment need not mean abandonment. It simply means keeping your own agenda out of the action. Think "Let go and let God," or the Zen-like advice to perform an action without attachment to the outcome.

Outcomes, however, are often more clear to a person with an Ajna focus because they are able to see and to create patterns. An Ajna focus armed with knowledge of the Inner Drives, for instance, will be able to assess what motivates other people and to use that knowledge to manipulate them, for good or for ill. Another example is of a person like yourself with a developed Ajna who is able to create exceptional story characters.

The Ajna focus has a clear idea of cause and effect and can project likely consequences out to third and fourth levels. They are great planners because they look in all directions, including backwards in time.

An Ajna character will be a powerful, fascinating character because they have each of the other Centers all balanced and integrated. Or not. As they occasionally drop-and-wallow in the other Centers you have great opportunity for exciting story points. As they rebalance and regain their higher perspective you have great opportunity for enlightening story points.

ARCHETYPES

Benevolent Dictator — A la Plato, this is the individual who takes control and manages things for the greatest good for the greatest number. Lee Kwan Yew, former Prime Minister of Singapore, comes close to this archetype in all the fabulously positive results he brought about in that city-state, though his restriction of political opposition and the press gave his administration a slight fascist twinge.

Commander in Chief — Like this officer in an organization, the pituitary controls all the other endocrine glands and ideally balances, integrates, and controls the other Centers. We see this position most often in the military, corporations, and organizations. Unfortunately not all people filling the role of CEO or CINC (Commander in Chief) actually have an Ajna focus, so they will fail to correctly support their workers/troops and/or will use their position for personal gain.

Fallen Ajna — Since the Ajna Center must be consciously built (in one lifetime or over many, some say), it must be consciously held in that higher position, receptive to higher consciousness. If someone's lower Centers overpower it, that incredibly effective, laser-like Ajna focus can drop and then — watch out. Now you've got an astute observer and manipulator of energies guided not by the Crown Center but by, say, the Lower Solar Plexus or the Sacral, maybe even the Root. Examples are Rasputin (Throat and Sacral), Hitler (LSP and Root), Jim Jones (LSP and Sacral), David Koresh (LSP and Sacral), Darth Vader (LSP), Hannibal Lecter (LSP and Root), Saruman (Root). The position of Chief Executive Officer is an Ajna position. Presuming they personally had developed Ajna Centers in the first place, many early twenty-first century CEOs scandalized American finance with their drops to the power-mongering of the Lower Solar Plexus and money-grubbing greed of the Sacral. Needless to say, this Archetype is a powerful story character.

Futurist — Alvin and Heidi Toffler, Faith Popcorn, Nostradamus… people who observe a broad range of past and present activities to draw conclusions about the future. Not included here are Isaiah and all those other Bible prophets since they are believed to have simply been mouthpieces for Jahweh rather than astute thinkers and analysts of trends and tendencies. Slipping into a trance and coming out with prophecies is very much *not* an Ajna Center activity. America's Sleeping Prophet Edgar Cayce falls in this category, although some would say he had developed a powerful Ajna Center in other lifetimes and didn't quite make it conscious in this one, so he had to access those abilities in the sleep state. Mmm-hmm.

Jedi Knight — Even the fallen ones will have developed an Ajna Center… that's what distinguishes them from regular warriors. But in the Darth Vader types, they've dropped their Ajna focus so it's no longer receiving guidance from the higher One Life, they're off on a separatist path. As Darth growled, "Soon you shall know the power of the Dark Side." The Rangers of the *Babylon 5* series are all very Ajna: We live for the One, we die for the One.

Magician — The esoteric definition of a magician is someone who can "See patterns where others cannot see them and create patterns where they did not exist before." Because of their abilities to see so much of the big picture and the details, the Ajna focused individual has an impressive grasp of situations, sees things developing and can influence them, and is able to assess other people's Center of Motivation and thus appropriately influence their actions as well.

Magic is about putting the right things together in the right order for a specific result. It is about manipulating the laws of nature. There are two types of Magic: Ceremonial and Creative.

Ceremonial Magic is moving around the stuff that's already here. It works from the lower Centers: Root = death magic (animal and human sacrifices), Sacral = sex magic (*Eyes Wide Shut*), Lower Solar Plexus = personal gain (chanting and daily affirmations), ASP = rituals of most religions (transubstantiation of the Host during High Mass), Throat = Alchemy and Science, which can look a lot like magic when you don't know it's science.

Creative Magic brings absolutely new things into being. This is often done by the artists of an era as they precipitate overshadowing and abstract concepts down into the physical dense world for the rest of humanity to use and work with. All artists have moments of inspiration, that's what makes them artists. But to consciously craft the inspiration into something new yet useful requires a developed Ajna focus. More than likely Wassily Kandinsky had an Ajna Center going; just read his books to see how conscious he was about his art. More than likely Andy Warhol did not have an Ajna Center going; his work is clever, yes, but there doesn't seem to be much conscious theory behind it.

Merlin, magician extraordinaire of the Arthurian tales, and Gandalf, Sauron, and Saruman, the high magicians of the Tolkien works, are of this archetype.

Man In the Head — Ancient drawings often show a miniature person residing in the skull, looking out through the eyes and controlling the body. My favorite modern rendition of this is in *Men In Black*, where in the city morgue the head of the human-looking wounded body opens up to reveal the tiny fellow inside the skull, the royal prince seated at the controls of the larger body. Another version of this, with added twists like gender-bending, is *Being John Malkovich*.

Renaissance Man/Woman — This person is adept in the arts, the sciences, language, sports, and the social graces. In classical times an adept was required to have proficiency in seven areas: Grammar, Rhetoric, Logic, Arithmetic, Geometry, Astronomy, and Music. The Jack-of-All-Trades is the junior version of the Renaissance Man but often gets short shrift in the modern rush towards specialization; we have created people who know one thing very well, but only one thing. Neuroscience is now proving what the ancients always knew: a broad range of activities and study improves every area of activity and study, all intermingled and interdependent, like a hologram.

SYMBOLS

Fertility Goddess — The voluptuous breasts and buttocks of goddess carvings, often in Neolithic stone and ivory, resemble the physical appearance of the pituitary gland.

Five-Pointed Star — The completed man/woman. Da Vinci's *Vitruvian Man.*

Golden Sun / Third Eye — The Hindu *bindi* mark falls in this category. At the end of the battle in *The Last Samurai*, Tom Cruise's Nathan Algren had a thick spot of blood right on his Ajna Center and in that movie, he was working hard to balance and integrate his physical, emotional, and mental bodies.

Pegasus — The flying horse symbolizes the pituitary for a couple of reasons. One is that he parallels the Centaur, that half-man half-horse of the Sacral Center; but Pegasus has risen above the limitations of being animal or human, freed entirely from the bonds of mere earthly existence.

The other is that the actual pituitary gland in the brain resides near the *turkis sellicas*, or Turkish saddle. As so often in the symbolism of esoteric anatomy, the symbol actually resembles the thing it symbolizes.

The winged horse Pegasus sprang from the blood of the beheaded snake-haired Gorgon Medusa, recently slain by the hero Perseus. Symbolically, the hero-soul separates the lower self below the neck from the higher self above the neck. Yet from the very essence of that old, lower self springs a marvelous new creature who will carry the hero-soul off on many great adventures. The lesson is obvious: transmute your old motivations and attachments and you will gain an elevated version of their qualities which will serve you rather than terrorize you.

Rainbow — It is the orderly and progressive combination and integration of all colors, just as the Ajna combines and integrates all the lower Centers. In the *Ring Cycle* operas of Richard Wagner a key element is the Rainbow Bridge which connects earth with heaven.

Rooster, Cock — It is the first animal to see the light of day, just as the Ajna Center is the first personality Center to receive the light of the higher energies which flow in from the Crown Center.

PLANET & ASTROLOGICAL SIGNS

Moon — The pituitary is seen as feminine and receptive, as is the moon.

Since the Ajna Center is about integration of the other Centers there is no one Astrological sign for it. Rather, a developed Ajna focus should ideally be able to access and express any aspect of all the other astrological signs at any time.

COLORS, SHAPES, MATERIALS

- Complementary combinations of other colors from the lower Centers, nothing clashing
- Monochromatic because of the blending and balancing aspects
- Rainbow
- Red & White together: remember the Royal Marriage, discussed in Mythic Meaning
- Rose: esotericists believe the pituitary begins to glow a rosy color when certain disciplines are applied

CLOTHING

- Three-piece suits
- Mix and match coordinates
- Monochromatic blending: creme skirt, oyster shirt, taupe vest, eggshell stockings, bone shoes, etc.
- Mélanges of complementary colors, fabrics, and styles a la a coat-of-many-colors (the Bible's Joseph and his coat of same)
- Patchworks, but always meticulously done and in good taste
- Seamless garments, such as the robes worn for magical or religious ceremonies
- Combinations of at least three symbols or styles from the lower Centers: a well-tailored lab coat (Throat) over a purple brushed-silk shirt (ASP) with black or burgundy reptile skin boots (Root)

STYLES OF SPEECH

Knowing that it takes many different styles to reach all audiences, the Ajna focused person will pepper their speech with words that trigger thinkers, feelers, and touchers.

"Consider this if you will, and see how it feels to you."
"All things considered...."
"On balance, this looks to be the best way to integrate our plans for...."
"Taking a rational perspective, it appears that...."
"Let's all put our heads together and...."
"Thank you for your input. Let's fold that into the system here and...."

A mantram of the Ajna Center is: Never Explain, Never Complain. Obviously there are some situations where you need to give instructions or are called upon to give a cause-effect analysis. But most of the time when we're explaining things we're simply trying to make ourselves right in others' eyes.

Physical Actions

- Controlled, precise
- Graceful, poised
- Touching or rubbing the forehead at the Ajna spot
- Leading with the eyes when moving
- Continually scanning the environment, hyper-aware of all that's going on, without being jumpy or a Nervous Nelly
- Nureyev meets Achilles meets Einstein meets Gandhi

Foibles, Phobias, Food

- When out of balance the pituitary can produce gigantism or stunted growth
- Migraines, headaches
- Hallucinations
- Clairvoyance (complex scenes are more Ajna, seeing auras around individual people is more Solar Plexus)
- Nerve problems
- Eye problems — right = higher alignment problems such as mental, relational, spiritual, etc.; left = lower such as the physical environment, the body, etc.
- Raging hormones — the onset of puberty with its surge from the pituitary gives rise to coming-of-age stories that usually focus on Sacral and Solar Plexus issues; hopefully in these stories we at least learn what a balanced and integrated personality would look like, even if the heroine/hero doesn't make it in this tale
- Exquisite blends and combinations of seemingly conflicting items: red chili jelly on cream cheese to spread on rye toast, parfaits, baked Alaska, paella
- Gazpacho
- Antipasto
- Smorgasbord

Wounds & Deaths

- Execution-style shootings could fit because there's a counterpart of the Ajna at the base of the skull.
- Wounds or fatal blows to the temples could work well.
- Blinded.
- And as you would suppose, any wound right between the eyes: knifing, gunshot, slingshot, arrow, blunt force trauma.

- Tommy Lee Jones' bad guy Stranix in *Under Siege* gets it in the eye; awfully close to the Ajna Center.
- Since the Ajna Center is about integration, getting dismembered or blown to bits would be good for a dropped Ajna character.
- Also, as the Ajna is control-central, paralysis would be its antithesis.

EXAMPLES

Characters

Neo in the first *Matrix* film takes an Ajna focus at the very end when, revived by Trinity's love, he accepts his identity, integrates all aspects of his selves, and becomes victorious over time and space. It's the consummate illustration of the acquisition of an Ajna Center.

Kate Beckinsale's Flora Poste in *Cold Comfort Farm* is an Ajna Center character on a comic vein, but with the requisite skills of seeing patterns and motives and being able to manipulate them for a specific outcome.

The Lion King on the other hand is mythologically incomplete. Young Simba should have spent his time in exile building an Ajna Center, developing his physical, emotional, and mental skills, but instead he just mucked about eating bugs and singing silly songs. He didn't even come up with the idea of going home on his own; his childhood sweetheart had to spur that action. It was more about entitlement than initiation. You certainly don't want to waste the opportunity of such a good setup in your own stories.

In the musicals *Hello Dolly* and *The King and I*, heroines Dolly Levi and Anna Leonowens both hold an Ajna focus and manipulate others, to the greater good.

Obi Wan Kenobi and Darth Vader are both on an Ajna Focus, but Darth's powerful abilities have dropped to a Lower Solar Plexus motivation.

You'll notice a paucity of examples listed for this Center. We need more Ajna Center characters and stories, particularly as humanity ventures into this incredible new era of scientific and technological advances. Ethics and values are lagging far behind the acquisition and promulgation of goods and services. The Throat Center seems too often to be at the service of the Centers below the diaphragm in their most separative sense: greed runs the global economy.

Balance and integration are lax if not non-existent in the large-scale issues of most civil societies and governments, from distribution of goods and finance to wasting the environment.

We need more stories of true Warriors who protect and defend the weak and the innocent, who promote the good, the true, and the beautiful.

We need more stories of Magicians who precipitate new things, ways, and means down from the planes of inspiration and creativity.

Storytellers, become the Magicians and take up arms as Warriors to bring about a better world. And I don't mean only goody-goody stories. We humans learn as much from tragedy and darkness as we do from happy endings and lightness… sometimes even more.

Films
A Man for All Seasons
Beckett
Cold Comfort Farm
Hello, Dolly!
Henry V
The King and I
The Lord of the Rings — Gandalf always has an Ajna focus; Frodo develops one as the story progresses
The Matrix
Patton
Pushing Tin — Ajna Centers (essential to do the job) dropped into hyper-competitive Lower Solar Plexus
Spiderman — at the end when he really takes up his mantle and gives up the girl
Star Wars trilogy — Obi Wan Kenobi and Darth Vader are both Ajna characters on opposite ends of that spectrum. Throughout the stories, Luke attempts to build his own Ajna Center with the assistance of Obi Wan and Yoda
The Truman Show — the concept of the observer. Jim Carrey's Truman Burbank goes from being the observed to being the knowledgeable observer
Under Siege

Musicals, Opera, Ballet & Theatre
The Firebird
Hello, Dolly!
Joseph and the Amazing Technicolor Dreamcoat
The King and I — Anna brings reason, learning, laws, and personal freedom into the King's dictatorial Lower Solar Plexus reign.

Books
The Crystal Cave — Mary Stewart
Eastern Approaches — Fitzroy Maclean, and other books by him
"If" — the poem by Rudyard Kipling
John Dee, advisor to Queen Elizabeth I — books by and about him
Kim — Rudyard Kipling
The Merlin Trilogy — Mary Stewart

Games
Largo Winch (all centers must be utilized for completion)

Music
I'll venture to say that film scores are Ajna since the composers must consider and combine so many aspects to affect both the visual and the aural to elicit precise emotional responses at certain times.

Historical
Alexander the Great's Empire

The Roman Empire

The British Empire

Leonardo da Vinci

Francis Bacon

Shakespeare

General George S. Patton, Jr. was a real Ajna Focus person. A warrior-poet, he saw what needed to be done militarily and often despite the objections and obstructions placed before him by competitive colleagues or dithering politicians, was able to achieve victory. There's a great story that he took a key town in Italy that had been earmarked for some other General who'd had problems getting there on time. When the high command was reprimanding him for stepping out of the allied pecking order, Patton offered to give the town back. His superiors (in rank if not in Centers development) were not amused.

People with dropped Ajnas have caused ever so much trouble: Hitler, Jim Jones and the Guyana Kool-Aid suicides, David Koresh and the Waco debacle.

Current Events
Air Traffic Controllers — while doing the job

Commanders in Chief — during battle

Media producers — while doing the job

You, doing a pitch or presentation, will want to be in your Ajna Center

B. The Practice
Now that you have a familiarity with this Center, it's time to put your new knowledge into practice.

1. FOR YOUR CHARACTERS

- Build their Character Profiles based on the above information
- Find photos of actors or people who embody the character you want to create
- Construct a Character Profile Collage
- Write up their ID Statement
- Note card — some intricate yet tasteful combination of aspects of other Centers' note cards: edging of velvet with computer wiring trim, foil with silk, etc.
- Do the Wash — check the various aspects to be sure you have integrity of character every time they appear on the page or on screen: food, dialogue, actions, others' reactions to them, etc.

2. FOR YOURSELF

This is where you Walk the Walk and *Act As If.*

- Observe, observe, observe! Keep a journal about how each of these activities affects your physical body, your emotions, your thinking. Watch everything from the energy rise and fall of consuming sugar or carbs, to your reactions to the news, to how you interact with others.
- Play 3-D chess.
- Wear a gold star on your forehead or wear a *bindi,* found in many ethnic stores and on-line, or glue a jewel on your Ajna Center.
- Imagine (or wear if you enjoy really playing dress-up) a full dress military uniform with pounds of decorations and awards.
- Wear a typical flowing magician's robe and wave a magic wand.
- For music, play film scores and/or watch your favorites to see how the score enhances and often actually tells the story.
- Eclectic blends of classical, world, and all other types of music.
- Create a concert for yourself that includes music typical of each Center but listen to it with a slightly aloof analytical awareness — the position of the observer. Note how you react internally to each different style.
- Note the various types of music in different public locales: quick and edgy in fast-food restaurants to keep you moving; slow, classical, and romantic in more up-scale restaurants; Geezer-Rock nostalgia in supermarkets to encourage comfort-food buying; bland yet perky in office building elevators; etc.
- Eat smorgasbord, as many different items as are palatable, but all well-balanced one with the others.
- Eat paella, gazpacho, antipasto.
- Have one ethnic food for breakfast, another for lunch, and yet a different one for dinner.
- Take a ride in a simulator.

- Get into a virtual reality outfit.
- Choose different activities from different Centers and do them all in one day. I once went to the *Los Angeles Times* Annual Book Award luncheon (Throat) and followed it up that same evening with a Motocross Rally at the Coliseum (Lower Solar Plexus).
- Dedicate two hours to doing something physical, emotional and mental, one right after another: a workout or brisk walk; playing with your kids, counseling a friend; being romantic with your loved one; balancing your checkbook without a calculator or reading a science text.
- Begin doing the Ajna Focus Meditation. (Many Wisdom Teachers in different disciplines offer classes.) MYTHWORKS offers a CD/tape.
- Determine what Inner Drives your friends, family, and co-workers are coming from. Chart it all out for a day. Or, choose someone you're around a lot and chart them individually at various times over a couple of days.
- Interview a CEO, a school principal, a military commander, a hospital administrator, a line producer or actual producer (not the nephew or girlfriend of the financing producer).
- Think of a situation that has upset you in the past and into which you could place yourself again. Perhaps an overly needy friend or a know-it-all boss. First determine a better, non-emotional way to handle it and rehearse that until you're comfortable with the new way. Give yourself a physical trigger to remind you to act differently in that situation, such as tugging your ear or clearing your throat. Then go into that situation as the observer and see what a difference it makes.
- Assess your own instrument and determine one aspect each to improve physically, emotionally, and mentally. E.g., cut out sweets, don't be so critical, and do the multiplication tables once a day; or clean out your closets, counter every self-defeating thought with a positive thought, free-style imaginative solutions to some major world situation.
- Attempt to see yourself from multiple perspectives, adding one after another and then holding them all at the same time: close up, extreme close up, medium shot, a low angle from below, a high angle from above, an over-the-shoulder shot from behind, etc.

3. EXERCISE

Complete your analysis from the "How To Use the Centers of Motivation" chapter on page 25.

C. Conclusion

An Ajna Centered character will have balanced and integrated their physical, emotional, and mental aspects. Such a person will have at their beck and call all the other Centers. You could think of a person with a developed Ajna as a modern Renaissance person. Though most of us would like to attain this for ourselves and would most likely like it if most other humans were focused here as well… well, very few of us actually are. More's the pity.

Watching a story character (like Frodo Baggins) strive for, build, and attain an Ajna Center focus can be quite compelling in that it embodies the initiatory aspects of growth and change in an individual's consciousness and actions and we will intuitively respond to this heroic journey with fascination.

Like many who achieve an Ajna focus, Frodo is also unable to fit back in to his regular life. Unlike Samwise Gamgee who marries and becomes a happy house-holder, the Ajna-focused Frodo is artistically competent (he completes his part of Bilbo's book) yet deeply discontented with the quiet life in the Shire. Like many who have seen the higher light, he wastes away in ordinary living and must press on towards some more elevated existence. As the old World War I song puts it about American soldiers coming back from Europe, "How ya gonna keep 'em down on the farm, after they've seen Paree?"

Watching Ajna characters drop into the lower Centers can also offer both cau-tionary tales and entertainment, like John Cusack and Billy Bob Thornton in *Pushing Tin*.

Some of cinema's most fascinating conflicts are between two Ajna Center char-acters, one of whom has dropped into a lower chakra, such as Obi Wan Kenobi and Darth Vader, or Gandalf and Saruman.

Recalling that the Ajna Center must be consciously built, there are now more opportunities to learn about it and it is actually being developed by more and more people. It would be really great to have more examples out in the media to inspire and instruct us — in very entertaining ways, of course.

So after the Ajna is built, what next? The Ajna Center is the highest human per-sonality Center of the major eight chakras, but there is still that other spiritual one, the Crown Center.

10.
Crown Center

Why does the Dalai Lama of Tibet choose flight rather than fight in *Kundun*?

For that matter, why has the Dalai Lama never spoken out in anger against the invading Chinese who forced him into exile and destroyed so much of his homeland?

When creating a Crown Center character you're giving a person such a higher perspective on human actions that they can see forward and backward to causes-and-effects that may not become apparent for centuries. These people, their Inner Drives infused with the spirit of a higher vision, are comfortable with the paradoxes of apparent reality.

Perhaps the driving of Tibet's spiritual leader and his inherent wisdom out of millennia of seclusion and into the world at large rates higher on the scale than preserving a medieval, insular culture into the twenty-first century.

Your Crown Center character takes direction from a higher source than humanity and will not be swayed by normal human emotions or concerns. Sort of like *Charlie's Angels* but with a really spiritual Charlie and with angels who kick karmic and socio-political hiney rather than actual criminal hiney.

A. The Theory

MOTIVATION: ENLIGHTENMENT

- Connection with higher energies, spirit, god, goddess, cosmos, etc.
- Highest, abstract thought
- Impersonal, big-picture, above compassion for individuals
- Long term, grand view

LOCATION

About three inches above the head. In Buddhist iconography it's that little top-knot on Buddha's head.

ENDOCRINE GLANDS & HORMONES

Pineal Gland — This pea-sized, cone-shaped body is of reddish gray color, located in the center of the brain, and is similar in structure to the eyeball.

The Pineal Gland is still not fully understood by Western medicine. It appears in the fifth week of the development of the embryo, is larger in children than adults, and is larger in females than in males. The Pineal Gland works with the Hypothalamus, a control-center for metabolism, heartbeat, and other body functions.

Hormone — There is no specific pineal hormone in humans that we know of. However, it does secrete melatonin, which has an effect on sexual development and on our circadian rhythms, including sleep patterns.

MYTHIC MEANING

The Crown Center is not a Center of the personality, but rather of the very elevated, awake, and aware soul. As one might expect we don't find many humans operating from this Center.

The pineal gland is said to be the place where spiritual and physical meet, where thought enters the physical realm. In addition to most Easterners, some Western scientists, from Aristotle to Descartes and on, have held this view. Some of today's most popular science books are those investigating the spiritual or intelligent nature of the cosmos.

Some reptiles have actual eyes buried deep within their heads; the chameleon's pineal gland is close to the surface of the skull beneath a scale that is transparent enough to admit light. Scientists continue to study the effect of light on reptiles as it relates to the pineal gland. Mesozoic dinosaurs apparently had an eye in the back of the head, but in humans this area (once an opening in the skull of the dinosaurs) has been closed over.

Some believe that the ability of young children to perceive "other worlds" is due to the workings of the pineal gland, not yet enclosed by the bones of the skull.

Manly P. Hall in his *Man, Grand Symbol of the Mysteries* posits the Egyptian use of the *uraeus* or cobra on the Pharaoh's royal crown may have been symbolic of the pineal gland's ability to see that which was not readily apparent to ordinary mortals.

The pineal gland is thought to have been much more active in the distant past. Its main value to today's humans is as a symbol of connection to higher non-physical realms. To esotericists this is more real than symbolic and the pineal is considered the "third eye."

The fabled Unicorn was said to dip its single horn into poison waters and transmute them into life-giving substance. In Frank Herbert's *Dune* novels the Bene Gesserit Reverend Mother transforms the poison of the sandworm into the Water of Life. These analogies mimic the action of the activated pineal gland with its horn-like protrusion, as it begins to vibrate and make changes in the cerebro-spinal fluid, that brain dew mentioned earlier. They also relate to the problems of the higher, spiritual consciousness fallen into the material world, aswirl in emotions (poison water). It's about reaching a dynamic balance between two dimensions (spirit and matter, energy and form) which are anathema to each other without some balancing and transforming action.

The Chinese, Egyptians, and American Indians all wear feathers positioned in crowns or headdresses that resemble the pineal gland. Scandinavian myths show an eagle in the top of their world tree Yggdrasil and a hawk sitting between the eagle's eyes, symbol of the pineal. In the Jewish Kabbalah the highest sephiroth of Kether is assigned to the pineal gland.

Recent scientific ponderings on string theory, wherein reality consists of eleven distinct dimensions made up of bundles of "strings," bear a striking resemblance to an ancient description of this Center where the physical and non-physical meet in *The Shatchakra Nirupana*: "like the roseate sun of the morning, possessed of sixteen attributes and as fine as the hundredth part of the string of a stalk of the lotus… as fine as a thousandth part of the human hair and as luminous as twelve suns." We may again find that the ancient Wisdom Teachings have preserved valuable information until humans are able to rediscover it.

Recent neurophysiological advances have identified the so-called "god module" in the brain, which gives the feeling of being outside the personal body and being connected with all creation. This is the experience of *satori* or bliss that is the goal of many spiritual practices.

ARCHETYPES

Buddha — With his multi-knobbed topknot resembling the pineal.

Cyclopes — These one-eyed creatures of myth and legend may well be the storification of our distant memory of this vestigial eye. Often however, they are cast as bad guys, leftovers from a bygone era desperately clinging to what little power they have left.

The most famous Cyclops is Polyphemus of Homer's *Odyssey* who was blinded by the clever Odysseus before he could devour all the sailors trapped in his cave.

Gods, Goddesses, Angels — In the chakra system, higher benevolent energies access the individual through the Crown Center; lower destructive energies like Freddy Krueger and Jason access through the Solar Plexus.

Recall the Ajna focus story of Arjuna and the blue-skinned god Krishna — Krishna represents the Crown Center.

In general, though, as humans tell the tales, not all gods and goddesses are benevolent and some even act from lower Centers. Just ask Xena: Warrior Princess about Ares, God of War. Or Hercules about Hera, Queen of the Gods. Or Job about Jahweh.

One way to tell gods from humans is that the accepted laws of physics do not apply. Another is that their normal home is above-and-beyond, or at least beyond, human realms.

Psychopomp — Traditional guide to other worlds, this character shows up in most spiritual systems, because without a *Lonely Planet* or *Hitchhiker's Guide to the Galaxy* in hand, most people will need a guide when traversing other realms. Shamans serve that role in many societies, Egyptians had the jackal-headed god Anubis, and fallen Norse warriors had the voluptuous, horse-riding war-rior-babe Valkyries. Many classical stories use the psychopomp device: Roman poet Virgil's Trojan prince Aeneas had a Sybil, and Italian poet Dante had Virgil in his *Divine Comedy*. Mohamed's night journey from Mecca to Jerusalem was on the psychopomp Buraq, a woman-headed horse with a peacock tail. In Sufism, angels accompany one's departing soul and in modern Near-Death Experiences, people report departed loved ones or spiritual beings meeting them in the tunnel of light.

Two-Faced Gods — The pineal gland is a connection between the spiritual realm and the physical realm and these gods symbolize that esoteric duality. Janus, the Greek god of doorways, and the Christian Saint Peter, who holds the keys to heaven, fill this office. So do some Hindu and Tibetan gods of many faces.

SYMBOLS

Dove — Take a look at the flood stories of many different cultures with this metaphor in mind. Those signature doves sent out to test the falling post-flood waters may be symbolic of the individual consciousness finally being free of the negative aspects of the emotions (water).

Halo — Many religious icons in many different religions have halos, symbolic of the radiant light (said visible to those with "psychic sight") given off by an individual in touch with higher realms.

Pinecone, Pineapple, Lotus, Pomegranate — All these items resemble the actual appearance of the cone-shaped pineal gland filled with grainy "brain sand."

Buddha is often shown with a top-knot on his head, or sometimes a lotus, signifying his developed Crown Center. The pinecone, pineapple, or pomegranate atop the medical symbol of the caduceus represents the Crown Center.

Single Eye — The Egyptian Eye of Horus symbolizes the pineal gland, as do the Eyes of Shiva on many of the Hindu gods and goddesses.

You can also see this symbol in the all-seeing eye of Masonry atop the pyramid on the dollar bill and in another reference to Masonic traditions, there's the spooky one-eyed idol in *The Man Who Would Be King* from the Mason Rudyard Kipling's short story.

Six-Pointed Star — Overlapping triangles: the inverted represents spirit descending into matter and the upright represents matter yearning up towards spirit. They're also symbolic of the union of male (upright triangle) and female (inverted triangle).

Staff or Spear — Because of the rod-like protrusion from the round body of the pineal gland, magical spears or staffs are often associated with its functions.

Topknot — Many gods and goddesses have topknots, including Buddha. The Maori trickster god Maui was presumed born dead and set afloat in the sea on his mother's shorn topknot. Turns out he wasn't dead after all and returned to wreak mischief on one and all. Perhaps the lesson is to pay attention to that voice from above lest it come back distorted and bite you in the hiney.

Tops, Dreidels — The ancient Greeks gave the god-child Bacchus a spinning top, and the Jewish dreidel is another manifestation of the shape and motion of the pineal gland. The sound of a whirring top is said to mimic the sound heard by a devotee when they have, by much practice and inner discipline, activated their pineal gland and thus their Crown Center.

Unicorn — The pineal gland has a phallic horn-like (masculine) protrusion extending towards the multiple lobed (feminine) pituitary gland. In most stories about unicorns they can only be tamed by virgins.

Winged Dragon — The serpent/dragon energy of the Root Center has been raised up and given freedom of flight in the Crown Center. It has encountered and is able to enter the realms of higher realities. It has wings. The fact that reptiles still carry the vestige of this once very active third eye makes the winged one a perfect symbol for mystical abilities.

PLANET & ASTROLOGICAL SIGNS

Sun — In the system that links the moon with the Ajna, the sun is that greater light which both feeds the solar system with radiated energy and holds it together with attractive gravity.

Like the Heart Center, the Crown Center is not related to the personality, but is an aspect of the overshadowing Soul. Therefore it is not affected by the astrological signs, which have to do with one particular lifetime or incarnation.

COLORS, SHAPES, MATERIALS

Sky Blue — One signal along the Path of Initiation is the appearance of a blue light in the head, often but not always seen during meditation. It's usually a blue dot that grows to fill the head, pulsing back down to a tiny dot, then growing again. Sometimes the color orange appears between the blue.

White — All colors combined. Light itself.

CLOTHING

- Fancy full drag royal garb: bejeweled crowns and scepters, ermine-trim capes, etc.
- Plain white or sky blue diaphanous robes

STYLES OF SPEECH

- Very spiritual, inclusive
- Very impersonal
- Not at all concerned with individual or earthly events
- Speaks in concepts and abstractions, not particulars
- Hollow, echoing, reverberations, otherworldly
- Calm. Very calm. Very… very… very… calm….
- Think Yoda

PHYSICAL ACTIONS

- Very ethereal, floaty
- Hovering above, levitation of self
- Disconnected, spacey. Think of someone who's just had a stunning "religious experience" and how distracted and un-physical they seem
- Graceful, barely touching physical things

FOIBLES, PHOBIAS, FOODS

- Perceives other realities, often to the consternation of other humans who do not
- Sensitivity to light
- Jet-lag
- Insomnia
- Melatonin is the drug of preference
- Crisis of faith — the dark night of the soul
- Mead - a honey-wine, given by the gods
- Ambrosia - food of the Greek gods, said to impart immortality. It's a popular dessert in the American South: a festive concoction of pineapple, bananas, oranges, grapes, coconut, pecans, and ginger ale
- Manna - food from heaven said to have nourished the Israelites in their desert wandering from Egypt to the Promised Land
- Milk and honey — a staple on the heavenly menu
- Pineapples, pomegranates — resembling the actual gland

WOUNDS & DEATHS

- Punctures or crushing blows to the top of the head.
- Decapitation.

EXAMPLES

Characters

1) Humans with an active Crown Center
The Dalai Lama, the Pope (ideally)

2) Other-worldly Crown Center characters
A questionably effective dramatic device is the *deus ex machina*: in classical Greco-Roman plays, a god would often be wheeled or craned in to resolve a situation. Modern storytellers sometimes do this and it's still just as clumsy.

The angelic creatures of *The Abyss* seem Crown Center: vastly superior and remotely benevolent.

Clarence Oddbody, the angel in *It's A Wonderful Life*, is a personable Crown Center being.

Cuba Gooding's character in *What Dreams May Come*.

John Travolta's chocolate-chip cookie-loving archangel in *Michael* was by office a Crown Center character, but by actions was more Sacral and Aspirational Solar Plexus.

Films

Angel movies — As "messengers of the gods" angels bridge realities. However, in many Western films angels have very human characteristics, such as John Travolta's *Michael* and Nicholas Cage in *City of Angels*.

Clash of the Titans
Cocoon
Dogma — with the decidedly fallen angels Loki and Bartleby
Gospel According to St. Matthew by Pasolini
Heaven Can Wait — both versions
Hercules stories (the gods)
Jesus dramas — but not Mel Gibson's *The Passion of the Christ*
The Last Temptation of Christ
Little Buddha (sort of)
The Mahabharata
Saint stories
Siddhartha
The Song of Bernadette
Touched by an Angel
What Dreams May Come
Wings of Desire - the Angels, until they become human
Xena: Warrior Princess

Musicals, Operas, Ballet & Theatre

Many works include gods and angels.

Angels in America
Orfeo ed Euridice — Gluck's gorgeous opera finds both the Goddess of Love and the God of the Underworld as major players. "The Dance of the Blessed Spirits" in the paradisical Elysian Fields is particularly lovely.
The Ring Cycle — These four operas by Richard Wagner deal with the War in Heaven theme with gods and goddesses passing in and out of power.

Books

Aeneid — Roman poet Virgil's dynamic puff-piece for the Roman Empire put the Trojan prince Aeneas under the guidance of the goddess Athena to leave defeated Troy and go found Rome, after lots of god- and goddess-manipulated adventures
Autobiography of a Yogi — Paramahansa Yogananda
Bhagavad Gita (part of the Mahabharata)
The Bible
Fingerprints of the Gods — aliens and ancient civilizations
Heaven's Mirror — more aliens and ancient civilizations

Iliad — in blind poet Homer's account, Greek goddesses began the whole thing with a rigged beauty contest, then various gods and goddesses continually pulled strings and meddled throughout the ten-year Trojan War

Koran

Mahabharata

Odyssey — Homer's sequel tells of Greek gods and goddesses meddling in Odysseus' journey home to Ithaca from Troy

Origin of Consciousness in the Breakdown of the Bicameral Mind — Julian Janes offers an explanation for the "voices of god" in early man, based on neurophysiology

Sacred scriptures of any religion. While obviously written down by human hands, believers feel that the words were inspired or dictated by gods, goddesses, and angels and that the humans were merely secretaries

Why God Won't Go Away: Brain Science and the Biology of Belief — Eugene G. D'Aquili

Games

Age of Mythology — those parts where the gods help or harm humans

Music

Harp, ethereal

Gamelan (Indonesian)

Gregorian chant

Historical

Debates rage over the existence or non-existence of gods, goddesses, angels, and other-worldly beings. To those who believe in their existence, many or all events have been orchestrated by these various beings. They are called upon for victory in love, war, and sports events.

Religious wars have plagued humanity probably since the first disagreement over cause and effect occurred, and many conflicts around the globe today are still based on religious differences.

Akhenaten and his chief wife Nefertiti tried unsuccessfully to bring monotheism to Egypt in the twelfth century B.C.E. but the system wasn't ready for it and after his untimely death, most evidence of Akhenaten's existence was eradicated from the records and removed from the temples.

Many humans claim to find connection to higher realms through prayer, meditation, and other spiritual disciplines. On the down side, some individuals who claim to be personally and often exclusively in touch with higher realms tend to be passive loners, ditzy meddlers, or crazies. These types tend to either cause trouble or get into lots of it, because "god told me to." And do be very skeptical of anyone claiming to have accomplished a fifth-level initiation and to be an ascended master. Not bloody likely. It's that old adage, "Those who know don't say; those who say, don't know."

Current Events

The Human Potential movement of the last half of the twentieth century aspired in great part to raise an individual's conscious awareness to the frequency of a "higher self," "god within," or "the greatest potential."

Much of the rise of fundamentalist religions in the midst of this age of science and technology can be attributed to a gut reaction against the onslaught of modernism, as Karen Armstrong explains in her book *The Battle For God*.

As more Westerners take up various forms of meditation and other Eastern spiritual disciplines adapted to Western thinking, the concept of the chakras allows more people to contemplate, aspire towards, practice at, and achieve a higher consciousness.

The mystic versions of Western religions are also enjoying a resurgence in popularity, from Sufism to Kabala classes, to the stepped-down information about mystic Christianity revealed in the popular novel *The Da Vinci Code*.

Brain studies on creativity, emotions, and the interpretation of our sensate world reveal the underlying neurophysiological workings of spiritual experiences. Much of this is strikingly similar to the poetic descriptions of mythology, the Wisdom Teachings, and the rituals of the world's Mystery Schools.

B. The Practice

Now that you have a familiarity with this Center, it's time to put your new knowledge into practice.

1. FOR YOUR CHARACTERS

- Build their Character Profiles based on the above information
- Find photos of actors or people who embody the character you want to create
- Construct a Character Profile Collage
- Write up their ID Statement
- Note card — glass, clear or stained, because it's about light passing through. Write on glass, or trim a card with bits of glass. Draw or apply the symbols onto it
- Do the Wash — check the various aspects to be sure you have integrity of character every time they appear on the page or on screen: food, dialogue, actions, others' reactions to them, etc.

2. FOR YOURSELF

This is where you Walk the Walk and *Act As If.*

- Play harp music, Gregorian chant, anything really ethereal

- Better yet, total, complete silence, so quiet you eventually hear your own blood pumping through your body
- Wear a crown, a tiara
- Carry a scepter
- Dress in angelic flowing white, or something regal like velvet capes, elegant fur-trimmed or bejeweled garb
- Attach your halo and wings
- If you do this around Halloween or Mardi Gras, go as an angel or a royal
- Eat ambrosia, drink mead (available in upscale liquor stores), sip honey mixed in milk
- Visit sacred spots of different cultures, the more formal or orthodox the better: Chartres Cathedral, a Native American sacred place, a Mosque, an Orthodox church, a Wiccan grove....
- Put William Blake paintings of angels above your computer
- Read William Blake and William Butler Yeats poetry
- Read some comparative mythology
- Interview a professor of theology and/or mythology

3. Exercise

Complete your analysis from the "How To Use the Centers of Motivation" chapter on page 25.

C. Conclusion

We have reached the pinnacle of the chakra system.

A Crown Centered character will most likely not be human. Humans can however receive input, insights, and inspiration from higher sources through the Crown Center that will influence their own Inner Drives.

It's rather a rare occurrence and you'll want to be certain that the story merits this type of event and/or character. If you are creating a story with a specific spiritual or religious message, do take care to make the appearance and actions of the Crown Center elements organic and not one of those clumsy *deus ex machina* situations where the gods step in to save the day just in the nick of time.

The tone of expression of a Crown Center focus will almost always be supernally calm and benevolent. They can have a calming and uplifting affect on the more normal, human characters, and can be inspiring to your audience.

I hope you have enjoyed exploring this rather rare, elevated Center and will use the information to great effect in creating those unusual instances when your characters, who are focused on other Centers, experience that bolt from the blue or find themselves in an unearthly realm.

Mythic Structure via the Inner Drives

III.

11.

$\mathcal{I}$ntroduction

From the first two Sections of this book you've gotten a grasp of the Eight Classic Centers of Motivation and what each of them means, how it expresses as Inner Drives through an individual, and how you can use it to infuse a unique identity into your characters.

Now comes another fun part — mixing and matching the Inner Drive Centers both within a character and between and among characters.

One of the basic tenets of storytelling is that "drama is conflict." You can see how putting together characters who are strongly focused on one or another of the Centers will bring about quite a bit of conflict, hence drama. Think of Neo in *The Matrix* on an Ajna Center focus and Agent Smith on a Root Center focus, or Rick (Lower Solar Plexus) and Ilsa (Sacral) in *Casablanca*. Even on the same Center there is a wide latitude of expression, just as Obi Wan Kenobi and Darth Vader were both Jedi Knights, supposedly on an Ajna focus, but they were definitely in conflict, mainly because Darth had seriously dropped to his Lower Solar Plexus.

This Section will explore many ramifications of the Centers in interaction with each other. It will also offer you some mythic paradigms for integration of character.

As you utilize the writing tool of the so-called "character arc" you can use the Centers as pivot points for your characters' growth and change. These specific shifts of physical, psychological, and philosophical focus will give your characters unique yet believable transformations throughout the story.

Needless to say you will also be able to apply these paradigms to your own life and affairs and to assess the Center focus of those around you.

There are a number of Mythic Character Structure situations to explore:

Sliding Scales — From the dark to the light, from the repressed to the overindulgent, how does a particular Center get expressed in various characters.
    Darth Vader and Obi Wan Kenobi in *Star Wars*

Pairs of Centers — Some of the most fascinating dramatic conflicts are between two characters occupying two different but linked Centers. In more character-driven stories, it is intriguing to observe one character as they themselves rubber-band between two Centers.
    Dustin Hoffman in *Tootsie*

Driving the Arcs — In the structure of a story your main character will usually hop about between Centers. Why? How? To what effect?

DeNiro's Captain Mendoza in *The Mission*

Ensembles — Whether you're doing a buddy movie, an ensemble play, or a straight narrative, there'll be Group Dynamics at work. Since every other character in your story is there to reveal something about the hero, what are some powerful and realistic ways to accomplish that goal?

The *Star Trek* series

Marilyns, Moms, and Muses — In romantic relationships women often tend to be categorized, and to categorize themselves, within a couple of Centers. The dynamics of these shifts are quite dramatic.

Diane Lane in *Unfaithful*

Peter Pans, Papas, and Pygmalions — Men in romantic relationships also get stereotyped, causing quite dramatic conflicts as the desires and expectations of their partners clash.

Kevin Spacey's Lester Burnham in *American Beauty*.

Raising the Dragon — Classic road stories usually include the hero making an incredible journey from the Root Center up to the Crown Center. So do some very good contemporary films. So can you.

Bill Murray's Phil Connors in *Groundhog Day*

12.

The Sliding Scale

A. The Theory

All life is a spectrum of dualities, a sliding scale of positive-negative, up-down, conservative-liberal, anima-animus, persona-shadow, good-evil.

This Mythic Theme of opposition repeats itself in most cultures in the guise of differing siblings: the Judeo-Christian Cain and Abel, the Greek Castor and Pollux, Romans Romulus and Remus, the African Dogon Nummo twins, the Hindu and then Buddhist Yama and Yami, and the Mesoamerican Hunaphu and Zbalanque.

Some of our best stories are those which pit two characters against each other only to discover that they are very much alike but at opposite ends of the spectrum of a Center. Many screwball comedies of the '30s and '40s do this, such as *Adam's Rib* with Tracy and Hepburn mainly at the Throat Center (they're lawyers), and *My Man Godfrey* with William Powell and Carole Lombard at seemingly opposite ends of the Sacral Center (he's a bum and she's a wealthy socialite). Shakespeare's *As You Like It* plays a fun Sacral Center sliding scale, as does *Love's Labour Lost* where the young men try to be on the dry side of the Sacral scale but simply can't hold out against the magnetism of the lovely ladies.

Psychiatrist Carl Jung did extensive work on the anima-animus, or the male-female within each person, regardless of gender. From the raging macho male to the shrinking clingy female there is a wide range of gender expression. Jung explored the light and dark within each of us and made popular the Shadow, that part of ourselves which if not expressed grows ever more powerful and uncontrollable until it bursts out in inappropriate ways. *Dr. Jekyll and Mr. Hyde* stories illustrate this very dramatically. So do the films *Dead Ringer* and *Dead Ringers* with Bette Davis and Jeremy Irons respectively, playing twins.

There is a dark side to every Center of Motivation. As an artist you are usually called upon to make a value judgment in your stories, though sometimes stories don't seem to take a position one way or another, such as *Natural Born Killers*. Discounting karma and the whims of the gods to punish mortals through each other, when a character's actions harm others, most societies consider that "bad" and make rules to control them. Even in the classical tragedies when the bad guys won, the point for the audience was to realize that wasn't the way it should have turned out.

To align your villain to match your hero and offer worthy opposition, or to give a character room to travel from one end of the Center spectrum to the other over the course of your story, simply stretch the "Foibles, Phobias, & Foods" section of the Center profiles to the extremes of the Sliding Scale.

The darker side of the Inner Drives can be seen in:

- Root — the battle-enraged soldier or the serial killer.

  Freddie Krueger of the *Nightmare on Elm Street* series and Daniel Day-Lewis's Bill the Butcher in *Gangs of New York*.

- Sacral — sexual debauchery, kleptomania, anhedonia (lack of pleasure in any activity), extreme poverty.

  In *A Streetcar Named Desire* Stanley and Blanche are at opposite ends of the Sacral spectrum. He is blatantly sexual and improves his financial status over the course of the story; Blanche is hypocritical about her own sexuality and has mismanaged the family money to the point of poverty.

- Lower Solar Plexus — the compulsive gambler, the doormat, the power monger.

  Michael Douglas's Gordon Gekko in *Wall Street* "Greed is good!" is the dark side of Charlie Sheen's Bud Fox.

- Aspirational Solar Plexus — the interfering do-gooder, the martyr. Since the ASP is more about being harmless and helping others, its Shadow is more about the inefficient or warped side of itself, often expressing as comedy.

  Whoopie Goldberg's Oda Mae Brown in *Ghost* comes to mind, as do Humphrey Bogart, Aldo Ray, and Peter Ustinov in *We're No Angels*.

- Heart — There won't be a dark side to a Heart Center focus because it isn't part of the individual personality but rather a higher spiritual aspect.

- Throat — the evil scientist, the blabbermouth gossip.

  Novelist Robin Cook's stories (*Coma, Invasion, Virus*, etc.) show the shadow side of science.

- Ajna — This Center is about balance and integration of the lower bodies under the direction of the higher self, spirit, god. It does not have a dark side per se.

However, a "dropped" Ajna is extremely dangerous. Just think, a person with conscious control and with access to higher realms. Darth Vader and others mentioned in the Ajna Chapter give vivid examples of the destructiveness of concentrated power under malevolent motivations.

• Crown — Like the Heart Center, there isn't a down side per se.

But there are plenty of stories of gods and goddesses gone bad, from the ancient Greeks to *Buffy, Angel,* and the *Charmed* sisters. When any character with lots of power drops to a lower Center, it's not a pretty picture.

B. The Practice

Examples of how you can use this concept:

Move a character through the course of the story from one end of the spectrum to the other, like Russell Crowe's John Nash in *A Beautiful Mind,* who moves from exceptional brilliance to pitiful delusion and back-and-forth between the extremes of the Throat Center.

Pit two characters on either end of the spectrum against each other like Brando's Stanley and Leigh's Blanche in *A Streetcar Named Desire* on diverse ends of the Sacral Center.

Whale Rider's drama derives from the surviving twin sister struggling to fulfill her dead brother's legacy against a system that suppressed female leadership. The heroine takes the high end of Lower Solar Plexus as she battles both her grandfather and the Maori societal expectations (lower, separative LSP) for the right to "be."

Other examples of characters on the opposites of the scale would be prisoners and prison guards, as expressed in ever so many boys-and-babes-behind-bars movies.

Pacino's detective Hanna and De Niro's thief McCauley in *Heat* are mirror images of each other, on either side of the law. Both men are very Throat Center. *Face Off* pulls the same sliding scale maneuvre with John Travolta and Nicolas Cage switching identities as well as faces. It's an interesting idea that could have been better developed, but it illustrates the concept well. Mythically speaking, how appropriate that Cage's character is named Castor Troy and his brother is Pollux Troy. Castor and Pollux are brothers in Greek mythology and the story of the Trojan horse — danger disguised as a gift — still carries cultural resonance.

In the animated film *Star Wars: Knights of the Old Republic* a warrior must choose between the Light Side of the Force and the Dark.

In *The Lord of the Rings* stories the wizards Gandalf and Saruman were once closer to each other on the Sliding Scale, but Saruman goes dark and Gandalf gets even lighter, going from Gandalf the Grey to Gandalf the White.

A perfectly balanced person may be desirable in real life but it isn't dramatically interesting. However, a position of balance is an okay place to end a story that has been about the person's ups and downs, allies and enemies, battles and victories along the Sliding Scale of the Centers.

C. Conclusion

So remember, do not limit your characters to just one aspect of the Inner Drives, for within each Center there is a broad spectrum of expression and experience. As the creator of characters you can take us all on an exciting ride along this Sliding Scale.

13.
Pairs of
Centers

There are three pairings of the Centers.

Root/Crown
Sacral/Throat
Lower Solar Plexus/ASP-Heart

The Ajna is the Center of balance and integration, so for our purposes here it has no pairing. In advanced spiritual disciplines there are more Centers within the head and the Ajna does link up with some of those in a number of ways.

As a person grows in conscious awareness they typically begin to elevate and transfer their Inner Drives from the Center where they are most focused up towards its higher counterpart. Some Centers Transfer simply happens in the course of evolution, but it can happen a lot faster if approached with conscious intent. The Mystery Schools teach disciplines such as meditation, mantras, and initiations to help aspirants accomplish this shift. As story-tellers we can use this same information to construct characters who reflect both the natural growth process as well as highly motivated changes.

Since the most interesting characters are those who change and grow before our very eyes, let's see how this process of Transfers between Pairs of Centers works and how you can use it to enrich your own characters.

A. The Theory

MYTHIC MEANING — ROOT/CROWN TRANSFER

The Root Center is about individual physical existence in this time and place. The Crown Center is our connection to higher consciousness, spirituality, and the One Life. Both are plug-ins to life-force sources: one really basic and the other more elevated, one earthly and the other spiritual. The Hindu god Shiva and goddess Shakti, the Egyptian god-couple Isis and Osiris, Christian Jesus and his bride The Church, and Greek hero Perseus and the Princess Andromeda are all examples of this pairing of Root and Crown Centers. The Hebrew Kabbalah designates these concepts as Kether at the very top and Malkuth at the very bottom.

The Fall in the Garden of Eden story, which appears in some form in most cultures' myths, is symbolic of the fall of spirit into matter and the rescuing hero sent to redeem this fallen energy. The serpent (Kundalini energy) tempts Eve (the creative Persona) with an apple (sensory experience). She then attracts Adam (overshadowing Soul), they both get kicked out of Paradise and an angel with a flaming sword is set to guard the gates. (Note the Root Center symbolism there.) And that, some say, symbolizes the beginning of the whole process of reincarnation, with its ultimate mission to redeem and uplift the fallen Kundalini.

One wonders why the powers that be felt the need to trick us and couldn't just say, "Hey, guys and girls, we've got a problem here and we need some brave volunteers for a really important mission." Perhaps they figured they wouldn't get many volunteers, so they used the old bait-and-switch ploy, and here we are.

Most stories set the fallen half as female since as givers-of-life women both represent Matter and are more bound to and reflective of the material world by their bodies (menstruation, childbirth, lactation, etc.). As in the Greek myth of Orpheus and Eurydice, where the immortal Orpheus attempts to retrieve his beloved wife from the underworld where all mortals must go when dead, the rescuers are usually male, since they are supposedly less earth-bound and represent Spirit. But just ask any guy if his body connects him to the material world (particularly in regards to sex) and you'll probably get the "every second of every day" reply.

In goddess-dominant systems the son-lover-brother may fall or be stolen away and must be rescued by the female, so that designation of earth-bound may well be more socio-political than physiological. Some of these more ancient versions include the Mesopotamian goddess Innana descending into the underworld to rescue Dammuz, and the Egyptian goddess Isis reclaiming the body parts of her slain brother-lover Osiris. She then gave a "special kiss" to one of his body parts and temporarily revived him, long enough to conceive their child Horus.

Modern tales using this older, flipped version of a Root/Crown pairing include Beethoven's opera *Fidelio*, where the wife dons drag and rescues the unjustly imprisoned husband; and *The Bodyguard*, where Whitney Houston's pop star redeems Kevin Costner's Secret Service agent who had fallen from grace.

In many stories with a Root/Crown pairing the burden of redemption is removed from the individual and taken on by a savior god. This Christ figure appears in many guises, from Buddha, Tammuz, the Norse god Balder, and Jesus to Jack Nicholson's McMurphy in *One Flew Over the Cuckoo's Nest* and Paul Newman's Luke in *Cool Hand Luke*.

MYTHIC MEANING — SACRAL/THROAT TRANSFER

The Sacral and Throat Centers are both about creativity. The former is unconscious creativity (gestating a baby while in a coma) and the other is conscious creativity. One is sensual, the other mental.

Half-human half-animals symbolize the Sacral Center because it's about our animal nature. It's instinct. It's relatively easy.

The Throat Center is symbolized by the eagle and the bull: one winged and free from the bonds of earth and the other the grounding of thought into physical dense reality. It's the intellect. It's imagination. And it isn't that easy. It takes effort, concentration, focus, training, and determination to do well. Just ask anyone who's written a script or put on a show.

As an individual awakens to the powers of their rational mind and imagination they begin to manipulate the environment via the Throat Center, rather than to be manipulated by it through their Sacral Center. They observe the patterns of nature and humanity. They learn to work with those patterns and then to control them. It's a move from instinct to intellect.

The shift in Inner Drives from Sacral to Throat Center is often marked as the beginning of civilization: agriculture, domestication of animals, metallurgy, writing, commerce, navigation, architecture, and so on. Most cultures have stories about teacher gods who came from a distant land, looked quite different from the locals, taught the people all sorts of valuable skills (including in one version, how to make and apply cosmetics), then for some reason or another left, promising to come back. Whether it's the Viracocha of South America, Quetzalcoatl further north, the Rishis or Kumaras in Hindu lore, Dagon on the shores of the eastern Mediterranean, or Thoth in ancient Egypt, there's usually a god or group of gods who help facilitate the Sacral/Throat Transfer and move people up the scale from primitive to civilized.

One school of thought interprets erotic carvings on the Hindu Khajuraho temple as more about electricity and chakra currents than simple sexual congress. Oral sex, connecting male and female currents at the Sacral and Throat areas, may be symbolic of the Sacral/Throat pairing and Transfer of energies. Then again, it could just be erotic art.

Regardless, as a creative person you have probably experienced the intense, rewarding, almost sensual joy of being in-the-zone of the creative process.

MYTHIC MEANING — LOWER SOLAR PLEXUS/ASPIRATIONAL SOLAR PLEXUS–HEART TRANSFER

This Transfer is the dichotomy between "me" and "we," "quantity" and "quality." LSP is about quantity, usually more-more-more; think conspicuous consumption and rampant consumerism. The ASP is about quality and community.

Other pairs of opposites between these Inner Drives are Ambition/Altruism, Exclusive/Inclusive, Agitator/Peacemaker, and Greed/Generosity.

Once someone starts waking up to the world around them and perceives their own affect upon it they typically become more considerate of others and concerned for the greater good. They will face opposition both from their own habits and from others who don't want them to change.

Stories about this Transfer will usually include an individual or a small group of people spreading out from their home base to interact with the wider environment. It is an expansion of the circle-of-life and if *The Lion King* had been more mythologically correct Simba would have learned useful things while in exile; he would have picked up tricks and concepts that would have made him a better leader, rather than simply an entitled one.

A mythic-historical figure who makes this Transfer is Gilgamesh, King of Uruk. He begins the story as an arrogant, power-hungry, selfish, womanizing king and by the end — after many trials, battles, loves, and losses — he is a true king, unselfishly concerned about and working towards the greatest good for his people.

In the New Testament the Jew Saul had been persecuting Christians and was on his way to Damascus to cause some more damage. Blinded by a bright light and confronted by Jesus' voice, he had a conversion, changed his name to Paul, and became a fervent Christian preacher. Most Transfers are not so speedy nor dramatic, but every now and again you find a character "blinded by the light on the road to Damascus," such as Jeff Bridges' air crash survivor Max in *Fearless*. These epiphanies make for dramatic turning points within a character.

An historical example of this Center Transfer is the Scandinavians. Hundreds of years ago they were the feared Vikings, marauding widely and wildly across the seas. Today Denmark, Norway, and Sweden are some of the most civilized, socially responsible, enlightened, and peaceful countries on the planet.

There's an interesting aspect of the dual nature of the Solar Plexus in the curious phenomenon of two similar movies coming out around the same time: *Saving Private Ryan* and *The Thin Red Line, Armageddon* and *Deep Impact, Dangerous Liaisons* and *Valmont,* and the like. Usually the tones of these pairs will be quite different. E.g., *Saving Private Ryan* and *The Thin Red Line* are both WWII films but the former is bloody, gory lower Centers all the way while the latter is poetic, aspirational, contemplative, and spiritual.

B. The Practice

1. MOVING BETWEEN PAIRS WITHIN THE SAME CHARACTER

Heroes need to change and grow throughout the course of a story for us to have any interest in them. In order to do this you must take a character from one focus to another, one point of view to another, one way of acting to another. It's really helpful to have a firm idea of where they are at the beginning and where you want to take them so you can then come up with all sorts of interesting ways for them to make that transition.

A really effective way to do this is to use the natural tendency humans have to bounce between a pairing of the Centers. Perhaps you know someone who seems to swing from one tendency to another, whether it's piety to debauchery like some fundamentalist TV preachers, or killer-instinct to leader-insight like General Patton, or selfish coolness to enlightened altruism like Samuel L. Jackson's Jules Winnfield in *Pulp Fiction*. These seeming about-faces can be explained by movement between Pairs of Centers, in either direction.

Perhaps the strict no-nonsense parent becomes a fun-loving older spouse once the kids have left the nest (Aspirational Solar Plexus to Lower Solar Plexus), or the retired aeronautics engineer takes up cooking or gardening (Throat to Sacral). In *The Accidental Tourist* William Hurt's writer Macon Leary (Throat) has shut down all emotion after the death of his son. Geena Davis' Muriel is a vibrant Sacral enticement who helps him connect with the delights and comforts of sensuality. A tragic version of this is in the Louis Malle film *Damage*, where Jeremy Irons' Stephen, a Throat Centered doctor and government minister, tumbles into a passionate, obsessive Sacral swirl with his son's fiancée, Juliet Binoche's Anna.

Perhaps the type-A businessman tosses it all over for life in a monastery (Lower Solar Plexus to Aspirational Solar Plexus). Jeff Bridges' Jack Lucas makes an LSP to ASP shift in *The Fisher King*, moving from a selfish know-it-all to a more truly caring man, willing to open up and give to others.

Maybe the military man becomes a grade school teacher (LSP to ASP) or the gang member leads a truce and creates neighborhood coalitions (LSP to ASP). In *Braveheart* Robert The Bruce tried to rise above his limited leader-of-the-nobles' interests and become a true king, but he never quite made it and broke William Wallace's heart. Later on, however, The Bruce did realize his aspiration and bravely freed the Scots from English rule. His actual heart was carried to the Crusades, hurled at the enemy, then buried back in Scotland, where supposedly it still remains.

Other examples of transfers within a character include:

a. Root/Crown

How about Jesus the Christ in Mel Gibson's *The Passion of the Christ*, where a god (Crown) is placed in a position of sheer survival (Root) and loses his earthly life. But as the story goes, he regains the higher position a la the Resurrection. The symbolism of dying and reviving Savior Gods takes on a new aspect when seen as Pairs of Centers.

In *Kundun* the Dalai Lama's escape into exile from Tibet to India places him, a very godlike man, in danger for his life.

• The Root/Crown dichotomy in your story line can be best expressed by these dualities in dialogue, sets, costumes, actions, and speech: dark/light, dead/alive, passive/active, vicious/benevolent, desperate/detached, earthy/ethereal.

b. Sacral/Throat

Much more common than the Root/Crown Transfer is the Sacral/Throat. It has problems as well as benefits and giving your characters some of these will flesh them out.

Physical problems inherent in the Sacral/Throat Transfer include congestion, allergies, and acne.

A person doing the Sacral/Throat Transfer will often be clairaudient and hear voices. This ties in with the poltergeist activity of the pubescent Sacral moving upward.

Enforced celibacy can bring on hyperthyroidism and goiter. Some psychologists, particularly of the Freudian bent, will credit the literary, musical, and artistic Throat Center accomplishments of medieval and Renaissance Catholic monks and nuns to the suppression of their Sacral Center sexuality.

In the classic film *Dr. Jekyll and Mr. Hyde* starring Spencer Tracy, he vacillates between the calm and logical Throat Centered Doctor and the Sacrally perverse and scary Mr. Hyde. This Robert Louis Stevenson story is a perfect example of a rough Inner Drives transfer.

Sacral/Throat transfers occur in *Shakespeare in Love* and also in *Dangerous Beauty*. In the latter, Catherine McCormack's Veronica Franco makes the transfer and link-up successfully as she becomes a supremely popular courtesan, poet, fencer, and unofficial diplomat — while she's expertly boffing most of the elite guys of Venice. True story, by the way. Alternatively, Oliver Platt's Maffio is thwarted.

He's plenty smart and talented, but his repressed Sacral expression results in him becoming a Catholic monk and persecuting Veronica via the Inquisition.

Computer hackers and self-styled geeks will often be stymied in the Sacral/Throat Transfer and stuck in the Throat Center. At the extreme it's all mind and no love life. Variations on this theme occur in many technology-gone-bad stories.

Frida Kahlo and Diego Rivera as portrayed by Salma Hayek and Alfred Molino in the bio-pic *Frida* is an intense revelation of two individuals both doing the Sacral/Throat Transfer, sometimes with success, sometimes with tragedy, always with incredible artistry.

- The Sacral/Throat dichotomy in your story line can be best expressed by these dualities in dialogue, sets, costumes, actions, and speech: passion/ration, moist/dry, emotional/mental, free-flowing/rigid, chaotic/ordered, passive/active.

c. *Lower Solar Plexus/ASP–Heart*

The adorable comedy *We're No Angels* arcs the escaped convicts played by Humphrey Bogart, Peter Ustinov, and Aldo Ray from Lower Solar Plexus to charmingly gracious and generous Aspirational Solar Plexus guys who help out the family they originally came to rob and kill.

In *Three Kings* American GIs out to commandeer Iraqi gold move from grasping, self-serving LSP to ASP when they encounter Iraqi civilians under persecution from their own government and abandoned by U.S. policy. George Clooney, Mark Wahlberg, and Ice Cube even have a Heart Center moment as they face down their own guns to defend the local civilians.

Schindler's List is a fascinating portrayal of a man moving from secure LSP to dangerous ASP. Given the enormity of the opposition, the Nazis, we might well say that at times he moved to a Heart Center focus.

The story-tool here is the discovery of otherwise unknown facts which tweak the heroes' sympathy and/or sense of justice and cause them to alter their Inner Drives.

- The LSP/ASP-Heart dichotomy in your story line can be best expressed by these dualities in dialogue, sets, costumes, actions, and speech: selfish/unselfish, greedy/generous, exclusive/inclusive, judgmental/accepting, introvert/extrovert, demanding/laissez-faire.

2. RUBBER-BANDING WITHIN A CHARACTER

Moving between the Pairs of Centers offers dramatic change and conflict for an individual character. Part of the conflict is that the Transfers are not always easy. Why?

There is a pattern called Rubber-Banding that occurs when a person is shifting their Inner Drives from a lower Center up to a higher one but hasn't yet made the full shift and keeps bouncing back and forth between the two. The more you think about this one the more you are likely to recognize it in yourself, in others, and in well-developed story characters.

When a character attempts to make a Transfer to a higher Center, they envision a goal or a new way of being. They learn more about it, find others who are doing it as examples or mentors, take up specific disciplines, and begin striving towards becoming/doing that.

There will be times of high success when they are able to "be" all they can be. And then, inevitably, will come a fall-back to the old ways, a "drop and wallow."

A typical rubber-banding situation is in young teens who are buffeted about by hormones just as they're called upon to develop their minds and prepare for their future.

This Rubber-Band Effect is where being on the Path to Enlightenment gets tricky. At first glance it seems like you will become Enlightened and then take a hike away from the Darkness, never to return to the nether realms. Hah. Would that it were so. Gurus often shrug and note that once you scale the mountain of Enlightenment all you really qualify for is to be a mountain-climbing guide for others making their way up.

So a character goes along, gets new info, new light, new insights. They work with these, begin to make them part of their lifestyle, and practice them. Then something comes along and phfoop! Down again. The trick is this — when a character is down there in the darkness, this time they have a flashlight. With their newfound Wisdom and Light, they can look around, see patterns, see what it's all about and begin to make enlightened choices about how to change things and deal with the stuff that drove them away from there in the first place. In story crafting, this appears as the thing-that-changes, be it Indiana Jones and the snakes, Eliza Dolittle and her speech patterns, or Demi Moore's *G.I. Jane* and her physical prowess.

This is the pattern Jesus set, too. During those three days between the cross and the empty grave, so the story goes, he descended into Hell and redeemed the souls who obviously wouldn't have heard about him before they died. A gracious act and a nifty way to get around that particular doctrinal dilemma. So, the "Harrowing of Hell" and then, voila, they're all off to heaven. It's a pattern to keep in mind when your character is in the deepest depths of doom or despair, or during those times we ourselves tend not to be as perfect as we aspire to be.

Some spiritual teachings say that the Darkness calls us because it wants to die, to be engulfed and transformed by Light. Remember the Fall and the need for Redemption? Darth Vader ultimately wants to be redeemed by his son Luke (whose name is a derivative of the Latin "lux" or light). Other systems say the Darkness is simply the other side of the Light and one would not exist without the other. People tend to argue these differences, often to the point of killing each other and proving, if nothing else, that Darkness does occasionally win. If your story deals with the Dark Side, one good way to explore it is through the Pairs of Opposites and Centers Transfers.

One of the most impressive and entertaining examples of Sacral/Throat Rubber-Banding is Willem Dafoe's performance as the FBI agent Paul Smecker in *The Boondock Saints*. He vacillates wildly between astute, opera-listening, Throat Centered crime-scene analysis and radical over-the-edge, fevered, fey-gay, well-dressed Sacral bitchiness. It's a magnificent, poetic performance.

a. How Rubber-Banding Works
The basic steps of a Centers Transfer are:

1. Activation of the lower Center
2. Awakening of higher Center, which begins to exert a magnetic pull, a new Inner Drive
3. Bounce around between the two Centers
4. Both rhythms going at the same time causes chaos as the differing Drives battle for control of the character
5. Eventually the higher Center gains dominance
6. Then the higher Center dictates the rhythm of the lower counterpart; it doesn't cut it off but rather controls it

A character will have a great thought, study a new thing, read an inspiring book, learn a new skill, have a great spiritual insight or experience. They are high, charged, jazzed with goodness and light and joy. Then as the laws of nature would have it, they get to go serve where most needed. An emergency will occur, a person in need will seek them out, a world or community situation will arise and because of their recent experience they are able to inject a fresh POV of wisdom. It's like going to school, learning stuff, then going out and practicing it. It's also like in the Hero's Journey when the Hero returns with that "boon" for the community.

And let's not make the mistake of condemning or repressing the "lower" Centers. The goal is to link them all under the conscious direction of the Higher Will which serves the Greater Good. Just as on a film set you need all parts of the body from the glorious and glamorous to the folks behind the scenes doing the hard physical labor, so too we need all the various parts of our selves working in concert, serving the Whole.

Because Frodo has wrestled with the dark power of the One Ring himself, he sees in Gollum what he might become if he does not complete his mission. He also gives recognition of Gollum's value as the opponent to keep him on the path to Mount Doom and even to the final moment when he himself falters once again. Often, characters will be motivated not to become like someone else — a parent, a rival, or an opponent.

b. Applying Rubber-Banding

When you do the Rubber-Banding within a character, you will want to have the initial shift be a short amount of time in the new Center. Then your character bounces back to their old ways and that lower Inner Drive takes over again. But, they carry some glimmer of the new way with them and it begins to take hold. With each successive challenge the story offers them, they get stronger and more grounded in their higher focus.

A sample time-line might go:

Old Center = ten minutes
New Center = two minutes
Old Center = six minutes
New Center = five minutes
Old Center = three minutes
New Center = eight minutes
Old Center = one minute
New Center = ten minutes

Not a hard and fast form, but rather a pattern to show the character's eventual stability in their new Center. Needless to say, all sorts of emotions and actions will accompany the shifts between Centers.

Eventually, it is the character's ultimate challenge to stay in the higher Center by giving up the draw of the lower Center, which includes the comfort zone and the expertise gained there from the long time living in it. Think of Eliza Dolittle in *My Fair Lady* or the same situation in *Educating Rita.*

In *Working Girl,* Melanie Griffith consciously works to move from Sacral to Throat and ultimately to Ajna.

Nick Nolte's artist in *New York Stories* is a perfect example of the Sacral/Throat Rubber Banding so typical for creative people trying to also have a "real life."

Sometimes the shift is from higher to lower as we watch a character fall deeper and deeper into the depths of Center darkness. Shakespeare's Othello comes to mind, as does Jeremy Irons, both as Claus von Bulow in *Reversal of Fortune,* and as Dr. Stephen Fleming in *Damage.*

Reactions and comments from other characters will help illustrate Rubber-Banding. "See, you always do that," or "Must you always…," or something to show that the hero is still perceived as being in the old Center.

A way to show them moving out of the old Center and into the new one is to have them begin an action in the old way — cooking, exercising, working, dealing with relatives or relationships, etc. — and then changing mid-stream to the new way. Dustin Hoffman in *Tootsie* and Robin Williams in *Mrs. Doubtfire* both illustrate this dynamic.

3. CENTER PAIRING BETWEEN CHARACTERS

A chief problem for new writers (and some more experienced ones as well) is making different characters really different. One effective way to do that is to craft two characters on different ends of a Center Pairing and use their conflicting Inner Drives to create dramatic tension.

This is also a helpful tool for crafting the Worthy Opponent. The Worthy Opponent is the Appropriate Opponent. The Protagonist and the Antagonist need to be matched up; not to be the same, but to have complementary Inner Drives in conflict one with the other. Using the Pairs of Centers is a very effective way to do this.

Opposites attract. Lovers often embody those things about ourselves we have not yet accepted, or those things we have not yet tried to do. These Pairs of Centers can play out into great dramatic conflict, from screwball comedies like *Adam's Rib,* to action adventures like *Romancing the Stone,* to torrid affairs like *Body Heat,* to sweet transformation like *The Accidental Tourist.*

a. Root/Crown

Though not very common in real life stories, this pairing is most often seen in fantasy and sci-fi, video and computer games. Having monsters go against the gods, pitting demons against the demigods, crazy creatures assailing the heavens, these are all examples of Root – Crown setups. *Clash of the Titans, Age of Mythology* computer game, *Xena: Warrior Princess, Hercules*, and the epic battles between Orcs, Uruk-hai, and humans, elves, and hobbits in *The Lord of the Rings*.

Review the dichotomies from B.1.a. above.

b. Sacral/Throat

In Greek mythology when Jason and the Argonauts got too close to the rocky shore where the Sirens (Sacral) sang their alluring songs, Orpheus (Throat) came to the rescue. He played and sang so well for his fellow sailors that they all ignored the seductive, deadly Sirens and sailed safely on to get the Golden Fleece.

Ariel in *The Little Mermaid* operates from an innocent Sacral but gives up her voice (Throat) to the wicked, conniving Sea Witch Ursula in order to marry the guy (Sacral). That is seriously "struck dumb by love." Often it goes the other way, as falling in love makes people poetic and prone to telling everyone who'll listen all about their new romance.

In *Body Heat* William Hurt's Ned Racine (Throat) is seduced by Kathleen Turner's vamp Matty Walker (Sacral). Part of Ned's problem is that although he's a lawyer, a Throat Center profession (though the confrontational practice of it is LSP), Ned is simply not very bright. Ned is on the weak side of Throat and Matty is on the very adept side of Sacral.

The dramatic tension in the romantic comedy *I.Q.* was set up by having Meg Ryan's Throat Center character Catherine manipulated by her uncle Albert Einstein (Walter Matthau) towards a more rewarding Sacral experience with Tim Robbins' gentle Ed Walters. The others manipulate Ed to make him more Throat Center but it doesn't take. It's a romantic comedy though, so all ends well.

Working Girl also plays off the Sacral/Throat disparity with Sigourney Weaver as the Throat Center character and Melanie Griffith as the Sacral Center character. Melanie then spent the movie integrating the two within herself. Her rubber-banding process leads to success.

The writer Christian (Ewan Magregor) in *Moulin Rouge* is a Throat Center character delightfully seduced by Nicole Kidman's ebulliently Sacral Satine.

Vladimir Nabokov's novel *Lolita* is a classic Sacral/Throat setup with the nymphet Lolita tempting college professor Humbert Humbert into relative ruin. Lolita's mom, best played by Shirley Winters, is driven man-hungry by Sacral scarcity and jealousy of her daughter.

Mira Sorvino's bimbo porn star and Woody Allen's composer in *Mighty Aphrodite* are a comedic Sacral/Throat coupling.

Once Were Warriors has the artistic teenage daughter at Throat Center pulled down to Sacral when her uncle rapes her. She can't handle the shift of this violent Center Transfer and drops even further into Root. She commits suicide.

Review the dichotomies from B.1.b. above.

c. Lower Solar Plexus/Aspirational Solar Plexus–Heart

Remember that the Solar Plexus is the home of the emotions and of dualities. It's that yin/yang of doubt and trust, love and hate, hope and despair, pessimism and optimism, fear and courage. In *The Mission*, Robert de Niro's Captain Mendoza is at Lower Solar Plexus and Jeremy Iron's Gabriel is Aspirational SP; the difference between the two offers dramatic conflict right up to the tragic end. Even when Mendoza gives his life for the local Indians he is doing it from a very warrior LSP focus.

In *Lawrence of Arabia* Peter O'Toole's Lawrence (ASP) serves as a catalyst to unite the squabbling Bedouin tribes (Lower Solar Plexus) long enough to take back Damascus from the Turks and help the Allies defeat the Axis in WWI.

In the sci-fi TV series *Babylon 5* the two Ambassadors G'Kar and Molari are at contentious odds in their own Lower Solar Plexuses for the first seasons but eventually join forces, transfer up to their Aspirational Solar Plexuses, and together fight the really bad guys for right and good.

Also in *Babylon 5* there are two groups of ancient super beings, the Vorlons and the Shadows. The Shadows are rather Nietzschean: all about power, control, acquisition. Very Lower Solar Plexus. Their mantra is "What do you want?" The Vorlons are more egalitarian, signed on to philosopher Jeremy Bentham's "greatest good for the greatest number." Very Aspirational Solar Plexus. Their mantra is "Who are you?," meant to spur an awakening to your true self. This could well be your guiding paradigm for writing characters on the Lower and the Aspirational Solar Plexuses: "What do you want?" = LSP, and "Who are you?" = ASP.

"Who are you?" links into the Grail question asked of the Knight Parsifal, "Whom does the Grail serve?" The Holy Grail, a cup designed to be held and used by one person at a time, represents that act of communion (i.e. community) wherein the individual connects up symbolically with the whole of humanity.

Review the dichotomies from B.1.c. above.

C. Conclusion

You have seen how to use the traditional Pairs of Centers (Root/Crown, Sacral/ Throat, LSP/ASP-Heart) to align the antagonist with the protagonist, create romantic couples with built-in conflicts, and to portray warring goals within an individual character.

When doing a Centers Transfer, character-driven story you'll want to explore the range of the Centers, how many different aspects you want your hero to explore, and whether you want them to end up in the higher Center or just know more about it but still yearn to be there.

In your own meeting-of-pairs stories you'll want to determine what triggers the two characters, how their goals and methods conflict, how they affect each other, and how much either of them changes from interacting with the other.

With this information you will be able to craft unique characters who undergo dynamic, believable changes both within and without.

14.
Driving the Arcs

Everybody talks about the "Character Arc" and I pretty much agree there ought to be one for lead characters, with a few exceptions like the Terminator, who was simply the Terminator throughout the whole story, one straightforward Root Center character with the Inner Drive to eliminate John Connor.

But say you want a character arc, how do you craft that? The Inner Drives offer an excellent paradigm for moving your character through various states of mind, emotions, and actions. In this section we'll explore the use of multiple Centers to identify a character's initial state, set up the change that will happen to her, align opposition and allies, and determine an ideal end state.

A. The Theory

There are basically three approaches to character arcs: up, down, or static. Each approach has its own particular Opposition and Assistance. One of the best ways to view this is via the Triangle of Assistance and Opposition.

OPPOSITION   ASSISTANCE

Your heroine's *Inner Drive and Goal* will be one of these:

1. *Static Aspiration*: to hold or perfect the current Center
2. *Upward Aspiration*: to attain a higher Center
3. *Fall & Redemption*: to regain a Center from which she was tempted or displaced

For dynamic tension a story needs complication and a heroine needs both Opposition, or Challenge, and Assistance, or Allies. *Opposition or Challenge* to your heroine will ideally come from:

1. The *Current Center*: the challenges of Mastery and others who are jealous or who guard the rewards of Mastery

2. A *Higher Center*: the challenges which must be met before the character quali-
fies for the next level; others who are jealous or dismissive of the heroine's
desires to rise

3. *Below*: the challenges of Temptation, or of being knocked or pulled down via
vicious intent by others who wish the heroine ill, or sometimes those personal
needs which pull her down

Just as in the Hero's Journey paradigm a heroine has *Allies*, you will want to set
up some *Assistance* from:

1. The *Current* Center, the present time: buddies, new friends, aids, increasing skills
2. A *Higher* Center: mentors, icons, idols, training
3. *Below, the Past*: what's been learned and incorporated, bad examples and/or
good advice from others in lower Centers

To align your payoff with your setup for a proper *Resolution*, by the end of the
story the heroine has:

1. Maintained her *Current* Center and/or gotten a new reward and/or broad-
ened her effect in that area

2. Gained the aspired-to *Higher* Center. You could also show that she'll need to
be careful up there lest a fall occur. (But then, that's an open door for a sequel,
right?)

3. *Reclaimed* the rightful, initial Center but with insights and abilities she will use
to help others in the same dilemma

4. Been *defeated* or failed but now knows where she should be and has some idea
how to get there. This version is not a Hollywood Happy Ending but should
be a Satisfactory Ending

B. The Practice

Here are examples of three different ways a character can arc through Inner
Drives, as well as suggestions on how you can utilize this paradigm. Keep
in mind what you've already learned in the Chapters on the Sliding Scale
and the Pairs of Centers and how those techniques can provide appropriate
Opposition and Challenges as well as aligned Assistance and Allies. Some stories in those chapters will show up here as well, since they are both methods
of arcing a character.

1. STATIC ASPIRATION

These stories will often be about sports, skills, or relationships. Many "chick
flicks" fall into this category, and if you're writing one, keep in mind that a

positive end result would have your heroine widening her sphere of influence, and/or finding balance and stability in the center of the Sliding Scale instead of being all over the place.

Waiting to Exhale is a good example of women attempting, with varying styles and levels of success, to resolve relationship issues.

The Robert Towne film *Personal Best* stars Mariel Hemingway as an athlete competing not only with others but also against her own record.

In the two classic novels *Anna Karenina* and *Madame Bovary*, the heroines struggled with perfecting a Sacral Center through illicit romances, but both failed tragically.

Most Martial Arts films are about simply holding one's own against all comers, which is not to say they aren't fun and exciting. Jackie Chan, Bruce Lee, and Jet Li movies are dynamic examples. Stephen Segal and Jean-Claude Van Damme movies also follow this paradigm — beat the heck out of the challengers and defend your position.

In a Static Aspiration story your character will certainly still have goals and desires, but they will be variations on the same Center. They could be in competition with someone else on the same Center. They could be seeking to master some aspect of the Center which has eluded them. There are plenty of variations within each Center to offer fascinating story-lines.

One particular pattern is the Eternal Puer, or Peter Pan syndrome. This is the male who simply will not go from boy to man. Hugh Grant in *About a Boy* plays this role with charm. The 1976 Sam Elliott movie *Lifeguard* captures it well for the baby boomer generation. Best I've seen in a long time was P. J. Hogan's beautiful, nostalgic *Peter Pan*. The story is about the difficulty of moving on from Lower Solar Plexus, whether it's into Sacral romance with Wendy, or taking on grown-up ASP familial responsibilities. Some say that the lack of formal initiation ceremonies in current Western culture has contributed to our Peter Pan syndrome. However, in the Mystery Schools the most effective initiations are those which are self-initiated. International observers often see America as a Peter Pan nation. It would be interesting to look back a couple hundred years from now and see how this Peter Pan era affected culture in the long term, if at all. Maybe it's just a blip in the evolutionary story of our own growth, a Static Aspiration paradigm for the race as we, supposedly, move onward and upward. Whatever, it makes for poignant and relevant story-telling.

2. Upward Aspiration

Many stories are about someone desperately wanting something they do not have, be it a person, a position, or possessions. In many instances that goal is a symbol for their Inner Drive to improve themselves, to reach a higher potential, to become all they can be. Meanwhile, it makes for good storytelling to watch them yearn and strive against the challenges and obstacles.

Norma Rae begins on the down side of the Sacral Center, simply struggling to get by. She is gradually drawn upward to the Aspirational Solar Plexus by the union organizer and a sense of what is correct. Defying convention, opinion, and the local law, she ultimately steps up and takes a stand which inspires others to rise as well.

Indiana Jones is also sucked up from LSP to ASP by outside circumstances as *Raiders of the Lost Ark* propels him to battle the Nazis for possession of the Ark.

Luke Skywalker leaves Yoda too soon, while still in his Aspirational Solar Plexus, not his heart. Throughout the rest of the *Star Wars* trilogy he is therefore prey to emotions, his own and others. The Heart Center is compassionate but impersonal.

In the musical *Annie* the little girl goes from orphan (Root) to ward of rich Daddy Warbucks (Sacral), to using the FBI (Throat) to search for parents, and then to stable LSP with a self-assumed identity, a new family, and a home.

Evita Peron was a streetwalker (Sacral) who marries a dictator (LSP) but then works to help the ordinary people (ASP).

Sometimes moving up is the source of the problem. In *The Story of Us*, two Throat Center writers marry but Michele Pfeiffer's Kate becomes so overly ASP with family responsibility that she has difficulties being romantic (Sacral) with husband Bruce Willis. A common marital problem when children arrive is the woman's inability to keep the Sacral Center active with her mate as she takes on the mother (ASP) role.

As your character arcs upward a Center or two, be sure to reveal somewhere the real Inner Drive behind all their action: a confession, a plea, a statement to a friend, a funny realization.

3. Fall and (Sometimes) Redemption

In this paradigm your heroine is either tempted down or forced down into a lower Center by their own weaknesses (addictions, foibles, etc.), by other people (temptation, abduction, war, etc.), or by events (floods, hurricanes, depressions, comets, etc.).

You'll first want to establish them at their current Center and show how they operate and how life is for them with this original Inner Drive. Then something happens to throw them out of this normal, pleasant existence and into a harrowing, dangerous situation from which they must extricate themselves.

If it's a temptation situation, then you'll want to have the tempter be so very attractive that the heroine can justly say, "It looked like a good idea at the time." But once she's a ways into the situation, oops, all heck breaks loose and she's too far in to easily get out.

a. Temptation or the Character's Own Weakness

A classic Fall and Redemption story is *Catch Me If You Can*. Based on a true story, Leonardo DiCaprio's portrayal of Frank Abagnale Jr. shows a young man at LSP being both seduced and driven to a Sacral Center by outside circumstances; he wants to bring in money to redeem his father's reputation and his family's status. Throughout the story he's mainly on a Sacral Center, but by the end of it he has risen, with assistance from Carl Hanratty (Tom Hanks), to aid the FBI and work on the side of the good guys (ASP).

In this Arc, a character falls, explores the new Center, but then rises even higher than where they were before, even though they hadn't had that in mind in the first place. They kind of surprise even themselves.

Robert De Niro's slave hunter Captain Mendoza in *The Mission* plummets down from LSP (Warrior) into Sacral when he discovers his brother having an affair with his fiancée. He kills his brother and then is given a chance to redeem himself by Jesuit priest Jeremy Irons. Mendoza really tries to establish himself at Aspirational Solar Plexus, and even does a self-sacrificing Heart action at the end in the fight to save the Indians, but basically, he reverts to being the Warrior once again and from his original, reclaimed LSP position, redeems himself.

The effective Character Arc here is that even though someone (Irons) tried to move someone else (De Niro) to their own Center (ASP), the hero was only really effective operating from his own very strong (LSP) Center of Motivation, the home of his Inner Drives. After all, Mendoza hadn't wanted to become ASP, he was just feeling guilty and remorseful for having dropped to Sacral and killing his brother.

Roxy Hart in *Chicago* begins at LSP, desiring greatly to be a star. She uses her Sacral to get what she wants but it turns out badly and she's propelled to the

Root Center. Through much manipulation of Root and Sacral she claws and dances her way back up to LSP.

Ralph Fiennes in *Quiz Show* takes a dive from Throat to LSP, trying to show off for the TV public and win his father's approval.

There is a human tendency to conform to societal norms and many cautionary tales (a la *Quiz Show*) illustrate why we shouldn't break the local rules. Your story can make an ethical point even if the heroine doesn't do the right thing — just let us see the social consequences. On the other hand, humans also tend to be rebellious and many stories are examples of how to break away and break the rules.

Fatal Attraction tells of someone who broke the rules, with bad results. LSP Dan (Michael Douglas) is easily seduced away from his ASP wife (Ann Archer) by the damaged-Sacral Alex (Glenn Close). Just in costumes alone you see the dramatic Center difference between the two women: the wife wears white cotton panties, the temptress wears… well, if anything, not white cotton.

In *Body Heat* William Hurt's Ned Racine is tempted from his lawyer Throat Center down to Sacral by Kathleen Turner's Matty Walker. Unfortunately, he doesn't redeem himself, but falls even further down into the Root Center and helps commit murder. No doubt in the end he's at Resolution #4, knowing what he should have done and resolving never to get in this situation again if he ever gets out. *Double Indemnity* resonates with the same frequencies.

The Maori princess Beth Heke in *Once Were Warriors* was seduced from her ASP position as leader of her people to a Sacral position by the irresistible sexual attraction between her and her husband Jake. The entire family is a study in Center Arcing, with the oldest son at LSP rising out of his gang activities to take on ASP tribal responsibilities. The artistic (Throat) daughter kills herself (Root) after being raped (Sacral) by her uncle. The younger son Boogie goes from a potential root Center through the assistance of a Maori mentor to ASP.

Elia Kazan's film *Viva Zapata* shows Marlon Brando's Zapata fall from ASP leader of a revolution to LSP when he becomes the very dictator he had been fighting. In this power-corrupts-absolutely karmic-flip-flop story, an opening scene with Zapata confronting the dictator is echoed at the end with Zapata behind the same desk, patronizing a peasant just as he had been patronized. A similar dynamic occurred when freed U.S. slaves emigrated to Liberia, dressed up like rich white Southern slave owners, and lorded it over the African locals.

The old Brer Rabbit stories remind us, "Don't fight with the tar baby" and Aesop's Fables observe that if we lie down with dogs we rise up with fleas. You can also use this effective psychological story-tool and show someone becoming the very thing they were fighting. Hazing and club initiations play on this tendency to do unto others as was done to us, and you can create emotionally tense situations for your characters by having them gradually become like their former persecutors… or not. *The Count of Monte Cristo* is a rich example of this process.

b. Other People or Human Events

Gladiator shows how an Ajna Center General is torn from his position by others and thrust into Root. The story is then about how Russell Crowe's Maximus struggles courageously and cleverly back up to an Ajna Center.

Russell Crowe's scientist Jeff Wygant in *The Insider* moves from Throat to ASP when he decides to speak out for the public about the dangers of tobacco. He is thrust down to Root, and eventually has Heart moments. When his wife learns he's been fired, she's very LSP and just asks about the money with no seeming thought for him. Granted she's a mom and instinctively should be protecting her children, but the lack of Sacral or ASP connection between husband and wife right there at the beginning foretold later marital problems. Throat Center news show producer Al Pacino continually recognizes Wygant's Center shifting and supports him in moving to and holding an ASP-Heart focus as he sacrifices his career, family, and personal well-being for the good of all mankind.

Tony in *West Side Story* moves tragically down from ASP to LSP to Sacral to Root. And he dies.

Cliff in *Cabaret* is a writer (Throat) who goes exploring down into the Sacral in exotic pre-war Berlin and as the Nazi threat grows, experiences those Root Center threats himself.

In *Witness*, John Book (Harrison Ford) is an LSP cop who goes to Root Center to help protect a little Amish boy who's witnessed a murder. Hiding out in an ASP Amish community, Book and Rachel, the little boy's mom, resist their mutual attraction and the strong temptation towards the Sacral. That yearning to move to a different Center and the social restrictions against doing so creates poignant dramatic tension. At the end of this story, Book leaves the Amish ASP milieu and realigns with his own strong LSP Inner Drive.

c. Force Majeure, Non-Human Events

Disaster movies wallow in this version, often to good effect. *Poseidon Adventure, Armageddon, Deep Impact, Day of the Comet,* and *Lord of the Flies* all show people from many different Centers thrust down into Root and then struggling to survive and/or to make their way back up again.

In *The Lord of the Rings* Boromir is tempted by the dark power of the evil Ring and falls, though he eventually redeems himself and pledges fealty to Aragorn with his dying breath. Bilbo and Frodo Baggins were often greatly tempted but did not completely fall. Whether by his own volition or not, there at the pinnacle inside Mount Doom when Gollum snatched it away, Frodo's valiant actions right up to that point brought about the destruction of the Ring and salvation to all of Middle Earth. Gollum is a sad case of one who was tempted, fell, and never did gain redemption.

The displaced young Chihiro in *Spirited Away* arcs from a childish, spoiled LSP to danger-threatened Root when her parents are turned into pigs in a magical kingdom. Through many trials and tribulations, learning courage and helping others, she makes her way up to ASP with a beneficent effect on all within her environment.

If you're doing a Fall and Redemption Arc, you'll want to be sure the temptation is attractive enough (*Body Heat*), the danger strong enough (*Deliverance*), and the rise back up difficult enough (*Gladiator*) to make a good story.

C. Conclusion

We've explored three basic Character Arcs related to the Centers: static, upward, and downward. As you create your heroine's progress through the story, remember to utilize all aspects of a Center profile to illustrate the changes, from wardrobe and speech styles to foibles and foods.

On the Static Arc the martial arts trophy shelf might get more crowded. On the upward Aspirational Arc the selfish person might become more generous. On the Fall and Redemption Arc you'd want to have one significant item or action the character did at the beginning that they couldn't do when in the lower Centers but were able to do once they had risen and reclaimed their position: perhaps eat a certain special food or have access to a technology. In *The Lord of the Rings* it's the return to the Shire. In *Groundhog Day* it's a return to the flow of normal time.

Mostly, you want to be sure to illustrate the changes in both the Inner Drives and the outer world as your heroine arcs through the story.

15.
Ensembles

Doing an ensemble piece? Working on a TV series? Want to be sure each of your characters is unique?

Use all the Inner Drives together as a template for aligning your various characters into a whole unit.

A. The Theory

Every "thing" has chakras, be it an individual human, a family, a business, a corporation (the Latin root 'corpus' means body), a nation, or a world. Years ago Theosophists identified Los Angeles as the Heart Center of America (processing the dreams and aspirations a la Hollywood), New Orleans as the Sacral (Mardi Gras and the Big Easy), Chicago the Solar Plexus (railroads, meat packing, and party politics), New York the Throat (finance and publishing), and Washington D.C. the inactive (no kidding) Crown Center. I've been unable to discover what city they considered Root.

Military structure mimics the Centers with its hierarchy. So do most businesses: a President (Crown and/or Heart), Vice President (varies according to the organization), Secretary (Throat), Treasurer (Sacral), a Sergeant at Arms or gatekeeper (Solar Plexus), and those who keep the physical plant working (Root).

Within a family the person holding the Heart focus processes the emotions of the group and the Throat focus is the spokesperson, or the gossip. Somebody is the best cook (Root), somebody is inappropriately sexual (Sacral), and the peacemaker (ASP) tries to mediate the trouble-maker (LSP). Check this out at your family's next Thanksgiving, wedding, or funeral, which may seem like a Robert Altman film.

Tribal roles of chief, shaman, jester, talker, trouble-maker, peace-maker, seducer, or charismatic are repeated in social cliques and groups of children. *Lord of the Flies* is a great example of how the Centers naturally form.

Small towns reflect the Inner Drives in the civic leaders, the corrupt official, whore-with-the-heart-of-gold, hypocritical preacher, village idiot, not-so-hidden homosexual, early bloomer gone stale, prodigal son, golden girl, etc. So strong is the tendency for Centers to form that they *must* be filled by some warm body or another. A college friend told me about his small home town where each generation has its bank embezzler. In his generation, a former cheerleader and golden girl was the one to abscond with the funds. It's one of those "It's a dirty job but somebody's gotta do it" situations, which I think is one reason a lot of people leave small towns: they sense this system at work and realize if they're not careful they're going to be molded into one of these stereotype Center expressions whether they like it or not. Watch Peter Bogdanovich's *The Last Picture Show* to see this at work.

B. The Practice

For your own story-telling, ensemble or not, it's effective to have at least one minor character represent each of the Centers, if only in passing. Every Center deals with situations differently, so by having characters on different Centers within a scene you can not only enrich the scene itself but also reveal a lot about each of the characters. A good example of that is a scene in *Galaxy Quest*, where writer David Howard has the TV actors-turned-space-heroes do a battle damage assessment of the starship, each with their own unique approach.

Screenwriter Steve Finly advises us to "Think of the hero as someone with layers of 'emotional clothing.' The purpose of the other characters and events is to reveal and remove one or more layers of the hero's 'clothing' until he's emotionally naked and his true self is revealed."

If you're doing an ensemble piece, consider placing each major character firmly on a different Center to help differentiate them and allow for more dramatic conflict. Certainly some of them can and will change (use the Sliding Scale, Pairs Transfers, and Character Arc chapters for guidelines) but the more complete your lineup of Inner Drives in the various characters, the more complex and rich your story.

Here are examples of Ensembles with varying representations of Inner Drives. Use the blank lists to fill in from your favorite shows and your own works.

Gilligan's Island

Crown	Captain
Ajna	If any of these characters were balanced and integrated, there wouldn't be a show
Throat	The Professor
Heart	Gilligan (only in the center of the group sense, not in the sacrifice for the greater good sense)
ASP	Mary Ann
LSP	J. Thurston Howell III
Sacral	Ginger
Root	Mrs. Howell (as a daft materialist and ditzy earth mother, but in a nice way)

Star Trek

Crown	Captain Kirk
Ajna	Mister Spock (though the Vulcan control of emotions does seem a bit unbalanced at times)
Throat	Lt. Uruha (in charge of communications)
Heart	Varies according to who's leading that episode
ASP	Doctor McCoy
LSP	Sulu and Chekov
Sacral	every Alien Chick who hooked up with Captain Kirk
Root	Scotty (the Engineer keeps the ship running)

Star Trek: The Next Generation

Crown	Captain Picard
Ajna	Commander Riker
Throat	Data
Heart	Varies according to who's leading each episode
ASP	Dr. Beverly Crusher
LSP	Lt. Worf (clannish Klingon, consummate warrior)
Sacral	Counselor Troi (she even has Sacral ESP qualities)
Root	Lt. Geordi LaForge (keeps the physical ship going)

Frasier

Crown	—
Ajna	Again, if any of these characters were balanced and integrated, there wouldn't be a show.
Throat	Niles
Heart	Varies according to who's leading the episode
ASP	Daphne
LSP	Frasier (could he be more me-me-me?)
	Martin (former cop, pleasantly ensconced in his nice little world of family and the policeman's bar)
Sacral	Roz
Root	Maybe Eddie the dog; he's pretty basic

The Lord of the Rings

Crown	Gandalf the White
Ajna	Frodo (builds an Ajna as the story progresses)
	Gandalf the Grey
	Saruman (falls to Root)
Throat	Elrond (logical, creative use of alliances)
Heart	Aragorn (as the King)

ASP	Arwyn (the Muse), Eowyn (noble warrior)
	Theoden (once freed from Wormtongue's influence)
LSP	Strider
	Samwise Gamgee, Merry, and Pippin (they're really only along because of Frodo)
	Boromir (negative, then redeemed)
Sacral	No real skirt action, no kissy face. Written for young teen boys, this is no surprise. But there is plenty of fear and lots of jealousy over the Ring.
Root	Orcs, Uruk-Hai
	Theoden (under Wormtongue's influence)

C. Conclusion

Use the charts below to assess your personal situations and gain a better understanding of your family and group dynamics. With what you've learned about the Inner Drives, you may have just the answer to bring about a positive change in difficult situations. It's also just a lot of fun to use the shorthand among others who know the language. And, it's humbling at times to find yourself doing a drop-and-wallow. But at least now you have another tool with which to bring about personal change.

In assessing your own stories, note where you're missing an aspect of the Inner Drives and craft out those Centers in your main characters, or via complementary characters, to make your story come fully alive.

Your Family Group
Crown
Ajna
Throat
Heart
ASP
LSP
Sacral
Root

Your Circle of Friends
Crown
Ajna
Throat
Heart
ASP
LSP

Sacral

Root

Your Professional Colleagues

Crown

Ajna

Throat

Heart

ASP

LSP

Sacral

Root

Story #1

Crown

Ajna

Throat

Heart

ASP

LSP

Sacral

Root

Story #2

Crown

Ajna

Throat

Heart

ASP

LSP

Sacral

Root

Story #3

Crown

Ajna

Throat

Heart

ASP

LSP

Sacral

Root

16.

$\mathcal{M}$arilyns, Moms, and Muses

Regardless of gender, an individual can experience any of the arcs already discussed. Just as the Peter Pan Static Aspiration syndrome generally applies more to males than females, so also there are a couple of particular patterns that tend to affect women in their romantic relationships.

- As a Marilyn (after Marilyn Monroe) a woman is sexy, sensual, seductive, romantic, Sacral.
- As a Mom she becomes the caretaker, protective of the offspring, possibly demanding, possibly the martyr, and depending on the size of the family and her own attitude, either LSP or ASP.
- As a Muse she is the elusive, often ethereal, yet passionate inspiration for Throat Center creativity, her own or others'.

Problems can occur when someone has begun a relationship in one Center and then moves or is forced into one of the others.

A. The Theory

A lot of these roles for females, and those for men in the next chapter, will seem stereotypical. That's exactly the point. Too often in so-called "love relationships" the people involved don't see each other as unique individuals with a rich panoply of characteristics. Rather, they pigeonhole the Significant Other into a proscribed role and insist they stay there, by god. Conflict, and hence drama, tragedy, and comedy can be the rich result for you as storyteller.

Notice that most love stories end at the wedding, before any "familiarity breeds contempt" details of domesticity and parenthood can take the bloom off the romance. A common complaint among fathers is that the romance goes out of the relationship when children arrive: the woman moves from Sacral/lover to Solar Plexus/mother and often forgets to maintain or revisit the Sacral. Michele Pfeiffer's mother-wife in *The Story of Us* causes husband Bruce Willis no end of grief because of this. He still wants to be Sacral but she is stuck in ASP and even treats him as one of the children.

You can tell a woman's gone from Marilyn to Mom when her comments about her man change from "Oh, he's so hot, he makes my toes curl!" to "All men are just little boys."

Part of the problem is the Madonna-Whore complex prevalent in many cultures. Simply put, it gives women only those two choices: Solar Plexus/asexual "good" or Sacral/very sexual "bad". Just like in Nathaniel Hawthorne's *The Scarlet Letter*, where Hester Pryne suffers social ostracism for illicit Sacral activity, so do movies from the Hays Code era (1930s to '60s) usually punish the bad girl and give the good girl the prize — the guy. Perhaps with tongue in cheek, but you can never tell with him, David Lynch's *Blue Velvet* gives hero Kyle MacLachlan first the Whore in Isabella Rossellini's Dorothy but then, typically, he ends up with the Madonna in Laura Dern's Sandy.

How fascinating by comparison are stories about a woman breaking away and expanding her options. Defending her bad-girl reputation, Jessica in *Who Framed Roger Rabbit* reminds us that there's more to a girl's character than just how she's drawn. Another fun example is in *Grease*, when Olivia Newton-John's good girl Sandy competes with Stockard Channing's bad girl Rizzo and then goes charmingly "bad" herself to win the guy.

The "Other Woman" is usually a Marilyn or a Muse. Most women in a relationship will admit they fear their man's involvement with the latter more than the former. The reasoning goes that sex is easy to get, and love is, thank goodness, relatively common, but a passion that also includes the mind and higher emotions is rare and precious.

Traditionally the Courtesan has been a glamorous combination of the Marilyn and the Muse, a sort of Renaissance woman who includes sexual skills in her repertoire of knowledge. As Venetian courtesan Victoria Franco explains in *Dangerous Beauty* to the boring straight-laced Moms (wives of men she's boffed and befriended), a woman's greatest asset is her intellect. That film is a gorgeous and well-done examination of Marilyns, Moms, and Muses dynamics and conflicts.

Many cultures dictate visible changes in a female's appearance to signal her availability for mating (a Marilyn) or to warn suitors away if she is already taken (a Mom). Hairstyles, facial markings, dress, and jewelry are codified to let people know her status.

Women's rights is a major international issue and we would all be served well by portrayals of men and women who dare to strive for equality and freedom for all individuals. In Varun Khana's film *Beyond Honor*, heroine Sahira is a medical student trying to express a healthy Sacral/Throat balance within an extended family tied to a repressive cultural system that denies the Sacral with horrific cruelty.

In *The Stepford Wives*, book and movies, we see the horrific downside of the Mom paradigm with its appendage Marilyn aspects. No Muse.

Anne Bissell's book *Memoirs of a Sex Industry Survivor* is creating a new archetype for feminism. Her heroic quest involves the search for the lost sacred feminine principle. The popular *Da Vinci Code* delves into the dark history of the repression of the feminine principle in Western culture.

In poet and historian Robert Graves' book *The White Goddess* he warns women who are Muses not to marry, because domesticity slays creative expression. It's hard to be elevated or romantic when you're arguing about the dry cleaning or the bank balance.

The underlying dynamic of the Chivalric era of the Middle Ages was that the Knight in Shining Armor would be in love with an unobtainable Lady, preferably one married to another man. The yearning of unrequited love and the desire to win her favors was supposed to spur him on to noble acts of honor. It was a system that sustained the Muse archetype through art and social codes.

The Muse herself is in a perilous position, up there on that pedestal. If she maintains the role, all that gets kissed is her feet. But sometimes the Muse combines the Sacral and Throat Centers for awhile. *Shakespeare in Love* ends however with Gwyneth Paltrow's Viola leaving the country, thereby assuring her unobtainable Muse status in young Shakespeare's pantheon.

The Hours plays with the Muse concept in three women's lives, none of whom quite seem to be able to hold their Centers.

Mexican artist Frida Khalo was her own Muse as well as husband and fellow artist Diego Rivera's, but as the film *Frida* illustrates, it was a very tempestuous Sacral/Throat relationship.

Civil societies are currently rewriting the role of women, and as artists we have a great opportunity to help formulate the next paradigm and bring about an improved status for and opinion of females.

B. The Practice

Typically, as your character shifts from Marilyn to Mom she might cut her long hair, lower her skirts, and raise her neckline. Often, the husband will require these changes.

A Mom going Muse could take up cello, painting, cooking classes, poetry, etc. The perfect-house syndrome would have less and less effect on her so you might see more dirty dishes, more dust, and more microwave dinners as she concentrates more on her art.

A Muse gone domestic (ASP) could go from eccentric to conservative, from creative to practical. The drama comes in with the conflict of trying to squeeze something big and dynamic into the straight and narrow confines of societal norms.

Jessica Lange's Carly Marshall in *Blue Sky* was, like many women in America in the 1950s, a Marilyn trapped in the Mom role. It's often theorized that perhaps that generation turned to drink and drugs so heavily because they had to anesthetize themselves against the pain of losing the freedoms they had had during World War II and of then being turned into Stepford Wives.

A Mom wanting to regain or explore the Marilyn or Muse modes might hire a babysitter and then make secret forays into sexy underwear or poetry readings. *Shirley Valentine* makes this shift in a sweet yet sensual way. Diane Lane in *Unfaithful* is also a perfect example of this Inner Drive shift as she slides purposefully down from Mom to Marilyn.

A Muse finally giving in to seductive Marilyn overtures after withholding her favors for a long time might either 1) find that her paramour now rejects her since she has "fallen from her pedestal"; or 2) find a sustained bliss between the dynamic tensions of their mental/creative energies and their sensual/creative energies.

A Sacral/Throat Marilyn/Muse rubber-banding could well be illustrated with an artist in love, like in the film *Frida*. Jayne Mansfield, a real flashy '50s Marilyn, was also a member of Mensa, the society for really really intelligent people, and an excellent example of that Center pairing.

Remember to use all the clothing, foibles, foods, styles of speech and action, and other characteristics of the different Inner Drives to dramatically illustrate your character's changes.

C. Conclusion

As restrictive traditions loosen and the true complexity of human relationships becomes more open, you have marvelous new opportunities to explore these issues. It would be fun to rewrite some of the old stories and let the bad girl win the guy because she's more flexible, more fun, and more fantastic than the goody-two-shoes girl.

Then again, these days she needn't win a guy at all. She could win another girl like in the Wachowski Brothers' stylishly decadent lesbo-mobster romp film *Bound*. Or she might decide she's actually better off on her own.

In your own stories, see how imaginative you can get with the Marilyn/Sacral, Mom/Solar Plexus, and Muse/Throat paradigms. Break through the stereotypes and offer us inventive new ways to experience the various Centers and the dynamics between and among them within an individual.

Explore positive new ways for us all to relate to each other. Which is not to say you can't still have fun showing us the ways that don't work. After all, tragedy and comedy can both be as effective as drama in getting across your mythical, social, and artistic themes.

17.
Peter Pans, Papas, and Pygmalions

Just as females in romantic relationships usually fall into one of the Marilyn, Mom, or Muse categories, so too do men in romantic relationships often get stereotyped into one of these next three categories.

• As the Peter Pan he is the eternal youth, the boy who refuses to grow up and clings charmingly but ferociously to his Lower Solar Plexus focus.

• As the Papa he takes on the breadwinner, protector role and usually becomes very serious as he shoulders responsibility for the family, usually from an Aspirational Solar Plexus Inner Drive.

• As a Pygmalion he takes on the project of remaking and molding another person to his own ideals in a Throat Center effort of conscious creativity.

Unlike with the Marilyns, Moms, and Muses, where problems can occur when someone has begun a relationship in one Center and then moves or is forced into one of the others, most problems occur for males and their partners because the men will *not* move. Nor will they ask for directions.

A. The Theory

You may be thinking, "But wait, where's the Don Juan-Playboy/Sacral Center in this relationship rundown?" Well, it's about relationships, remember? The only thing a Don Juan has a relationship with is his own — um, er... So anyway, these three stereotyped roles are played out in meaningful, longer-than-one-night encounters and seldom encompass men who're *only* interested in sex.

Besides, it's a rare woman who can let a man remain for long in the Lover/Sacral role without trying other hats on him, like husband, father, or provider.

In Western culture, as societal norms and economic realities shift, more women have the freedom to link up with a man simply because she wants to, rather than because he's a good match, can take care of her, will be a good father, etc. As a commercial producer friend of mine once observed about a sexy but flaky man she was dating, "An eccentric man is a luxury, and right now I can afford one."

More women these days have boy-toys, but for the most part these are still not considered "real" relationships. Think Samantha in *Sex and the City*.

No matter what planet they spring from, one major cause of rifts between men and women is "commitment-phobia." She wants him to commit; he resists. But why, mythically speaking?

The development of an individual consciousness must necessarily go through that Lower Solar Plexus phase of leaving the tribe, the family, the animal nature, the lower self, and rising up to stand alone.

For people (both men and women) who are not yet solid in their own individuation, the commitment of a single, monogamous relationship with its societally imposed responsibilities and compromises can feel like a step back down the chakras rather than what it ideally could be, a step upward. It can feel more like a closing down than an opening up. It can feel like that "ball and chain" of the marriage jokes, rather than the liberating freedom of a balanced relationship.

Fear of commitment can often be the need to continue to establish that individualization so necessary for personal growth as our consciousness initiates itself by moving up the chakras. A person may well realize (consciously or not) that their most important task at this time is to develop their individuality, not their ability to couple. Yet most people are terrified of solitude and much coupling occurs because of fear, rather than desire.

This attitude to hold on to one's uniqueness is exemplified by the Peter Pan, or Puer as he is known in mythic circles, the Aeternal Youth. He is favored for his charm and his idealistic optimism, but may also be denigrated for his inability to see and assess the hard facts and multiple facets of a situation.

The Peter Pan is visionary, he goes exploring, he is naïve and selfish with a purity that is almost admirable, were it not so disturbing to the cultural status quo. Parsival is a Peter Pan in those early stages of his Grail Quest, as is the youth portrayed on the Fool [0] card of the Tarot deck.

In the chapter "Driving the Arcs," we see examples of how the Peter Pan might act under the "Static Aspiration" section.

The Peter Pan clings to his egocentric position as if it were a matter of life-or-death and in a way, it is. He resists the efforts of others to manipulate and control his reality. Some examples of the Peter Pan/Puer are:

About a Boy — Hugh Grant plays a man who ducks responsibility until it serves his desires, and discovers personal truths about both freedom and commitment.

Against All Odds — Jeff Bridges' Terry Brogan battles his own Peter Pan nature to save the woman he falls in love with.

The Big Lebowski — Jeff Bridges' "Dude" Lebowski is a thoroughly endearing, White Russian-drinking, pot-smoking slacker Peter Pan.

Die Hard — Bruce Willis' John McClane is a Peter Pan in conflict with his wife Bonnie Bedelia's Mom; Holly wants him to move to Papa, he's resisting.

The English Patient — In the bathtub with Katherine after their first sexual encounter, Count Amalsi admits that most of all he hates "ownership," a typical Peter Pan position.

Indiana Jones — The scene with Marion in her Tibetan bar where they talk about why Indy isn't still her sweetie is pure Peter Pan.

Lifeguard — Sam Elliott's portrayal of the eternal youth is pure and heartfelt in this 1976 movie about a man who doesn't want to leave his job as a lifeguard, grow up, and sell Porsches... but he wants the girl who wants him to.

Peter Pan — Need I say more? Please do see the 2003 P. J. Hogan version, it's fabulous and ever so poignant.

Romancing the Stone — Jack T. Colton is a Peter Pan, still refusing to grow up until his desire to link with Joan Wilder transforms him, somewhat. But you must admit, that yacht down the streets of New York is pure Lower Solar Plexus show-off.

Streets of Fire — Michael Pare's Tom Cody is the eternal, unattached Peter Pan. He even says to his true love Ellen Aim (Diane Lane) that he won't carry her guitars around for her, but if she ever needs him, he'll be there. And check out Willem Dafoe as the outrageous Raven.

On the down side, Peter Pans/Puers can also be Mama's boys. Not the Norman Bates kind; he's on a Root Center focus. More likely they'll be the kind of men who simply cannot deal with grown-up women, or in a grown-up way with any woman. Like Danny DeVito in *Throw Mama From the Train* or Sam Rockwell's obnoxious Guy Fleegman in *Galaxy Quest*, who gets rebuffed by a girl with the snub, "Ew, you live with your mother!"

The Papa paradigm is all about responsibility. At times it's the taking on of responsibility; at other times it's the shirking of same. Though many TV sit-coms portray dads as bumbling fools, some have upheld the higher aspects of the Papa Inner Drive. Feature films usually give a broader and deeper range of character to the Papa stereotype.

Though romantic comedies and bedroom farces take couples through Sacral romps, their ideal ending is a move to the Papa and Mama situation.

Observant people will not be surprised to know that scientific studies have recently shown that when women are in their fertile days they are attracted to strong, macho-esque manly men of LSP and Sacral demeanor, and when not fertile they tend to pair-bond with softer, gentler protective men of Papa type ASP demeanor. Even in many animal species, the females will bond long term with the comfortable Papa males but will have secret hot sex with the Alpha-male high-testosterone guys.

Perhaps part of a man's resistance to going from Peter Pan to Papa is the secret sense that he's being emasculated, in a subtle, often unconscious way.

Some examples of the Papa paradigm are:

American Beauty — Kevin Spacey's Lester Burnham threw off the shackles of his Papa role and reverted to the Peter Pan, reclaiming, against society's rules, his own identity.

The Cosby Show — Bill Cosby's Dr. Huxtable, a rather healthy Papa.

Father Knows Best — an idealized Papa.

The Great Santini — a twisted Papa.

Jacob's Ladder — Tim Robbins' Jacob Singer cares about many people, but his most passionate connection is with his dead son, Gabe. He desperately wants to be a good father, again.

Leave it to Beaver — Ward Cleaver was put up as the perfect mid-twentieth-century Papa.

Mr. Mom — Michael Keaton's Jack Butler struggles to be perfect, with comedic effects.

Mrs. Doubtfire — Robin Williams' Daniel/Mrs. Doubtfire gives credence to that positive, nurturing side of the Papa paradigm, even if as a woman, supposedly.

Shine — Geoffrey Rush's talented pianist David has a real problem with his own father/Papa who is also a Pygmalion and is overbearing and at times, quite cruel.

The Story of Us — Bruce Willis yearns to be Sacral with his wife but she demands he' hold the Papa position.

What Dreams May Come — Robin Williams is a sorrowful Papa who lost both his children. Even when he enters the underworld in hopes of saving his suicided wife, they seem very familial together, not passionate.

In Greek mythology, Pygmalion was a talented sculptor disappointed in romantic love. Shunning real live fickle females, he carved a statue of the perfect girl and worshipped her to the point of obsession. He dressed her up, talked to her, had tea parties with her, tucked her into bed at night… you get the picture.

A gift from the love goddess Aphrodite brought his statue Galatea to life. The desire to remold the often imperfect "what is" into the supposed perfection that we wish it to be is the core issue of Pygmalion stories.

It is often seen as a sign of our inherent divinity that we have this powerful urge to create. Creating works of art is one thing; creating and controlling other humans, a la Pygmalion, can be dicey. Unlike statues, real women tend to have their own personalities and agendas.

Yet how many times do women, especially young women, take up the hobbies and activities of their latest sweetie in order to emulate them, fit in, and be accepted. If a girl dates with any sort of variety she can learn a lot about music, art, sports, literature, business, and adventure simply by being a Galatea to her current Pygmalion.

Sugar Daddies. In all times and places these elementary versions of Pygmalions tend to be on the down side of the paradigm, manipulating the females (or males) to fit their own Sacral or LSP desires. And, too often because of the constraints of societal norms, women see men as meal tickets and fall in with the dynamics of the Sugar Daddy role. Sometimes a woman has no choice because she isn't allowed to have a profession, to work outside the home, to support herself and her children in any way — she is totally dependent upon the man. He becomes a Pygmalion by default and often, if history and current events serve as evidence, a rather mean and suppressive one.

But, many women desire to be taken care of — oh, who doesn't at times? It's a main underlying motivational factor in both conspiracy theories and religion: "Please, let there be *somebody* in charge here." These women will elevate a man and give him power over them, even if he doesn't want it or deserve it. This is more prevalent when women do not have equal rights and freedoms and must find succor and protection through men.

These situations, Pygmalions and its Sugar Daddy aspect, can be treated comicly as well as dramatically. Some examples are:

Born Yesterday — The Pygmalion role goes awry when the girl falls for her tutor instead of the Sugar Daddy who's paying the bills.

Professor Higgins in *My Fair Lady*.

Richard Gere in *Pretty Woman* transforms Julia Roberts's Viv Ward and lifts her, with his money, from the gutter to the penthouse.

Svengali — In the early versions of the story this Pygmalion used hypnosis to entrance Trilby and make her a successful singer.

Bob Hoskins in *Mona Lisa* is an ex-con failed Pygmalion-Sugar Daddy who tries to redeem himself by saving high-dollar call-girl Simone.

Streets of Fire — Rick Moranis' Billy Fish was singer Diane Lane's manager-boyfriend. He took Ellen Aim out of the Bowery and into rock-and-roll fame in a typical Pygmalion feat of transformation.

B. The Practice

If you're creating a man in a romantic relationship, here are some aspects to keep in mind as you move him around the chakras... or not.

A Peter Pan/Puer forced into the Papa responsibility mode against his will is going to suffer deeply. Often he will cause those around him to suffer too, through his petulance, depression, and/or violence.

His freedom as an individual has been thwarted and, like any cornered animal, he will fight back in whatever way he can, albeit sometimes with that maddeningly frustrating passive-aggressive behavior.

In his more immature aspect, the Peter Pan/Puer would sport that bumper sticker, "Whoever dies with the most toys wins." He'll be into watching and/or playing sports. Boys' night out is six nights a week and girls are either strictly entertainment or danger to be avoided.

These guys may be great pals to girls, but we're only talking here about romantic relationships.

On the romantic aspect, Peter Pans can be dashing and daring, those Pirates whose adventuresome natures can be ever so alluring. Think Errol Flynn, Tom Cody, Jack Colton, Indiana Jones, and Johnny Depp's Jack Sparrow. Peter Pan/Puers all, but oh, my, hearts do flutter.

As a Peter Pan moves to a Papa focus he will become more sedate, more expansive, more altruistic. He'll become protective of his widened field of interest, usually a family.

Papas often call their wives "Mom" or "Mother" and are called in turn, "Dad" or "Pops," rather than using first names.

Many Romance novels transform a Peter Pan into a Papa, usually through the irresistible allure of the leading lady in a combination of Marilyn and Muse. This often unrealistic "taming" of the man is presented as a dream to women, a blessing for the men. Yet comedians have played havoc with this situation and portray the "taming" as a nightmare trap to the men.

Certainly if a man consciously chooses to move his main Inner Drive focus to the Papa position, that's all well and good. But storywise, keep in mind that you can cajole, seduce, or force someone to act differently… only for a while. But until their consciousness itself alters, the old Inner Drives will resurface, causing all sorts of conflict. And luckily for you… drama.

In a midlife crisis, men often move in the other direction and go from Papa to Peter Pan, shrugging off all that responsibility and starting to live for themselves again. Divorces, retirements, job changes, Harley Davidsons, little red sports cars, new trophy wives, and very young mistresses often exemplify this Center shift as the middle-aged man attempts to recapture his lost youth. Dramatically speaking, this shift is likely to be stronger if he was forced into the Papa role without having grown there on his own. *First Wives' Club* is a rather vitriolic look at women whose men are jettisoning their Papa roles, and the tailspin into which their wives are thrown when the paradigm is tossed aside.

One positive way to portray the Papa role is to have the man expand his awareness, influence, and responsibility out into his community, city, nation, or some larger noble cause. You could have him fretting over the responsibilities at first and then get inspired and motivated by the altruism and rewards of the ASP position.

Men in the Pygmalion role see the potential in others and arrange to foster it. This can be a very good thing, as young talent really needs assistance to break through the structure of the system. Too often though, like Rodin's mistress-student Camille Claudel, the Pygmalion soon finds himself in competition with the person he has created. It's that trouble-making situation where the student overtakes the teacher, very ripe for drama.

Granted, some Pygmalions work their magic just for the sake of exercising their creativity, but often they want something specific in return: gratitude, servitude, sex, a share of the profits, to bask in the glow of youth, beauty, or talent. You can create quite dramatic situations when his desires for rewards are thwarted by the Galatea he has created. *A Star is Born* is an example of a tragic Pygmalion story.

Like the young man in the myth, Pygmalions are often picky and judgmental, demanding perfection and refusing to settle for less. Benedict in Shakespeare's *Much Ado About Nothing* embodies this type.

C. Conclusion

In your stories, you may well bring us more insight into the Peter Pan/LSP, Papa/ASP, and Pygmalion/Throat Inner Drive motivations and the conflicts that arise when their significant others and society demand changes before the guys are ready to move.

As we all, hopefully, become more aware and self-aware, and as economic demands and cultural norms widen our needs and choices, both men and women will find it necessary to be more integrated than these stereotypes afford. It's unlikely anyone will live just one or two roles anymore.

As some societies become more egalitarian, traditional men's roles are less set and secure. Many movies exploring this cultural phenomenon are comedies a la *Mr. Mom*. Not many tragedies about this have been produced, though a number of nonfiction books posit the redundancy of males.

You could well experiment with various tones and approaches to the blurring borders between masculine relationship roles and the discomforts that arise when people no longer know what's expected of them and they are allowed to make up their own rules.

It would be very interesting to see a man who combines all three of these Inner Drives, plus a healthy Sacral Center, as he builds an Ajna Center focus.

18.

Raising the Dragon

If you're creating a character-driven story, one of the most ancient and powerful paradigms is what I call "Raising the Dragon."

In this pattern the hero journeys from the Root Center all the way up to the Crown Center, hitting most of the other Centers along the way. Ideally they will meet obstacles, gain abilities and allies, overcome challenges, and absorb the lessons of each of the Centers of Motivation. As they add the values of each Inner Drive to their personal tool kit they become more capable and more enlightened, until by the end of the story they are close to perfection — whatever that might look like in each particular story.

A. The Theory

"Raising the Dragon" is a character journey that shows up in many myths. In fact, a lot of journey myths reflect a rise up the Centers.

In Mesopotamian legend the goddess Inanna journeys down into the underworld. At each step along the way she must shed an item of her identity until she finally stands stark naked before the doors of the underworld. On the way back up she reclaims the aspects of the Centers but with renewed respect and appreciation of each.

The Greek heroes Hercules and Odysseus both take journeys up the Centers. Recall from the "What Are the Inner Drives?" chapter that two energy currents twine up the spinal column: one female, one male. In the Root Center chapter we learned that Hercules strangled two snakes sent by jealous Queen Hera to kill him in his cradle. One of his Labors involved cattle (Throat Center) and from another he wears a lion skin (Heart Center). Hercules' twelve Labors also reflect the signs of the Zodiac.

Odysseus' journey from Troy back home to Ithaca touches upon the Centers: the fall into Root in the Land of the Lotus-Eaters; breaking out of Root at the cave of the Cyclops; Circe and the pigs is Sacral, as is resisting the seductive call of the Sirens; he passes between the conflicting Solar Plexus polarity of Scylla and Charybdis; and so on until he makes it home and regains his Crown as King of Ithaca.

The serpent or wingless dragon coiled at the base of a tree symbolizes the Kundalini energy of consciousness coiled at the base of the spine, the Root

Center. As the Kundalini rises up through the various Centers it eventually reaches the top and takes flight into higher realms. The winged dragon in its many forms is symbolic of this achievement. In Chinese symbology the winged dragon was reserved for the Emperor alone.

The medical symbol of the caduceus is that rod with the snakes twining up it. The winged caduceus symbolizes the completely raised and integrated Kundalini energy — an enlightened being. The wings symbolize the Ajna Center and the pine cone symbolizes the pineal gland, the Crown.

Another symbol of raised Kundalini is the oroborus, the snake with its own tail in its mouth. In Egyptian iconography the winged globe symbolizes the raised Kundalini and sometimes there's even a cobra atop the globe. The Mesoamerican feathered serpent Quetzalcoatl symbolizes raised Kundalini.

The twenty-two Tarot cards of the Major Arcana are seen as a guide to enlightenment, from the first card The Fool/0 to the final card The World/21. This system echoes the Hebrew Kabbalistic Tree with its own twenty-two paths, the Root Center Malkuth, and the Crown Center Kether.

There's a protective webbing between Centers and responsible teachers carefully guide their students' rise up through the Centers; it's well known in Eastern systems that if you go too fast you can burn out. Writer Bruce Joel Rubin is a teacher and student of Buddhism so may well have intended a spider web in *Jacob's Ladder* to symbolize this etheric webbing.

You could create setbacks for your character by taking them up the Centers too fast. A mythic example is Icarus, who rose up from the dark (Root) trap of the Minotaur's labyrinth towards the sky, but then disobeyed his father Daedalus' instructions and flew too close to the sun (Crown). The wax on the youth's wings melted, the feathers fell off, and Icarus plunged into the sea (Solar Plexus emotions) and perished.

B. The Practice

Some "Raise the Dragon" films are *Apocalypse Now* (especially *Apocalypse Now Redux*), *Groundhog Day*, *Jacob's Ladder*, and *Under Siege*. All take the main character on a dramatic ride from a drop down to the Root Center, then back up through most of the other Centers, to the very top.

Following are plot point analyses with correlative Centers for three of these films so you can follow the characters' rise through the Centers, the transformations of their Inner Drives, and how they express their shifting goals. You will see how whether it's a comedy, a drama, an action-adventure, etc. you can craft a rise up the Centers of Motivation to create compelling character-driven stories.

As you chart out your character's rise, review the section on the Centers to select particular characteristics, foibles, challenges, and expressions for each of the Centers.

GROUNDHOG DAY

This charming film tells the story of a man who redeems his own flawed nature through trial and error, moving through and up the Centers, shifting his Inner Drives, and becoming a more whole, enlightened person.

Phil Connors begins as a selfish, arrogant, mean man. He gets stuck in time and relives the same day over and over again. First he goes wild and breaks rules, then he falls prey to despair. Gradually, inspired by love and desiring to relieve his own suffering, he learns the lessons of the various Centers and eventually masters them all. Along the way he develops many talents, helps alleviate the sufferings of others, and begins to value himself and other people. At the end of the story Bill Murray's Phil has integrated and balanced his own Inner Drives and has consciously chosen to live his life for the greater good under the direction of his higher self.

Mythic notes: February 2nd, Groundhog Day is also the Celtic holiday *Imbolc*, the beginning of the new year. Andie MacDowell's Rita is always ASP; she is the magnet that attracts Phil up from his lower focus. Insurance Salesman Ned Ryerson is all Sacral: insurance is all about fear and money, right? Producer Rita and Cameraman Larry both wear blue, the color of relationship. The repeating radio-alarm music "I got you, Babe" reflects inspirational (ASP) romantic linking. The last song contains a lyric about having a smile for the whole human race.

Note the Rubber-Banding as Phil strives to rise through the Centers and how the other characters on various other Centers help illustrate Phil's flaws and offer challenges and assistance.

CENTER	ACTION
Lower Solar Plexus	Phil Connors starts out arrogant and judgmental, a selfish show-off.
LSP	Days 2-4 Phil is short and snobbish to people in the B&B where he's staying, and to townspeople.
LSP	Day 5 Phil realizes there are no consequences to his actions, punches out the annoying insurance salesman, eats tons of pastries and doesn't floss, pumps Nancy Taylor for personal information.
Sacral	Day 6 Phil drops to the Sacral, seduces Nancy.
Sacral	Day 7 Phil robs a bank truck, buys a Mercedes, and takes out a different girl.
LSP	Day 8 Dissatisfied with his shallow Sacral adventures, Phil chats up his producer Rita, finds out what she likes.
LSP	For days on end, Phil pursues Rita with his inside info and she starts to fall for him. Then he makes a mistake, moves too fast, and Rita pulls away. She slaps him, accusing him of not loving anyone but himself. Phil retorts that he doesn't even *like* himself. Angry that he made her care for him, Rita slaps Phil — over and over again.
Root	Rejected by Rita and increasingly despondent over the repetitiveness of his life, Phil smashes the clock, kidnaps the groundhog, and drives off a cliff to crash and burn. But he still wakes up the same way the next morning.
Root	Trying to escape his maddening existence, Phil tries to kill himself by tossing a toaster into the bathtub, jumping in front of a truck, diving off a bell tower… nothing works. He's stuck.
LSP	Beginning to see a way out by using what he's learned, Phil tells Rita he's "a" god. To prove it he reveals intimate knowledge of many townspeople.
Ajna — just beginning	Phil has accepted his situation and is becoming an objective witness to his own life. It's the beginning of building an Ajna focus. Now he needs to pick up all the loose threads from the various Centers.
ASP	Rita spends the night for the first time, but no sex, just sweet sleepiness. Phil speaks tenderly to her as she sleeps, but wakes up alone, again. Yet he knows he's made romantic progress and that inspires him.
Root/Sacral	Phil gives the old bum money.
LSP	Phil brings coffee to his co-workers Larry and Rita, helps carry equipment, is a team player.
Throat	Phil begins piano lessons.
ASP	Phil is kind to the guy on the B&B stairs, even quotes him some poetry.
Throat	Phil carves an ice angel… he's getting much more creative.
ASP	Phil hugs the insurance salesman, rather terrifying the obnoxious man.
ASP	The old bum dies and it devastates Phil.
ASP	Phil feeds the old bum, and gives him mouth-to-mouth as he lies dying.
Throat	Phil quotes Chekhov to the B&B crowd, kindly, without his former arrogance.
ASP	Phil saves a kid falling out of a tree, again. He fixes a flat tire for old ladies, again. He saves a man from choking in a restaurant, again, and chivalrously lights a woman's cigarette. Yes, again. Rita notes Phil's kindnesses.

Ajna	At a town party Phil plays the piano really well and graciously receives thanks from the many townspeople he has been helping. Rita is really impressed by Phil now. He's gallant, talented, and well-liked — the town hero.
Crown	At the party auction, Rita buys Phil. Mythically, this is the reunion of those male and female Kundalini currents in the head. That "wedding" is the crowning achievement of the "Raising the Dragon" paradigm.
Crown	Phil wakes up with Rita still in bed with him. It's a brand new day.

JACOB'S LADDER

The alternate title for this troubling film is *Dante's Inferno*. You can find resonances among the Tibetan and Egyptian *Books of the Dead*, the *Epic of Gilgamesh*, the Bible, Dante's *Divine Comedy*, and John Milton's *Paradise Lost* and *Found* books. Nowadays many movies also show us versions of the afterlife; this one closely follows the ancient, classical tradition. Don't watch this film alone: the images are frightening and the confusion troubling. But if you watch it with "Raising the Dragon" in mind, it all begins to make perfect sense.

Because writer Bruce Joel Rubin studied and teaches Buddhism, we may well suspect he consciously utilized the Centers of Motivation as plot points in the story structure and shifting Inner Drives of hero Jacob Singer, played by Tim Robbins.

Jacob Singer doesn't make a swift one-by-one rise through the Centers but has to keep going back down and solving issues before he can progress upwards again. It's two steps upward, one step back; or sometimes, one step upward and two steps back. According to many traditions, including the Tibetan and Egyptian, both of whom have guidebooks for it, the Death Process includes a series of scenarios revisiting important aspects of an incarnation until the departing soul "gets the point" of that particular lifetime.

The death process also often includes a Psychopomp to guide the departing soul to and through the underworld. In this story it's Jacob's chiropractor Louis, played by Danny Aiello. Chiropractic adjusts the spinal column to restore the free flow of energy along the nerves, to the various plexuses, and to their organs, and so is a perfect profession for a Psychopomp.

Mythic notes: there are a lot of Biblical names and parallels.

Jacob the dreaming prophet — the hallucinating hero climbing the ladder of the Centers of Motivation.

Jezebel the temptress — his lover.

Sarah the wife of Bible patriarch Abraham — Singer's ex-wife (To follow more closely the Bible, she would have been named Leah or Rachel, as both these sisters were the Old Testament Jacob's wives.)

Gabriel the Archangel messenger of the end of the world — Jacob's dead young son who calls him into the light and an acceptance of death.

See the William Blake painting of Jacob's Ladder with its spiral staircase and the angels ascending and descending.

Also note the Rubber-Banding in Jacob's journey up the Ladder of the spinal column and the Inner Drives.

CENTER	ACTION
Root	VIETNAM Jacob Singer is a soldier in Vietnam, coming under fire, struggling for sheer survival.
Root	NEW YORK Jacob is on a near-empty subway, an ad reads "Hell," a man has snake parts on him… it's obviously the underworld. Jacob's exit is closed and he crosses the tracks to try and get out. The tracks could well symbolize those Ida-Pingala-Sushumna currents running up the spinal column.
Sacral	NEW YORK Crying babies, showering with his girlfriend Jezebel… the sex-reproductive aspects of Sacral.
Root	VIETNAM Jacob is wounded, crawling through the jungle. Light glistens through a spider web. Recall that protective webbing between Centers; this might symbolize his struggle to rise up the Centers.
ASP versus Sacral	NEW YORK With words about having sold his soul, Jacob and Jezzy affirm their sexual bonding. He reminisces over his family photos (ASP), she later burns them.
Crown	NEW YORK Chiropractor Louis (Danny Aiello) is Jacob's Psychopomp, attempting to help him rise up through the Centers. Jacob even calls him an angel and a lifesaver.
Sacral back to Root	Like the Sirens from Odysseus' journey, girls on a stoop sing "Mister Postman" just before Jacob is almost run over by a car and is forced into yet another tunnel.
Throat	NEW YORK At the Veteran's Administration Hospital Jacob searches for Dr. Carlson to solve some mysteries for him. But Carlson's dead and a nurse shows signs of ugly demonic growths on her head. Jacob stumbles into a group session and the VA Shrink offers to help, but Jacob flees.
Sacral	NEW YORK In bed with Jezzy, Jacob mentions seeing demons; she plays with his spine. At a party, various symbols of the situation appear to Jacob: a skinned animal head in the refrigerator (Root), a caged bird (the trapped soul). A palm reader tells him he's already dead and he hallucinates Jezzy dancing with and being sexually ravaged by a creepy demon.

Root	VIETNAM Jacob flashes on dots of light, a typical phenomenon in meditation and in crossing over from life to death.
Root	NEW YORK Fever-ravaged Jacob is plunged into an ice bath by Jezzy and neighbors. In this delirium he reaches up to….
ASP	NEW YORK In bed with his former wife Sarah, Jacob complains of the cold from an open window, confesses to a dream of that sexy girl from the Post Office (Jezebel), and does sweet daddy things with his three sons. It's a warm picture of domestic love and bliss.
Root	VIETNAM & NEW YORK Jacob alternates between a stretcher in Vietnam and the icy bathtub. Again he wonders if he's dead, but Jezzy reassures him he's right there with her — holding on to life.
Throat	NEW YORK Attempting again to intellectualize his experience, Jacob reads books on witches and demons. Jezzy, the Sacral, storms out, perhaps realizing the threat that knowledge poses to mindless sensuality.
LSP	NEW YORK Jacob meets a buddy from Nam who's having similar experiences. Both are paranoid over what happened to them that night (in the first scene). Small groups of Warriors will usually be at that exclusive, tight LSP Focus. This scene is even set in a boxing gym-pool hall, very LSP.
Root	NEW YORK & VIETNAM The buddy's car explodes — Jacob's back in the Viet's chopper where blood explodes onto the windshield. The VA Shrink pulls Jacob away from the NY street explosion, then leaves.
LSP	NEW YORK At the buddy's funeral, the rest of Jacob's company from Vietnam discuss their common paranoid hallucinations of death and demons.
Throat	NEW YORK Jacob and Company consult a lawyer to find out what the Army did to them, attempting to use intellect to solve a situation.
LSP	NEW YORK Conflict is typical of the Solar Plexus. The angry attorney reveals that Jacob's buddies backed out of the suit and besides, records show they were never in 'Nam, just war games in Thailand. Jacob argues with his buddies, reminds them they're all in it together, but they deny it.
Root	NEW YORK Yet again, Jacob is assaulted, kidnapped, and warned off his investigation. He barely escapes, then is robbed by a sidewalk Santa. The forces of darkness and inertia are certainly working to keep this soul imprisoned.
Root	NEW YORK Paralyzed on a gurney, Jacob is rolled through a wretched, terrifying bedlam of twisted ruined people. A wrecked bicycle catches his attention.
Ajna	NEW YORK Jacob is told he's dead and there's no way out. A needle goes into his Ajna Center. This is his first episode this high up; it signals a change in Jacob's approach to his problems and the assistance he gets.
ASP	NEW YORK Jacob's ex-wife and the two older sons visit him in hospital. They assure him he is not dead and he is very much loved. The support of this Center often strengthens the individual as they re-enter the fray in lower Centers.

Crown	NEW YORK Chiropractor Louis, the Psychopomp, frees Jacob from the VA hospital. Symbolically, the Law of Grace overrides the Law of Karma and helps one rise up out of suffering.
Ajna and Crown	NEW YORK Louis adjusts Jacob's spine and they discuss philosophy. Jacob is putting all the pieces together here, integrating his experiences and pulling in wisdom from above. Louis gives the Lesson Statement of this film: Whatever you won't let go of as you are dying binds you; those demons ripping away your life are simply trying to free you. When you shift your perspective and see them as angels liberating you from earthly existence, the whole experiences changes.
Sacral and ASP	NEW YORK With acceptance and increasingly detaching love, Jacob, at his home with Jezebel, reminisces over the family photos and a note from his youngest son Gabe, who was killed in a bike accident. Jacob relives the accident, accepting it.
Throat	NEW YORK Jacob meets the Psychiatrist who explains he was a hippie, busted for making acid, then drafted by the Pentagon. He came up with an acid variant called "The Ladder," which sent guys straight to the Root of aggression. Against the inventor's warnings Jacob's Company was given the acid, they all flipped out and tore each other to pieces. This is the information that Jacob needs to resolve the Throat Center mystery.
Ajna	NEW YORK Many myths posit a ferryman across the river of death; in the Greek myths it's Charon. Jacob's Charon is a cabby, and Jacob calmly asks to be taken "home." He has balanced and integrated his Centers, made his resolutions, and is ready to go.
Root	VIETNAM Jacob is bayoneted by one of his buddies in the acid-aggression frenzy.
Crown	NEW YORK Unfazed now by Root Center activity, Jacob arrives at his fancy high-rise home and is greeted by the doorman as "Dr. Singer." He has reclaimed more of his higher Throat Center identity.
	At home with Sarah and the kids, Jacob views it all with love as rain falls against the windows. There's still sadness, but he is accepting it.
	Gabriel, the youngest son who died in the wreck, is on the stairs. He hugs his father, invites him to go up, and leads Jacob upstairs into the light.
	VIETNAM Around the bright light above the field hospital operating table, the doctors realize Jacob has died. They comment on the helluva fight he put up. Jacob Singer looks peaceful.
	He has successfully made, through furious and dangerous struggle and with the assistance of his Psychopomp Louis, the journey up through the Centers from Root to Crown.

UNDER SIEGE

This action-adventure movie follows a "Raising the Dragon" paradigm as undercover Navy Seal Casey Ryback (Steven Segal) serves as special cook to the battleship's Captain, much to the chagrin of second-in-command Commander Krill (Gary Busey).

Krill is in cahoots with exiled over-the-edge Commando Stranix (Tommy Lee Jones) to hijack the nukes from the battleship for their own nefarious ends.

Locked in the galley freezer (Root Center) by Krill, Ryback makes his way out and up through the levels of the battleship, wreaking mayhem on the bad guys and rescuing the good guys. He defeats Stranix, saves Hawaii from nuclear attack, and is rewarded in a shipboard Crown Center ceremony by the President of the U.S. Echoing the Royal Marriage and union of those male and female Ida-Pingala Kundalini currents, Ryback also gets the girl, or at least a kiss.

There isn't much psychological development in this movie so it's a pretty straightforward boom-boom-boom rise up the Centers, but that's alright because it works and it's fun.

Symbolically the ship is an individual afloat in the waters of the emotions and Ryback is the Consciousness. By picking up the chick in the Sacral Center he makes a more balanced Rise through the Centers. Interestingly, it is Playboy Centerfold Jordan Tate who demands he take her along and who later helps save the day. She evolves from a Sacral "skirt" to a unique, valued individual of female gender.

Trivia Note: Dick Cheney appears at the end of the movie in the stock footage aboard the USS Missouri with the first President and Mrs. George Bush.

CENTER	ACTION
Root	Symbolic of the fallen Soul trapped in matter because of some disapproved action, Chief Ryback has been demoted. He is separated from the Captain (who continues to champion him) and now works in the survival center — the kitchen.
	Ryback is locked in the meat freezer by the bad guys and makes a fire-bomb to escape.
	There are echoes here of Odysseus breaking out of the Cyclops' cave, Jesus' tomb with the stone rolled away from the door, and Brunhilde asleep on the rock surrounded by fire.
Sacral	Bad guy Commander Krill has dressed up as a woman for the Captain's birthday party and signifies distorted sexuality. He kills the Captain.
	The Playboy bunny, drugged and locked away, is freed by Ryback. Ryback wants to leave her safe below but she will not be abandoned; he takes her along. This strong female position illustrates a healthy balance between the Ida-Pingala male-female currents rising up the spine.
LSP	Ryback calls Pentagon command and identifies himself; recall that LSP is about individualization and recognition. It's also his first connection to the top/Crown.
	Ryback finds a chopper. He could escape on his own, but rather than following that selfish LSP path he stays to fulfill his higher mission.
	Ryback finds and frees six trapped guys. This new little tribe sets out to save the ship and defeat the bad guys. It's a conscious decision to move up to Aspirational Solar Plexus.

ASP	With group awareness, the little tribe sets out to save their fellow crewmen locked in the hold which is being flooded with water. Recall that water always symbolizes the emotions.
	Ryback rescues some Navy Seals who're trying to rescue the ship.
Ajna	Ryback cuts off the bad guys' power.
Heart	Ryback discovers Stranix's nuclear threat to Hawaii and humanity. Ryback risks his own life to stop the bombs.
Throat	Ryback, Tate the skirt, and the small tribe use their skills and coordinate their efforts to make bombs, and re-rig the torpedo tubes.
	Tate does a Rubber-Band move when she consciously overcomes her Sacral ultra-girly tendency and kills some bad guys to save Ryback and via him, the day.
Ajna	Ryback and Stranix meet in the battleship's control center. They were former colleagues, now enemies.
	Balancing and integrating the three bodies, Ryback:
	1. Physically defeats bad guy Stranix — physical
	2. Frees the crew from the flooded hold — emotional
	3. Uses the intellect to defuse the last missile — mental
Crown	Up on deck in full dress uniform, Ryback is reinstated to his former status, receives new honors, and is awarded by the President of the U.S.
	He also gets a kiss from the girl, who has herself risen from the Sacral to the higher Center.
	This symbolizes successful re-union of the Root/Center pair, successful raising of the male and female energies, and therefore successful enlightenment.
	Then again, it's also just a fun action-adventure movie.

Apocalypse Now and *Apocalypse Now Redux* both have "Raising The Dragon" runs. The former is lacking some Centers that the latter fills in. On your own, analyze both those movies — which take the hero Captain Willard from Root Center, up-river (the spinal column) through varied adventures and misadventures to Colonel Kurtz (the wounded Crown Center). In a shift of polarities, it's also Willard who is the fallen Crown Center and who goes upriver to sacrifice and redeem the fallen Root Center Kurtz. Sound confusing? They are mirror images of each other: Willard tells us at the beginning that to tell Kurtz's story is to tell his own. Both movies are fascinating "Raising the Dragon" paradigms.

C. Conclusion

As you have seen from the above examples there are a number of ways to Raise the Dragon, depending on the nature of your story. If you're doing a plot-driven story it's probably cleanest to construct a rather straightforward run up, like *Under Siege*.

If you're doing a character-driven story you'll have more psychological complexity with a Rubber-Banding rise like *Jacob's Ladder* and *Groundhog Day*.

Either way, your main character will arrive at the Crown Center after incredible adventures, revelations, challenges, and accomplishments. Be sure to let us actually hear in words from someone's mouth what the hero has learned: we are all connected and are responsible for each other (*Groundhog Day*), detachment from earthly existence transforms demons to angels and makes dying easier (*Jacob's Ladder*). Also be sure to have the reward be large enough to support the concept: the accomplishment of an important mission to defeat an evil situation (*Apocalypse Now (Redux)*), a huge awards ceremony from the President of the United States (*Under Siege*).

Conclusion

IV.

Conclusion

You have just completed a mythic journey exploring many aspects of the Inner Drives, that ancient system of character analysis and development that is behind many of our best-loved stories.

In Section One you learned the background of the Eight Classic Centers of Motivation, those physiological, psychological, and philosophical sources of our Inner Drives. You also saw how knowledge about these Centers has been applied throughout history, mythology, and in many forms of art.

Now when you listen to classic stories, visit religious sites, view art, or observe human relationships you'll be able to apply another paradigm to them, that of the Inner Drives. You now have the tools to make you a Magician, someone who can "See patterns where others do not see them, and create patterns where they did not exist."

In Section Two we explored each of the major Centers in depth and you now have a rich range of attributes from which to build authentic characters.

Your character descriptions can now be more evocative as you stay away from specific skin and hair colourings, heights, weights, racial or cultural characteristics, etc., (unless they are story-specific). Instead you'll use Inner Drive descriptions like "nervous," "in control," "chatty," "sedate," and the like. You'll also be able to imply backstory: "Has settled into his role as conservative businessman," or "Relishes the weirdness of her New Age circle," or "Resents both his dad and his stepmom for the changes in his life," etc.

The Centers of Motivation are also wonderful tools for directors and actors in crafting unique characters. Designers can use the information to offer subtle cues about the nature of character.

By using the Inner Drives to observe yourself and others, you can become a more conscious creator of character, a myth-maker on the order of those ancient storytellers whose stories still entertain and inspire us.

In Section Three we examined Mythic Structure as influenced by the Inner Drives. Using the Centers of Motivation in their different aspects and in different combinations opens up vast arenas for dramatic conflict and character development.

A fun way to explore the effect of the Centers upon each other and in combination, is to rewrite scenes from your favorite films and put a character on a different Center to see how that changes things. We saw this shift from *Terminator* to *Terminator II* when Arnold's character went from Root Center to ASP. But think, what if Stanley Kowalski were Throat Center instead of Sacral? What if Norma Rae ran off to "love jail" with the union organizer? What if Frodo succumbed completely to the temptation of the One Ring, as had Gollum? This exercise vividly illustrates the power of the Inner Drives in determining character and action.

I hope you have really enjoyed learning more about the Inner Drives and how they work.

Plato observed that "Those who tell the stories rule society." They also construct, challenge, and change society. But perhaps most important of all, they entertain and inspire society. Now you, like the ancient myth-makers and classic storytellers, have a powerful Mythic Tool with which you can create unique, authentic characters.

As an added bonus, you have some ancient Wisdom you can apply in your own life, relationships, and work.

So, use these Inner Drives to write and create marvelous characters, tell great stories, and make great myths!

Bibliography

Adams, Jeremy. *Grammatical Man: Information, Entropy, Language and Life*. New York: Simon and Schuster, 1982.

Bailey, Alice. *A Compilation on Sex*. New York: Lucis Publishing Company, 1980.

—. *Esoteric Healing*. New York: Lucis Publishing Company, 1953.

—. *Esoteric Psychology I*. New York: Lucis Publishing Company, 1936.

—. *Esoteric Psychology II*. New York: Lucis Publishing Company, 1942.

Beinfield, Harriet and Efrem Korngold. *Between Heaven and Earth: A Guide to Chinese Medicine*. New York: The Ballantine Publishing Group, 1991.

Bentov, Itzhak. *Stalking the Wild Pendulum: On the Mechanics of Consciousness*. Rochester, VT: Inner Traditions International Ltd., 1988.

Blavatsky, H. P. *The Secret Doctrine: The Synthesis of Science, Religion, and Philosophy*. London: The Theosophical Publishing Company, Ltd., 1888.

Blum, Deborah. *Sex on the Brain: The Biological Differences Between Men and Women*. New York: Penguin Group, 1997.

Budge, E. A. Wallis. *The Egyptian Book of the Dead*. New York: Dover Publications, Inc., 1967.

Bulfinch, Thomas. *Bulfinch's Mythology*. New York: Random House, 1998.

Campbell, Joseph. *The Flight of the Wild Gander*. New York: HarperCollins, 1990.

—. *The Hero With a Thousand Faces*. Princeton: Princeton University Press, 1972.

—. *The Inner Reaches of Outer Space*. New York: Harper & Row, 1986.

—. *The Masks of God*. New York: Penguin Books, 1964.

—. *The Power of Myth*. New York: Doubleday, 1988.

—. *Transformation of Myth Through Time*. New York: Harper Perennial, 1990.

Cavendish, Richard. *Legends of the World*. New York: Barnes & Noble Books, 1994.

Cedercrans, Lucille. *The Nature of the Soul*. Whittier, CA: Wisdom Impressions, 1993.

Chivalry, The Path of Love. San Francisco: Chronicle Books, 1994.

Crowley, Aleister. *The Book of Thoth: Egyptian Tarot*. York Beach, Maine: Samuel Weiser, Inc., 1944.

Cumont, Franz. *The Mysteries of Mithra.* New York: Dover Publications, Inc. 1956.

Damasio, Antonio R. *Descartes' Error: Emotion, Reason and the Human Brain.* New York: Grosset/Putnam, 1994.

Diamond, John. *Your Body Doesn't Lie* (aka *Behavioral Kinesiology*). New York: Warner Books, 1989.

Gray, Henry. *Gray's Anatomy.* Philadelphia, PA: Courage Books, 1999.

Easwaran, Eknath. *The Bhagavad Gita for Daily Living.* Petaluma, CA: Nilgiri Press, 1979.

Evans-Wentz, W. Y. *The Tibetan Book of the Dead.* New York: Oxford University Press, 1960.

Fillmore, Charles. *The Twelve Powers of Man.* Santa Cruz, CA: Unity Press, 1930.

Fitzgerald, Edward. *Rubaiyat of Omar Khayyam.* New York: Random House, 1947.

Fortune, Dion. *The Mystical Qabalah.* York Beach, Maine: Samuel Weiser, Inc., 1984.

Frazer, James G. *The Golden Bough.* New York: Gramercy Books, 1981.

Gibbs, Laura, trans. *Aesop's Fables.* New York: Oxford University Press, 2002.

Goleman, Daniel. *Emotional Intelligence: Why It Can Matter More Than IQ.* New York: Bantam Books, 1995.

Graves, Robert. *The White Goddess: A historic grammar of poetic myth.* New York: Farrar, Straus and Giroux, 1948.

Haich, Elizabeth. *Initiation.* Aurora Press, 2000.

—. *Sexual Energy and Yoga.* Aurora Press, 1991.

Hall, Manly P. *Man, The Grand Symbol of the Mysteries.* Los Angeles, CA: The Philosophical Society, Inc., 1972.

—. *Secret Teachings of All Ages.* Los Angeles, CA: The Philosophical Society, Inc., 1928.

—. *Super Faculties and Their Culture.* Los Angeles, CA: The Philosophical Society, Inc., 1939.

Hamilton, Edith. *Mythology: Timeless Tales of Gods and Heroes.* New York: Warner Books, Inc., 1999.

Hodson, Geoffrey. *The Kingdom of the Gods.* Madras, India: The Theosophical Publishing House, 1952.

Jaynes, Julian. *The Origin of Consciousness in the Breakdown of the Bicameral Mind.* New York: Houghton Mifflin Company, 1976.

Johnson, Steven. *Mind Wide Open: Your Brain and the Neuroscience of Everyday Life.* New York: Scribner, 2004.

Leadbeater, C. W. *The Science of the Sacraments*. Madras, India: The Theosophical Press, 1920.

Maciocia, Giovanni. *Foundations of Chinese Medicine: A Comprehensive Text for Acupuncturists and Herbalists*. New York: Churchill Livingston, 1989.

Muldoon, Sylvan and Carrington. *The Projection of the Astral Body*. New York: Samuel Weiser, Inc., 1970.

New Larousse Encyclopedia of Mythology. New York: Prometheus Press, 1972.

Norretranders, Tor. *The User Illusion*. New York: Viking Penguin, 1998.

Pert, Dr. Candace B. *Molecules of Emotion: The Science Behind Mind-Body Medicine*. New York: Touchstone, 1997.

Pomeranz, Bruce and Stux. *The Basics of Acupuncture*. New York: Springer, 1985.

Purce, Jill. *The Mystic Spiral: Journey of the Soul*. New York: Thames and Hudson, 1974.

Rudel, Anthony J. *Tales from the Opera*. New York: Simon and Schuster, 1985.

Shattuck, Roger. *Forbidden Knowledge: From Prometheus to Pornography*. New York: St. Martin's Press, 1996.

Shlain, Leonard. *The Alphabet Versus the Goddess: The Conflict Between Word and Image*. New York: Penguin Group, 1998.

Talbot, Michael. *The Holographic Universe*. New York: HarperCollins Publishers, Inc., 1991.

Schwaller de Lubicz, R. A. *Symbol and Symbolic*. Brookline, MA: Autumn Press, 1978.

—. *The Temple in Man: Sacred Architecture and the Perfect Man*. Rochester, VT: Inner Traditions, 1949.

Weblinks

Carter Center *www.cartercenter.org*
Center for Enhanced Performance *http://www.dean.usma.edu/CEP/*
DARPA: Defense Advanced Research Projects Agency *http://www.darpa.mil/*
Joseph Campbell Foundation *www.jcf.org*
Institute of Noetic Sciences *www.noetic.org*
Theosophical Society *http://www.theosophical.org/index.html*
Massachusetts Institute of Technology's Media Lab *http://www.media.mit.edu/*
Mindship *www.mindship.org*
MYTHWORKS *www.mythworks.net*
Philosophical Research Society *www.prs.org*
Science Week *www.sciencenews.org*

$\mathcal{G}$lossary of Terms

Alta Major — this Center of Motivation (chakra) is not one of the major seven/ eight. Sometimes called "the mouthpiece of god," it is located at the base of the skull. In later stages of spiritual meditation and disciplines it comes into relation- ship with the Ajna. The Alta Major is said to access the past, or unconscious, or past lives.

Ancient Wisdom — universal insights and information that show up in most cultures, mythologies, and spiritual systems. Often attributed to the gods, ancient civilizations, or simply wise humans, the Ancient Wisdom offers advice and disci- plines on personal enlightenment and ethics, social systems, planetary and species history, and prophecies. Though the truths are evident in various writings and oral traditions, there is no rigid structure or dogma. If there is any dogma at all, it's not to form dogmas.

anima — this Latin word means the life principle, or soul. Dr. Carl Jung used it to designate the feminine principle of the psychological unconscious self, particularly in a man. Note the anima/animus dichotomy of soul/mind, passion/reason.

animal man — the prototype for humans before self-consciousness and self-identity took hold. Higher primates. Some mythologies (including hints in the Bible) say the gods mated with these primitive creatures to produce us.

animus — this word in Latin means mind, animating force. Dr. Carl Jung used it to designate the masculine principle of the psychological unconscious self, particularly in a woman. Note the anima/animus dichotomy of soul/mind, passion/reason.

archetype — a personification of a psychological aspect said to be accessible to all humans via the collective unconscious. Most mythologies have slightly different versions of the same archetypes: warrior, lover, trickster, mother, etc.

bindi — Hindus wear a spot of red pigment or often jewels at the Ajna Center, on the forehead between and slightly above the eyes. Originally meant to symbolize Shakti, the female energy, the *bindi* can range from a very spiritual symbol to a simple fashion statement and is worn by men and women alike.

caduceus — symbol of the medical profession, this staff was carried by the Greco-Roman Hermes/Mercury, god of medicine (and messages, commerce, and trickery). A wooden staff symbolizing the spinal column has two serpents symbolizing the kundalini currents (*Ida*–feminine and *Pingala*–masculine) twining up it. At the top is a set of wings symbolizing the Ajna Center and sometimes a pine cone, symbolizing the Crown Center. Each crossing of the serpents indicates an activated Center of Motivation.

Centers of Motivation — the chakras: physiological, psychological, and philosophical Centers that affect and effect our bodies, emotions, and thinking.

chakra — a Sanskrit word meaning "wheel." *Prana* (vitality or life energy) is said to spin through and around each of these Centers. Each chakra is a *ganglia*, or grouping of nerves, and connects to an endocrine gland which produces certain hormones which bring about changes in your body, emotions, and mind. Some spiritual disciplines teach the use of consciousness to affect the chakras and thereby the thinking, emotions, and body.

chi — the vital force that animates the physical body. It's said to flow along certain *nadis* or channels, and to gather at the Centers or chakras. With training, the chi can be controlled. Sometimes called *gi* or *ki*.

circadian rhythms — an individual's physiological rhythms associated with the 24-hour planetary day; includes sleep, digestion, glandular, and metabolism cycles.

dharma — duty, the law, everyday responsibilities. Social, familial, and professional harmony and virtue.

endocrine gland — secretes a hormone carried through the blood or lymph system to some part of the body which it then controls or regulates.

endocrine system — the main ductless glands include Luschka's gland, the testes and ovaries, the adrenals, pancreas, spleen, thymus, thyroid, pituitary, and pineal. They secrete hormones which affect the functioning of the body.

energy work — the various uses of conscious attention to affect the physical state of the body, usually to improve health. Though sometimes using hands—on applications, stones, crystals, herbs, needles, etc., energy workers also claim results from a distance with no physical contact with their patient. The basic principle is that consciousness affects the physical world.

esoteric — hidden, open only to tested and approved initiates; opposite of exoteric which means out in the open and available to anyone.

etheric body — the energy pattern that is the mold for the physical matter that makes up our bodies. Chakras are part of the etheric as well as the physical body. Think of it as both a blueprint for and a different-dimensional foundation of your physical body.

exoteric — information freely available to anyone.

ganglia — groupings of nerves along the spinal column.

hajj — the Moslem pilgrimage to Mecca in Saudi Arabia during the month of Ramadan. This trip is one of the five pillars of Islam. Everyone who can afford to is supposed to make the journey at least once in their lifetime.

hormones — chemical substances produced in the endocrine glands which have effects on the physical body and in turn, on the psychological self. For example, testosterone, estrogen, adrenaline, etc.

Ida — the feminine kundalini current residing in the Root Center and capable of twining up the spinal column to the Crown Center as consciousness is raised up through the Centers of Motivation.

Kaaba — the large central structure in the mosque at Mecca, site of the yearly *hajj* pilgrimage and the place to which Moslems face when praying five times a day. Symbolizing the oneness of Allah, the huge cube is draped in black and contains a small stone said to have been given by the Angel Gabriel to Abraham. Many aspects of the mosque resonate with pagan symbolism: the original 360 idols housed there were destroyed by Mohammed before he made the place a holy site of Islam.

Kabala — developed by Jewish rabbis, this mystical doctrine holds much of Ancient Wisdom. It influenced alchemy, the Rosicrucians, and Masonry. Using numerology, symbolism, archetypes, and analogies, the Kabala offers instruction in personal enlightenment as well as an understanding of the universe.

kanda knot — the primitive knot of cells from which the spinal column develops; esoterically, the egg where the kundalini resides.

karma — the Hindu version of the law of cause and effect. Often analogous to Isaac Newton's 3rd law: For every action there is an opposite and equal reaction. Karma (both positive and negative) is said to collect and be paid out over many lifetimes. Think of it as a character's "ghost," big time.

kundalini — a fiery, spiraling power that rises up the spinal column, energizing the various chakras. Best raised by conscious effort under the guidance of a trained teacher, if done too quickly or incorrectly, raising the kundalini can "fry the circuits" and damage the nerves and the person.

Law of Grace — enlightenment, being "born again," baptism, forgiveness are all examples of this Law in action. Once you get the point of life, existence, and the consequences of your actions, then supposedly you don't need to pay back the debts since it was all about getting you to become conscious and then stop creating karma.

Law of Karma — cause and effect. You reap what you sow, positive and or negative, now or in another lifetime.

manvantara — Sanskrit word for the physical manifestation in the life—cycle of a planet, a solar system, a galaxy, a universe. It's the awake time as opposed to the *pralaya* or down-time.

metaphysics — the study of first principles of reality; abstract reasoning; the origins of the world and how it works. Modern physics, astrophysics, and paleology are technically "proving" many things formerly considered "above" physics, or metaphysical.

Mithra(s) — ancient Persian god of Light and Truth. A popular god with the Roman Army, the Mithraic religion had seven levels of initiation. Many of the teachings migrated over to Christianity.

Muladhara — name of the Root Center in Sanskrit.

Mystery Schools — teach the Ancient Wisdom, the Physics of Metaphysics: how things, people, and systems really work; the nature of reality; the nature of consciousness and the unconscious; the interdependency and reciprocal workings of the soul-mind-brain-body connections. Modern physics, astrophysics, and paleology are technically "proving" many things these Schools have always taught. There is no structure, no bureaucracy, no set curricula, and most of the Wisdom is imparted orally from teacher to tested-and-proven pupil. The inherent Truths are so universal, however, that you can recognize them across the globe and across the ages, once you know what you're looking at. Though usually kept secret and opened only to sincere seekers, the Wisdom Teachings are now being given to the world in general, in hopes of affecting positive changes in humankind.

mysticism — the emotional, feeling approach to life, initiation, character and spiritual growth; as opposed to the mental, rational, occult approach. Most religions have a mystic branch: Gnostic Christians, Sufi Muslims, Jewish Kabalists, etc.

mythology — the stories we tell ourselves to explain the world around us and within us. It's said that a "true myth" will resonate with truth on at least seven different levels such as: physiological, sociological, psychological, historical, philosophical, geological, cosmological, astrological, astronomical, chemical, evolutionary, and now with the incredible revelations of sub-atomic physics and quantum mechanics.

Namaste — Sanskrit word of greeting, used by Hindus and others, meaning "I honor the Divine within you." The bowing gesture places the hands together, symbolic of uniting the dualities of existence. Sometimes the hands are held over the Heart Center, sometimes at the Ajna Center, and sometimes at the Crown Center.

occult — means hidden. It does not mean evil. The information used to be kept hidden because it is powerfully effective and if done without proper training and motivation can be dangerous to the self and others. To be on the Occult Path implies study, mental work, step-by-step logical progression as opposed to the more emotional Mystic Path.

Persia — the old name for the country called Iran since 1935. Persians are not Arab/Semitic; they are Aryan and thus related to Indians and Caucasians/Europeans.

persona — the individual personality of a singular lifetime. The eternal soul's projection into one particular time and place. The combined physical, emotional, mental, and spiritual bodies. Much of the Wisdom Teaching is to align one's persona with one's soul and to encourage continuity of consciousness before, during, and after an incarnation — not that the persona itself lives on, but its lifetime contributes to the soul's experience and wisdom. Think of the soul as the actor (Meryl Streep) and the various personas/lifetimes as the roles (Karen Blixen, Sophie, Lindy Chamberlain, Suzanne Vale).

Peter Pan syndrome — males who refuse to grow up, named after the main character in J.M. Barrie's eponymous 1904 play.

Pingala — the masculine kundalini (life energy) current residing in the Root Center and capable of twining up the spinal column to the Crown Center as consciousness is raised up through the Centers of Motivation.

plexus — a twining, braiding, network of nerves, as in the Center named the Solar Plexus.

pralaya — a period of inactivity in the life cycle of a large system such as the universe. The down-time or darkness, quiescence, entropy, dissolution; as opposed to the *manvantara*.

prana — the general life force of the planet, said to be plentiful in trees and water, scarce in cities.

puer — Latin for "boy," childish.

Sahasrara — Sanskrit name for the Crown Center; the thousand—petaled lotus.

Sanskrit — the sacred language of old India. Some say its words were designed to have specific effects, so mantras and names are "magical." The same is also said of Latin. The liturgy of the Catholic Mass was also supposedly designed to have certain affects via the sounds of the words.

SETI — Search for Extra Terrestrial Intelligence. An organization conducting scientific research on life in the universe with an emphasis on intelligent life.

shadow — an individual's animal instincts, that pre-conscious part of the self.

shaman — a priest, usually in relatively unsophisticated tribal systems, who uses ritual drugs, dancing, drumming, etc. to affect a shift in states of awareness for the purpose of healing, hunting, divination, or other service to the tribe.

shamanic tree — similar to other mythologies' world trees, this often has seven roots and seven branches, each with different meanings, obstacles, lessons, and rewards. In their altered states, the shamans journey along the tree.

Shakti — the female energy of a Hindu deity; usually personified as the wife or consort, as in Shiva and Shakti, the couple separated by the Fall as mentioned in Section Three, Chapter 13.

Shiva — third aspect of the Hindu Trinity: Brahma the Creator, Vishnu the Preserver, and Shiva the Destroyer. Also seen as the Regenerator since life comes out of death.

***siddhi* powers** — special abilities said to result from spiritual disciplines associated with the various chakras. For example, knowledge of past-present-future, astral projection, shape shifting, invisibility, control of fire-water-wind-poisons, etc.

soul — conscious awareness, sentience.

spirit — the animating life force.

Sufi — a member of the mystical order of Islam, seeking direct union with Allah, the Merciful, the Compassionate.

Sushumna — Sanskrit name for the central spinal column around which *Ida* and *Pingala* twine.

thalamus — means "bridal chamber" in Greek. A chamber in the center of the head where the pituitary and pineal glands reside in proximity. The activation and synchronization of these two glands is called the Royal Marriage in alchemy and other mystic systems.

Vedas — the most ancient and most sacred Sanskrit works.

Wisdom Teachings — see Ancient Wisdom and Mystery Schools.

About the Author

PAMELA JAYE SMITH is a mythologist, writer, consultant, speaker, and award-winning producer-director with twenty-five years experience on features, TV series, commercials, music videos, documentaries, corporate, and military films.

Pamela holds a BA from the University of Texas at Austin in English, Latin, and Film, and is randomly pursuing a Masters in Military Studies and Intelligence. She has eight years formal study in Comparative Mysticism and is a certified teacher of the Mystery Schools.

In her early career Pamela spent four years in production at Universal Studios, including time with Sherwood Schwartz, creator of *Gilligan's Island* and *The Brady Bunch*, and with director Joel Schumacher.

MYTHWORKS is Smith's consultation company offering "Applied Mythology for more Powerful and Fulfilling Reality" to individuals, organizations, the media arts, and the military. Her story consultation clients include screenwriters, novelists, playwrights, nonfiction authors, directors, designers, actors, and development executives.

Besides story consulting with a mythic spin, Pamela also does Image Consulting based on Archetypes, using the wisdom of myths to help people accomplish career and personal changes and enhancements. She also consults with organizations on design, missions, teamwork, leadership, communication, and stress management.

Pamela was media spokesperson for Microsoft's PC game "Age of Mythology" and appeared on the international TV series "Forbidden Secrets" as an expert in mythology.

She has taught at RAI-TV Rome, UCLA Extension Writers Program, American Film Institute, USC Film School, Screenwriting Expo, Pepperdine University, National Film School of Denmark, Thot Fiction in Marseilles France, Women in Film, and many other venues. She also judges screenwriting contests and presents at a number of film festivals.

Other international clients and credits include Paramount, Disney, Universal, National Association of Broadcasters, GM, Boeing, Hughes Space & Communications, the FBI, ROTC Cadet Corps, and the U.S. Army.

During the Clinton administration Pamela was a member of the U.S. Army's Advanced Warfighting Working Group and recently contributed to two classes at the U.S. Army Military Academy at West Point: "Ethics in Leadership" and "Mental Skills for the New American Warrior." She attended Air War College and Army War College National Security Forums.

Pamela serves on a Boeing Space & Communications Think Tank on Science and Technology Education, and did an analysis and recommendations paper for the National Committee Against Youth Violence media campaign.

She appears in a museum exhibit at the George H.W. Bush Library in Texas, alongside JPL head Dr. Charles Elachi on a project using space shuttle technology to locate her uncle's lost WWII plane high in the Himalayas. The Chinese and U.S. governments have collaborated on the project.

Various projects have taken Smith to the Arctic, the Andes, Southeast Asia, and New Zealand. She has filmed on the largest offshore oil rig in the Gulf of Mexico, slept in grass huts and eaten guinea pig under Ecuador's highest volcano, caught her own sushi breakfast in the Leyte Gulf, and rappelled into the jungles of Mindanao searching for lost WWII Japanese gold.

Pamela is an avid reader, drives a '77 Bronco, and enjoys opera. A dilettante approach to sports has included surfing, skiing, snorkeling, flying, go-cart and auto racing, and driving an offshore oil rig and an Army tank — both under close supervision.

You can learn more about MYTHWORKS and contact Pamela Jaye Smith at: www.mythworks.net

THE WRITER'S JOURNEY
2ND EDITION
MYTHIC STRUCTURE FOR WRITERS

CHRISTOPHER VOGLER

BEST SELLER
OVER 116,500 UNITS SOLD!

See why this book has become an international bestseller and a true classic. *The Writer's Journey* explores the powerful relationship between mythology and storytelling in a clear, concise style that's made it required reading for movie executives, screenwriters, playwrights, scholars, and fans of pop culture all over the world.

Both fiction and nonfiction writers will discover a set of useful myth-inspired storytelling paradigms (i.e., "The Hero's Journey") and step-by-step guidelines to plot and character development. Based on the work of Joseph Campbell, *The Writer's Journey* is a must for all writers interested in further developing their craft.

The updated and revised second edition provides new insights and observations from Vogler's ongoing work on mythology's influence on stories, movies, and man himself.

"This book is like having the smartest person in the story meeting come home with you and whisper what to do in your ear as you write a screenplay. Insight for insight, step for step, Chris Vogler takes us through the process of connecting theme to story and making a script come alive."

> — Lynda Obst, Producer
> Sleepless in Seattle, How to Lose a Guy in 10 Days
> *Author*, Hello, He Lied

"This is a book about the stories we write, and perhaps more importantly, the stories we live. It is the most influential work I have yet encountered on the art, nature, and the very purpose of storytelling."

> — Bruce Joel Rubin, Screenwriter
> Stuart Little 2, Deep Impact, Ghost, Jacob's Ladder

CHRISTOPHER VOGLER, a top Hollywood story consultant and development executive, has worked on such high-grossing feature films as *The Lion King, The Thin Red Line, Fight Club*, and *Beauty and the Beast*. He conducts writing workshops around the globe.

$24.95 | 325 PAGES | ORDER # 98RLS | ISBN: 0-941188-70-1

MYTH AND THE MOVIES
DISCOVERING THE MYTHIC STRUCTURE OF 50 UNFORGETTABLE FILMS

STUART VOYTILLA
FOREWORD BY CHRISTOPHER VOGLER
AUTHOR OF *THE WRITER'S JOURNEY*

BEST SELLER
OVER 15,000 UNITS SOLD!

An illuminating companion piece to *The Writer's Journey*, *Myth and the Movies* applies the mythic structure Vogler developed to 50 well-loved U.S. and foreign films. This comprehensive book offers a greater understanding of why some films continue to touch and connect with audiences generation after generation.

Movies discussed include *The Godfather, Some Like It Hot, Citizen Kane, Halloween, Jaws, Annie Hall, Chinatown, The Fugitive, Sleepless in Seattle, The Graduate, Dances with Wolves, Beauty and the Beast, Platoon,* and *Die Hard.*

"Stuart Voytilla's Myth and the Movies *is a remarkable achievement: an ambitious, thought-provoking, and cogent analysis of the mythic underpinnings of fifty great movies. It should prove a valuable resource for film teachers, students, critics, and especially screenwriters themselves, whose challenge, as Voytilla so clearly understands, is to constantly reinvent a mythology for our times."*
— *Ted Tally, Academy Award Screenwriter,* Silence of the Lambs

"Myth and the Movies *is a must for every writer who wants to tell better stories. Voytilla guides his readers to a richer and deeper understanding not only of mythic structure, but also of the movies we love."*
— *Christopher Wehner, Web editor*
The Screenwriters Utopia *and* Creative Screenwriting

"I've script consulted for ten years and I've studied every genre thoroughly. I thought I knew all their nuances - until I read Voytilla's book. This ones goes on my Recommended Reading List. A fascinating analysis of the Hero's Myth for all genres."
— *Lou Grantt,* Hollywood Scriptwriter Magazine

STUART VOYTILLA is a screenwriter, literary consultant, teacher, and author of *Writing the Comedy Film.*

$26.95 | **300 PAGES** | **ORDER # 39RLS** | **ISBN: 0-941188-66-3**

24 HOURS | **1.800.833.5738** | **WWW.MWP.COM**

THE HOLLYWOOD STANDARD
THE COMPLETE AND AUTHORITATIVE GUIDE
TO SCRIPT FORMAT AND STYLE

CHRISTOPHER RILEY

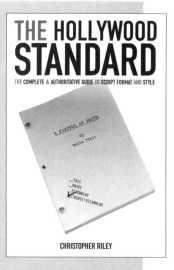

Finally, there's a script format guide that is accurate, complete, and easy to use, written by Hollywood's foremost authority on industry standard script formats. Riley's guide is filled with clear, concise, complete instructions and hundreds of examples to take the guesswork out of a multitude of formatting questions that perplex screenwriters, waste their time, and steal their confidence. You'll learn how to get into and out of a POV shot, how to set up a telephone intercut, what to capitalize and why, how to control pacing with format, and more.

"The Hollywood Standard *is not only indispensable, it's practical, readable, and fun to use.*"
— Dean Batali, Writer-Producer, That '70s Show; Writer, Buffy the Vampire Slayer

"*Buy this book before you write another word! It's required reading for any screenwriter who wants to be taken seriously by Hollywood.*"
— Elizabeth Stephen, President, Mandalay Television Pictures;
Executive Vice President Motion Picture Production, Mandalay Pictures

"*Riley has succeeded in an extremely difficult task: He has produced a guide to screenplay formatting which is both entertaining to read and exceptionally thorough. Riley's clear style, authoritative voice, and well-written examples make this book far more enjoyable than any formatting guide has a right to be. This is the best guide to script formatting ever, and it is an indispensable tool for every writer working in Hollywood.*"
— Wout Thielemans, Screentalk Magazine

"*It doesn't matter how great your screenplay is if it looks all wrong.* The Hollywood Standard *is probably the most critical book any screenwriter who is serious about being taken seriously can own. For any writer who truly understands the power of making a good first impression, this comprehensive guide to format and style is priceless.*"
— Marie Jones, www.absolutewrite.com

CHRISTOPHER RILEY, based in Los Angeles, developed Warner Brothers Studios script software and serves as the ultimate arbiter of script format for the entertainment industry.

$18.95 | 208 PAGES | ORDER # 31RLS | ISBN: 1-932907-01-7

COULD IT BE A MOVIE?
HOW TO GET YOUR IDEAS OUT OF YOUR HEAD AND UP ON THE SCREEN

CHRISTINA HAMLETT

Includes a 50% discount certificate on professional script coverage – a $450 value!

Movies. No matter their theme, budget or cast, they all start out in pretty much the same way: with dreamers – just like you – sitting in darkened theaters around the world and imagining what it would be like to see their names scrolling up the credits after the words, "Screenplay Written By..."

Is there a movie inside of you that's been yearning to get out but you don't know where to begin? Before you stock your shelves with books on how to write a film, take this roadmap to determine if film is the best destination for your creative ideas.

This detailed book will teach you:
- How to identify whether your plot packs enough punch to be a hit movie.
- How to acquire and adapt pre-existing material for a feature length screenplay.
- How to find today's hot markets for the kind of films you want to write.
- How to predict what tomorrow's audiences will want to see.
- How to find and land an agent.

"The single most important thing about a screenplay is the basic concept. And the single most important thing an aspiring screenwriter can do is read this book before he or she starts writing."
> — Pamela Wallace
> Academy Award Winner (Witness) and Author

"Hamlett has culled together essential screenwriting information and integrated it with her wise industry counsel. Both will get you pointed in the right direction for being a successful screenwriter, and keep you there once you've arrived."
> — John E. Johnson
> Executive Director, American Screenwriters Association

CHRISTINA HAMLETT is an award-winning author and script coverage consultant whose credits include numerous books, plays, musicals, optioned features, and screenwriting columns.

$26.95 | 280 PAGES | ORDER # 21RLS | ISBN: 0-941188-94-9

24 HOURS | 1.800.833.5738 | WWW.MWP.COM

ORDER FORM

MICHAEL WIESE PRODUCTIONS
11288 VENTURA BLVD., # 621
STUDIO CITY, CA 91604
E-MAIL: MWPSALES@MWP.COM
WEB SITE: WWW.MWP.COM

WRITE OR FAX FOR A FREE CATALOG

PLEASE SEND ME THE FOLLOWING BOOKS:

TITLE	ORDER NUMBER (#RLS _____)	AMOUNT

SHIPPING _____

CALIFORNIA TAX (8.00%) _____

TOTAL ENCLOSED _____

PLEASE MAKE CHECK OR MONEY ORDER PAYABLE TO:

MICHAEL WIESE PRODUCTIONS

(CHECK ONE) ____ MASTERCARD ____VISA ____AMEX

CREDIT CARD NUMBER _____

EXPIRATION DATE _____

CARDHOLDER'S NAME _____

CARDHOLDER'S SIGNATURE _____

SHIP TO:

NAME _____

ADDRESS _____

CITY _____STATE _____ZIP _____

COUNTRY _____TELEPHONE _____